AN EAGLE'S FLIGHT

A BIOGRAPHY OF BRIGADIER GENERAL ERNEST K. WARBURTON, U.S. AIR FORCE

BY

JAMES P. COYNE

BEST WISHES TO
HENRY SALEM, A
SUPERIOR HOST —
Jim Coyne
06/21/01

DORRANCE PUBLISHING CO., INC.
PITTSBURGH, PENNSYLVANIA 15222

For information or to order additional books, please write:
Dorrance Publishing Co., Inc.
643 Smithfield Street
Pittsburgh, Pennsylvania 15222
U.S.A.
1-800-788-7654
Or visit our web site and on-line catalog at *www.dorrancepublishing.com*.

DEDICATION

To Anna, the Eagle's Wife, and Their Seven Remarkable Children.

FOREWORD

From the earliest days of military aviation, flight testing has been the most important—and most dangerous—phase of aircraft development. Ernest K. Warburton began flying in the 1920s and soon became a test pilot in the 1930s and 1940s—a period of tremendous change in flight. During his career, top aircraft flying speeds increased from about 100 miles per hour right through the speed of sound to more than 3,000 miles per hour. It was an era during which the basics of aerodynamics were still being refined. Computers did not exist. Engineers and designers could produce an aircraft and calculate what they thought its performance should be, but a test pilot would have to take the finished product into the sky and "wring it out" to determine its capabilities and limitations. Often, the airframe or engine would be found wanting, a plane would crash, a test pilot would be killed.

When the aircraft companies were satisfied with their products, they were turned over to the military flying services for "real world" testing. Did an aircraft live up to its design specifications – would it really do what the manufacturer said it would do? Would it prove to be just a good flying machine, or one that could fight in war?

Military test pilots like Ernest Warburton had the challenging job of finding out whether the new aircraft met the rigorous standards of the military services in the life-or-death world of actual combat. An anonymous observer once wrote "All a test pilot was expected to do was combine the judgment of Solomon with the speed of a vibration." It was often dangerous work and relatively few pilots had the flying skills, proficiency, and desire required for the job. Ernest Warburton possessed these qualities and was born with the courage needed to face harrowing situations thousands of feet up in the sky.

He was a contemporary of famous test pilots like Jimmy Doolittle—men who willingly risked their lives in the early days of modern aviation. They, and many more like them, daily tempted fate in the air, flying the most advanced airplanes of the Twenties, Thirties and Forties. Many did not survive, and their names grace the streets and buildings of the famous Air Force test centers at Wright Patterson Air Force Base, Ohio and Edwards Air Force Base, California, and the Navy's Patuxent Naval Air Station, Maryland. General Warburton and men like him were the foundation of today's aerospace world.

which has superb fighting planes for war as well as peaceful space vehicles that can take mankind to the moon and beyond. They and their work must be remembered, for without them, aviation could not have advanced.

ACKNOWLEDGMENTS

The author gratefully acknowledges the assistance, advice, counsel and support from the following:

Col. Nathan R. (Rosie) Rosengarten, USAF (Ret.), of the "Wright Stuff Association" and Irma Rosengarten, at Wright Patterson AFB, Ohio, Col. Ralph Hoewing, USAF (Ret.), Riverside, California, Col. Ellis J. Wheless, USAF (Ret.) and Doris Wheless, San Antonio, Texas, Maj. Gen. Osmond J. Ritland, USAF (Ret.), Rancho Santa Fe, California, Lieut. Gen. Emil L. Sorenson USAF (Ret.), Canyon Lake, California, Maj. Gen. Homer L. Sanders, USAF (Ret.), Albuquerque, New Mexico, Lt. Col. Harvey Kuntsman, USAF (Ret.), El Paso, Texas, Ralph Royce, Lone Star Flight Museum, Galveston, Texas, Dave Menard, Researcher, Air Force Museum, Wright Patterson AFB, Ohio, Dr. James Young, Chief, Flight Test Center Historical Office, Edwards AFB, California, Dr. A. Timothy Warnock and Col. Richard S. Rauschkolb, Air Force Historical Research Agency, Maxwell AFB, Alabama, Elizabeth Andrews, Library Archivist, Massachusetts Institute of Technology, Cambridge, Massachusetts, Jack Nowling, Alexandria Bay, New York, Mrs. Anna M. Warburton, Hardwick, Massachusetts, Dr. Keeling Warburton, Charleston, South Carolina, Joanne Warburton Smith, Brunswick, Maine, Sally Warburton Morris, Kailua, Hawaii, Ward Warburton and Darby Warburton, both of Ware, Massachusetts, Dr. Mark Warburton, High Point, North Carolina, Frank Warburton, Newtown, Connecticut, Charlie Angell, Hardwick, Massachusetts, and Lt. Col. Arch Lorentzen, Kalispell, Montana.

A portion of the proceeds of this book will be donated to the Wright Patterson Air Force Base Educational Fund.

CHAPTER ONE

October 8, 1929—First, there is only the sound. The children in the Hardwick school, with their youthful sharp ears, are the first to hear it. All eyes turn from textbooks and blackboards to gaze out windows, riveted on the sky. It is just a faint buzz in the air. Then it becomes a hum, and finally, the unmistakable drone of an approaching airplane. The children know what that sound means, and they wait eagerly for the exciting show to begin. They squirm in their seats, hoping for a brief recess in the open air. Then, teacher says, "All right children, you may go outside." In an orderly line, they eagerly move out the door.

Swiftly riding the air currents 3,000 feet above them, strapped securely into his seat in the open cockpit of his black and yellow U.S. Army Curtiss Hawk biplane, the young pursuit pilot smiles in anticipation of what he is about to do. He is outfitted in regulation dark leather flying suit, boots, helmet and goggles, and his white silk neck scarf flutters back in the slipstream. He looks down through fleecy, scattered white clouds upon the villages, neat stone-fenced farms and verdant wooded hills of Massachusetts. Lieutenant Ernest K. Warburton is about to pay another airborne visit to his home town.

With his gloved hand, he shoves the throttle forward. Smoothly coordinating the movements of control stick and rudder pedals, he simultaneously lowers the nose of his craft and rolls over into a steep dive towards the villages below. As his airspeed rapidly increases in the descent, the steady throb of his powerful engine changes to a thundering roar. He watches the houses of the small villages of Hardwick, Gilbertville and Ware rapidly grow larger in his windscreen. At the last moment, he pulls out of the dive at 200 miles an hour and streaks down Gilbertville's Main Street, just above the housetops. Now, people begin to stream out of their houses into the streets and back yards. They, too, await the show. Then, with slipstream screaming in the plane's struts and guywires, Ernest climbs, dives, zooms, loops and rolls his nimble plane in sun-splashed blue skies. As usual, it is a show to remember.

Ernest Warburton spent his boyhood in Gilbertville, roaming the waters and woods of the surrounding countryside. Although his family moved to Boston when he was halfway through high school, he never lost

1

his love for the small town, his relatives and the townspeople. Until he finished college, he returned often for visits and spent summer vacations working there. Then, for the rest of his career as a fighter pilot and top military test pilot, advancing to the rank of Brigadier General, living enough heroic aerial exploits along the way to fill a book, he returned often for visits to his home town, both on the ground and in the air.

After becoming a pilot in the U.S. Army Air Corps in the late Twenties, Ernest took every opportunity to fly back over the area and put on aerial demonstrations for his relatives, old friends and neighbors.

In 1929, the mere sight of an airplane droning overhead brought excited comment from gaping people below. Ernest's airshows electrified them. "Oh, well," says Charlie Angell, Ernest's first cousin and best friend, who is now in his nineties, "He gave Gilbertville some shows they'll never have—never again. When *he* came over Gilbertville—you knew it. I mean, you *knew* it!

"One time, he came down the Ware River, so *low* that—well, there's a stone wall going up the side of New Braintree Road, and I've got a picture taken by a guy standing on top of the wall and you can see Ernie in the cockpit *down below*, just skimming along the surface!

"And there are people in Gilbertville who say he flew under the Ware River bridge. 'Course, he couldn't have, his wings would probably have been clipped off by the bridge supports. But, you see, they'd be standing on the bridge, knowing he was coming, because he'd just made a pass over Gilbertville. Well, he comes streaking down the river, his gol-blamed wheels just skimming the water, and he's coming straight at them. They think he's going to hit them! So they crouch down and duck their heads. They lose sight of him! He flashes over them, so close the roaring sound of the airplane seems to be everywhere. Zoooom, the sound is overwhelming as he goes by! Then he's gone, curving off down the river. He couldn't have—but even the Chief of Police says Ernie went under that bridge. Whew! And Ernie—well, he never would say whether he did, one way or the other.

"I remember one time he came over Gilbertville," Charlie Angell continued. "He'd just been in the Cleveland Air Races—and he had come in second. Ernie could really fly, no doubt about that. He'd had a special propeller installed for the races, and that airplane made a helluva noise!

"My father was chief engineer in the woolen mill powerhouse. There were two General Electric turbines in there, I forget how many horsepower they had, but they made a lot of noise. My father listened closely to the sound of those turbines, because if it changed, that might mean something was going wrong, like a bearing burning out. So he was attuned to every noise he could hear and every vibration he could feel.

"All of a sudden, my father told me, the whole place shuddered. Mr. Dorman was the boss fireman, and he came running up the stairs. 'Mel,' he said, 'one of the boilers, I think it's going to blow!' Then, while the two men stood staring at each other, one of the coal-passers came running up. The coal passers worked outside, where they loaded the cars for the firemen. 'Holy smoke!' he said. 'An airplane just went around the chimney!' 'Around?' my father asked. Just then, they heard a 'zooom!' and they knew Ernie was overhead on his second pass!

"Every time he came," Charlie continues, "after the first pass, everybody would be outside, and Ernie's disappeared again. What did he do? He'd go way the hell up high and then he'd dive back in, picking up more speed. They tell me that Andrew Baker was out in his yard, waving a broom to make sure Ernie saw him. When he saw Ernie diving back in, right at him, Andrew dropped that broom and ran like hell for the house!

"Everybody was out—oh, everybody! One time, when they knew he was coming, Mr. Holt, one of the big bosses at the George H. Gilbert Manufacturing Company, let the school out to watch Ernie. He let Gilbert's mill out, too! He figured, nobody's going to be working in here anyway, so he gave permission for everybody to stop work at their machines and go outside. Ernie always gave them a good show. He'd make three or four passes in about fifteen minutes, and then he'd be gone.

"The noise was something to hear! One time, I didn't know he was coming and I was standing on the back steps, and all of a sudden I heard this roar—Holy smoke! Right on top of me! I don't think Ernie was more than 50 feet over the top of my house, and when he got there, he went right up—just like that! And I remember seeing him in the cockpit! I could see his brown helmet, his goggles and his white teeth as he smiled and he waved to me, looking back over his shoulder as he went straight up. Oh, boy, he was going! And then, a few seconds afterwards, the leaves are coming down. It was autumn. I think he blew all the leaves off the trees around my house! Golden, red, yellow and brown leaves, swirling everywhere! And then, he was gone again."

One standard part of Ernest's show was to fly upside down over the woolen mill in which his father spent much of his life as a superintendent of wool sorters. The wool sorters worked in a huge, glass enclosed room on the top floor of the mill. They needed plenty of light for sorting. The sorters reported they could look up and see Ernest pass overhead, upside down, his plane's chrome yellow wings with the two big stars almost scraping the roof. He would be so low they could glimpse the top of his brown helmet, his goggles, and his leather-gloved hand on the control stick as he flashed overhead.

It should be noted that, in those days, in the early years of military aviation, aerial demonstrations by responsible pilots were not discouraged by the military authorities, because they sparked public interest in military aviation and helped the Army recruit pilots and mechanics. Civilian audiences loved these aerial demonstrations, as exemplified in a letter of appreciation, written the day the school children were let out to see Ernest perform.

Dictated by the above mentioned Walter W. Holt of George H. Gilbert Mfg. Co., dated Oct. 8, 1929, it reads:

> "My dear Earnest (sic),
>
> "You will, no doubt, be surprised to receive a letter from me, as I haven't seen you since you were a rather small boy, that is, to speak to, but today you surely did announce your coming as well as your presence in town, and believe me, you have no reason to be ashamed to enter your home town in such a noisy manner.
>
> "It is needless for me to say that the entire town's people had the thrill of their lives and that your name is on the tongues of all of the residents this afternoon, your Aunt Jane no doubt the proudest of them all, but we all share her pride in you and hope that some day you will again pay us a visit.
>
> "Perhaps you noticed that in your honor I had all of the children in the Gilbertville School dismissed so that they could see you in your excellent performance over the town and they could realize that you once attended the same schools and roamed in the same streets and woods.
>
> "In the last hour I have talked with a large number of our people and the subject is always aviation with you playing the leading role, and I am quite sure that you would pile up a big score in a popularity contest just now.
>
> "I could go on but I would only repeat myself and I am taking the liberty, on behalf of the town's people to say nothing of the school children, to congratulate you on your ability and wish you a long and successful career.
>
> "Very truly yours,
> (signed)
> Walter W. Holt"
> (*The letter is reproduced in its entirety at Appendix 1*)

The Nov. 27,1929 issue of the school newspaper, *The Melting Pot*, in the "Social Activities" column, carried this item: "About a month ago the school was most ably entertained by Mr. Ernest Warburton, formerly a student of the Hardwick High School. He is now a lieutenant in the United States Army Flying Corps. Mr. Warburton was on his way from Boston to Detroit, and spent about twenty minutes over the school and then made his way onwards."

Ernest, at that time, was stationed at Selfridge Field, near Detroit, Michigan. The entry in his flight log book for Oct. 8, 1929, reads "Cross country to Buffalo and Boston," and he logged four hours and 35 minutes of flying time. In the "Detail of Work Done" section, he listed, simply, "XC (cross country) home. Landed at Mansfield." Mansfield was a small field near Hardwick.

CHAPTER TWO

On a hill above one of the mills in Gilbertville, the pupils of Hardwick High School watched Ernest's thrilling demonstration on that bright October day in 1929, as they had watched his other shows. Among these cheering students waving handkerchiefs at him was a petite, pretty blond sophomore named Anna Miriam Ward.

While both Ernest and Anna had grown up in the Hardwick area, they had not met. Ernest had graduated from high school in 1922 and from Massachusetts Institute of Technology in 1926; Anna would not graduate from Hardwick High until 1931, so there was a nine-year difference in their ages. But Anna, like all Hardwick area residents, knew who this local celebrity—the famous, dashing Lieutenant Warburton—was, although she didn't know him personally.

Later, they would meet and marry, but on October 8, 1929, she had no such wild dream. Nor marrying anyone else, for that matter, not at that stage of her young life. Nor did it seem likely they would ever meet, because Ernest and his family had moved from Hardwick to the Boston area before he finished high school. Their parents knew each other, however. Her father was superintendent of the woolen mill in town, and Ernest's father had been superintendent of wool sorters in that mill.

Both families had emigrated from England to America, but in different eras—the Wards in the 1600s and the Warburtons at the beginning of the 20th Century.

It is easy to see that Ernest did not become a pursuit pilot by accident—by family background and upbringing, he was destined to follow a demanding, exciting life. Excitement was in his genes, and his youthful experiences fed the venturesome fires that smoldered within him.

Ernest Keeling Warburton's family originated in England. Ernest's father, Joseph Warburton, was born in Bootle, a suburb of Liverpool, on October 12, 1875. He grew up in the village of Milnrow and became a leather dresser, like his father and his maternal grandfather before him. His schooling ended in about the fourth grade, when, like other working class English children, he entered the workplace at the age of ten.

He went to work for his future wife's Grandfather, known as "Old John" Whitehead. Old John owned the Whitehead works, where sheepskins were

6

processed into wool and leather. Joseph was first a tanner and then learned to be a wool sorter. In those days, wool sorting was the most important step in wool processing. When a sheep is shorn, the wool is called a fleece. Each fleece, even though it comes from one sheep, contains several grades of wool, varying from fine to coarse. Cloth woven from the wool reflects the fineness of the fibers. The best and strongest wool cloth, called worsted wool, contains a specific mixture of fine, soft, fibers and coarser but longer fibers. The sorters identified and separated out the different grades of wool to be woven in the mill. Men like Joseph Warburton brought their expertise to America when they emigrated. "Throw a fleece out there," Charlie Angell says of the sorters in the Gilbertville mills, "and they could pull eight or ten different kinds of wool out of it, just by feel."

When Joseph was fourteen, he fell in love with Betty Whitehead, one of Old John's granddaughters. She was thirteen. They made quite a contrast, according to an essay written by Betty Warburton Rizzo, Ernest's niece: Joseph was taciturn and quiet, although he liked a good, slow conversation— "probably what entranced him was her bubbly sense of fun, and her spirit." He may have looked at other women, but he loved only Betty Whitehead.

Betty's father, Mark Whitehead, was a restless, adventurous man who worked in the Whitehead woolen mill until he decided in the 1890s to leave for Central America. He worked there as a ship's engineer and was involved in the ill-fated scheme to build a canal through Nicaragua. Mark Whitehead left his wife, Amelia, and four children to fend for themselves. He wrote a final letter in October 1889, and was never heard from again. The family assumed he had been struck down by fever, as were so many people in the American Tropics (*Full text of Mark Whitehead's letter at Appendix 2*).

Although Joseph was quiet, he was not a shrinking violet. He owned an inexpensive bicycle that had no brakes. He was a member of a bike riding club that visited other towns on weekends. He acquired a reputation as a daredevil, and was locally famous for having ridden down the steep Blackstone Edge, the mountain just outside Yorkshire, without brakes. In his off-work hours, the wiry young man became a bicycle racer, and won many prizes and considerable renown. On weekends and time off from work, he sometimes rode 100 miles a day.

In his old age, he once gave a silver watch chain he had won in a race to Frank, Ernest's elder brother. "He was a lean and light man," Frank Warburton later wrote, "but with enormous stamina and strength."

Joseph's fame as a daring bicycle rider notwithstanding, Betty did not return his adoration. She was vivacious and flirtatious, and as the years passed, had many admirers. But she accepted no one as a serious suitor, much to the chagrin of her mother Amelia. Herbert Hurst, Joseph's closest friend, courted Ada, one of Betty's sisters. They became engaged. Following Mother Amelia's guidance, Herbert and Ada would invite Betty to accompany them on walks, during which they would "accidentally" meet Joseph. At home, the whole family talked up young Joe as the good husband he would undoubtedly make, if only Betty would see the light and marry him. Joseph's mother told Amelia how much he loved Betty and hoped he could marry her.

Unfortunately, Joe didn't impress Betty himself, because in her presence he was shy and almost speechless, and his naturally laconic manner prevented him from returning her playful banter. She felt he wasn't interesting and didn't want to marry him.

But all was not lost for Joe—emigration saved the day for him. The movement of skilled workmen from England to America had been underway for some time and almost everyone knew someone who had gone there. Herbert, still engaged to Ada, traveled to Norwood, Mass., and worked in a tannery for a year. He returned, married Ada on May 30, 1900, and took her back across the sea to Norwood.

After some months, Ada wrote that she was pregnant. Betty was already anxious to follow in the footsteps of other relatives who had emigrated to Pittsburgh and Connecticut. She became obsessed with the idea of going to America to help her beloved sister in her pregnancy (Probably, Ada had written to her, asking her to come). Her mother insisted she could not go unless she was a "decent, married woman." Under this condition, and being pressured by everyone in the family to marry Joe, she consented to be wed.
The couple were married in St. James's Church in Milnrow on Dec. 17, 1900. They departed Liverpool for America on the steamship *New England* on December 20. Ernest's brother, Frank, later eloquently wrote, "For the bride, marriage was the price of admission to America. For the groom, America was the price of admission to marriage."

The trip was no honeymoon. Joe and Betty traveled separately—Betty up on the top deck in First Class, while Joe worked his way over in steerage, by tending cattle down in the bowels of the ship. Betty never mentioned to the other First Class passengers that her husband was on board. She later related she had enjoyed a flirtation with a Canadian cannery magnate who expressed great regret that she wore a wedding ring. Elder son Frank wrote: "This aspect of her honeymoon was one of the high spots of her life."

Joe found immediate employment in the same Norwood tannery in which his best friend, Herbert, worked, and the Warburtons settled down there, but only for a short time. Their first child, Frank, was born September 15, 1901 in Norwood. Soon after, the little family returned to Bootle, Joe's birthplace, where they lived for about two years.

Then, they returned to America and Ernest Keeling Warburton was born in Norwood, July 12, 1904. This was the year in which Teddy Roosevelt won his second term as U.S. President and articulated "The Roosevelt Corollary" to the Monroe Doctrine. He soon enunciated his foreign policy, which was to "speak softly and carry a big stick."

These policies depended on the availability of a strong Army and Navy and brought the armed services into the public spotlight. Recruiting programs over the next several decades, as well as glamorous reports of America's "knights of the air" in World War I would emphasize the attractiveness of a military career for young men—young men like Ernest, who had in his genes his father Joseph's daredevil qualities as well as the adventuresome spirit of his mother's father, Mark Whitehead. These undoubtedly played a large part in his decision to enter military aviation at a time when it was viewed as a particularly exciting and dangerous profession.

CHAPTER THREE

Not long after Ernest's birth, the Warburtons moved to Gilbertville, follow-ing the lead of Herbert Hurst and his brother, who had found employment in the prosperous woolen mill run by the Gilbert family. By this time, Joseph had become a Master Wool Sorter. His industriousness and leadership did not go unnoticed by management and he soon was made superintendent of wool sorters. Joseph Warburton was a man of prodigious energy. During the time he and his family lived in Gilbertville, the factory work week was 54 hours. Factory workers started work at 7 A.M., took an hour off to go home for lunch between noon and 1 P.M., and then worked until 6 P.M. They put in four hours on Saturday morning. After that, most men needed to rest. But not Ernest's father. Joseph worked those hours and then put in more hours, trekking a mile uphill each day to care for chickens and rabbits he kept on a farm owned by a friend, Arthur Goodfield.

On the Goodfield farm, Joseph did all kinds of maintenance work—fencing, milking the cows, whatever had to be done. On occasion, with his son Frank, he peddled the Goodfield's milk from door to door. "I remember being up there with Ernie when his father was putting up a windmill," Charlie Angell says.

The windmill stands today. Most of the time, Joseph was not paid, because Arthur Goodfield seldom had money to spare. But Joseph put in the hard work anyway, because he enjoyed working. Then, too, it was a way for him to pay Goodfield for permitting him to keep his chickens on the farm.

Joseph was a natural born practical mechanical genius. "He could build or make anything" recalls Charlie Angell. "He was one of the first men to put in a milking machine—at a time when there was no electricity on that farm. So everything was run by a gasoline engine. I remember being up there when Ernest's father hooked up the gasoline engine, the driveshaft, the overhead, the pulleys and belts, the milking pump and everything else, on Goodfield's farm, and it worked just like clockwork."

Joseph had always worked with tools. As a boy in England, he built a model steam engine out of pipes and scrap metal. It was one of the things he brought to America with him, along with his tools. "He used to put the boiler on the stove and run it for us," Charlie Angell remembers. He collected tools and had a workshop in the attic in Gilbertville. During slack times at the mill, when there was not much wool sorting to be done, he worked with Jim Leach, the maintenance man, from whom he learned a great deal about building.

He was not only energetic—although slight and lean, he was strong. The men in the woolshop often had competitions in which they would put heavy weights in a bucket and see which man could hold it out at arm's length for the longest period of time. Joseph always won the contest, showing he was strongest of all. He was courageous—Charlie Angell remembers once seeing him face down a large, drunken man who was armed with a knife, forcing him to get off Goodfield's farm. "When he was in his prime, he was afraid of nothing and would tackle anything. He never saw any danger."

In his spare time, usually on Sunday, after church, Joseph took Frank and Ernest berry picking and walking in the woods, and he went swimming with them in the Gilbertville swimming hole. When the boys were old enough to ski, he made skis for them, by steaming maple slats in a big copper boiler, and then bending up the tips. He made a bobsled for the boys. One of his grandsons, Darby, has that bobsled today. He kept their bicycles in working order. In some respects, he was a man ahead of his time—in his attic workshop, he built a stationary bicycle which he rode for exercise—and the word "aerobics" had not yet been coined.

Joseph especially enjoyed looking over farms for sale. "It was his dream to buy a farm," Frank remembered. But his wife, his mother-in-law, Amelia (who immigrated to Gilbertville about 1905, not long after Joseph and Betty returned from their sojourn in Bootle), and sister-in-law continuously and vociferously opposed his dream. "They just ganged up on him," Charlie Angell says.

There were several prospects, but Joseph didn't buy any of them. "The Boynton place, for example, is just outside of town on Upper Church Street in Ware. Ward Warburton (one of Ernest's sons) built his home on part of that land."

If Joe had fulfilled his ambitions and gotten a farm in Gilbertville, he would have employed son Frank, and probably Ernest as well, to help him run it. In that case, neither boy would have gone to college, and Ernest probably would never have become a flyer. It was Betty, their mother, who was determined her boys were to have a college education, although she hoped it would be Divinity School. Her brother convinced her that electricity was the wave of the future and that a degree in electrical engineering would be their key to success outside the mills. So both Frank and Ernest matriculated at Massachusetts Institute of Technology in Boston.

Frank enrolled at MIT after graduation from high school in 1919. For the first school year, he boarded with a family in Boston. In 1920, in the aftermath if World War I, work began to slack off at the Gilbertville mill, and, coincidentally, Betty "didn't think that Frank was getting the right food, or the right treatment," Charlie Angell remembers. "She insisted that my uncle go to Boston, and find a job."

Frank wrote, in an essay, "She determined that the entire family should move to Boston to look after me properly. Joseph found a job wool sorting at Francis Willey's in Boston, where the work was piece work. This was much to his advantage, because he was not only a master wool sorter, but he could do the work of two men. He found a row house on a street of houses that had been built for officers at the Watertown Arsenal in the Civil War. After 14 years in Gilbertville, the family settled down for another 14 years in Faneuil, a Boston suburb."

Years later, after he retired from the wool business in Boston, Joseph finally was able to buy a farm in Westboro, Massachusetts.

CHAPTER FOUR

Growing up in Gilbertville, young Ernest lived the life of a typical small town boy. He developed into an intelligent, tall, well-muscled young man, with the strength, daring and drive of his father and the lighthearted but steadfast style of his mother. He was handsome, especially when he smiled, and his hazel eyes were direct and honest. In the summer and fall, he swam and fished in the Ware River and nearby lakes, and roamed the woods, camping and hunting. In winter, he skied, ice skated, and sledded. He attended Gilbertville schools through his sophomore year, and in Charlie Angell's words, was "good-natured and full of fun." Well liked and respected, he was a leader among the boys of the town.

He also worked. Like most Gilbertville boys, when he reached fourteen years of age, he became a doffer in the woolen mill. Doffers worked before and after school hours in the spinning room. In the summers, they worked in the mill full time. In the spinning room, the wool thread created from the fleeces was wound by machine on dozens of spindles. A doffer's job was to change a spindle when it was fully wound with thread, replacing it with an empty spindle. The full spindles were then wrapped in foil, and deposited in large wicker baskets. When the doffers were not changing spindles, they carried the baskets to another part of the mill. They constantly swept floors, keeping the mill clean. Ernest started work each morning at seven, when the mill opened, attended school starting at nine, and after school returned to the mill until six in the evening. In summer, he worked in the mill full time.

On Saturday mornings, Ernest's job was to clean out his father's chicken coop. That took about an hour. "From then on," says Charlie Angell, "you couldn't tell what he was going to do because there was a big gang of boys in Gilbertville in those days, and they found their own amusement. We used to go up the river often. We'd bring some potatoes from home, and on the way up the river, we'd try to catch some fish. If corn was in, we'd borrow a couple of ears from a farmer's field. Then, we'd build a bonfire, and cook up a meal fit for a king."

"Ernie wasn't interested in organized sports, like baseball. He never talked about girls.— wasn't interested in them back then. He loved nature, hunting, fishing, and just roaming the woods. And mechanical things. He

13

loved to play with old alarm clocks, taking them apart, finding out how they worked. Anything mechanical fascinated him."

Ernest started hunting at an early age. From the start, he had a great respect for guns. His father, who was not a hunter, gave him an old shotgun with a 30-inch choked barrel that must have been intended for duck hunting. "Of course, we'd be in heavy brush, and that long barrel made it difficult for Ernie to bring it to bear when a partridge flew. Not only that, the choke kept the load so concentrated, it could take the bark off a tree twenty feet away. I never saw him get one bird, never, not with that gun. If partridges were out in fields, and one went up a hundred feet away, he might have had a chance, but he had no chance in thick brush. Never got a one. But he never stopped trying!

"He sure took good care of that gun. Like I say, it was an old, old gun. When he'd finished hunting, he'd clean it, then he'd put a cork in the breach, fill the barrel full of oil, and put another cork in the muzzle. To keep it from rusting. Oh, he took care of that gun!"

Then there was the case of Ernest's pet skunk, which brother Frank remembers, "though not descented, it was totally not aggressive."

Except once.

Ernest and Charlie first saw the skunk near the chicken coop one morning and Ernest decided to make it a pet. "Ernie got the skunk in a barrel, and nobody got hit with the spray. He did the maneuvering, and I did the watching." After a few days, Ernest had tamed the skunk. It lived under the chicken coop.

"When skunks get excited and throw their scent, it comes from two little vents, one on either side of their tail end. You can see the stuff come out, and the two sprays mix, and that's what makes the awful stink. There's some kind of green fog, and if it hits you, you've got it! Well, one Saturday morning I was fooling around somewhere, and Ernie had that little skunk sitting on his shoulder. It had been real tame. Anyway, I came around the corner of the coop fast, and the skunk saw me, and was startled.

"The little skunk was pointing towards me, and his tail was pointing towards Ernie. Well, the stuff hit Ernie right in the neck. Was he mad!" Ernest's mother had to wash his clothes in vinegar to neutralize the odor, and Ernest had to wash with vinegar, too. After that incident, because the little skunk was a pet, Ernest's father arranged for a local trapper to remove its scent bags. Unfortunately, it did not tolerate the operation very well and died a week later, probably from postoperative stress.

Ernest got into mischief, like any youth. "The night before the Fourth of July used to be a big night. Boys would play practical jokes. Ernie and I used to try to get into the school and ring the bell. Sometimes we got in, and sometimes we didn't. If we did get in, we'd pull on that rope and ring the bell ten or twelve times, and then we'd run like hell! Nobody ever caught us."

Even after Ernest moved to Boston with his family, he came home in the summer to work and earn money at Gilbert's. One summer, Ernest and

Charlie built a boat. "I told Mr. Leach, our neighbor, that we wanted to build a boat. He was a boss carpenter, and he said 'figure out the number of square feet of lumber you want, and I'll get it for you.' Well, he did more than get the lumber, he sawed it all out, so all we had to do was put it together. Ernie and I spent several evenings putting the boat together. My father asked what color paint we wanted, and Ernie said 'red,' so he got us a quart of red paint, and oakum to seal the hull, and everything else we needed." The boat became the vehicle for many happy days on the Ware River.

Ernie only got angry on occasion. He was, after all, "good-natured, full of fun." After the skunk, the only other time he got mad, Charlie recalls, "We were up the river with our boat. A kid named Leo Parker was with us. We were trolling, and I got a pickerel, maybe fourteen or sixteen inches, on the line. A pickerel takes the bait, and then you have to wait for it to swallow it. It you try to pull it in too soon, it spits it out and you lose your fish. On the other hand, it might chew through the line. I was waiting. Ernie says 'pull it up, pull it up, pull it up.' I said, 'no, I'm not pulling it up. I'm waiting til I'm damn sure I got it.' Ernie says, 'he's going to chew the line.'

"Ernie, behind me, stood up. He starts to walk, one foot in front of the other, and I can feel him coming. I know when he gets to me, he's going to make me pull up the fish. I waited as long as I could, and when I figured Ernie had just about gotten to me, I gave a hell of a yank and jerked that pickerel out of the water and back over my head.

"The fish hit Ernie right in the face! Naturally, he jerked back to avoid it! Splash! Well, I turn around quick and I see the fish is on board but Ernie is over the side! He's up to his neck in the water! Then he stands up, soaking wet. It isn't quite to his waist. Without a word, he stalks ashore. He is mad as hell! Leo and I are trying to keep from laughing, but not doing a very good job of of it. Ernie wouldn't ride home with us. He wouldn't even talk to us. He walked home along the railroad tracks. Ernie was all through with us for that day.

"A couple of years ago, I was at a funeral at St. William's Cemetery in Ware. Leo Parker, who I had not seen in thirty years, was there. The first thing he said to me was 'Remember when Ernie fell off the boat?' We had a good laugh, again."

Ernest was intelligent, and he was well read. "Once, a bunch of us were in the woods, and we came upon a dead woodchuck. We couldn't figure out what killed it, but it was dead. Ernie decided to give us all an anatomy lesson. So we sat down on a stone wall while he lectured us. He cut open the woodchuck and he started to dissect it, taking out parts, one by one. He would give each piece of woodchuck a name, hold it up so we could see it, and set it aside. He was putting us on! He didn't know the names of those organs anymore than we did! He was making up names as he went along, and he sounded like one of those wonderful, learned doctors you hear on the radio today. Oh, he had a quick mind and a vivid imagination. Where he got those names from, I don't know. But Ernie was quick, and he had a wonderful sense of humor."

On the other hand, Charlie Angell says, "He could be stern. He was a taskmaster when it came to work or business. But outside of that, he always had a big grin."

"The last time he tried to get into mischief Ernie had moved to Boston, and he was home for summer vacation. The night before the fourth, we planned to ring the schoolhouse bell, as we had done when we were growing up. Unfortunately for Ernie, his older brother, Frank, had gotten into trouble the year before. He'd pulled the pegs out of somebody's tent and the tent collapsed on them, and they found out who had done it, and Ernie's mother didn't want any shenanigans this time. We went to bed just after dark, planning to get up and sneak out after everybody else was asleep. Well, we weren't in bed more than an hour, when his mother came in and took his pants! That ended that."

CHAPTER FIVE

How does a future pursuit pilot, with his eyes on the clouds and his mind in the sky, perform in school?

Ernest's report cards show his marks in Hardwick schools were at first about average for an active boy, but they improved as he progressed through the grades. In first grade, he received marks of "Good" for arithmetic and language, "Excellent" in writing and music, but only "Fair" in reading and "poor" in spelling. His deportment was "Fair."

By fourth grade, it became apparent his best subjects were arithmetic, language, history and drawing. He did well in all subjects, varying slightly lower, each year, in spelling. In seventh grade, the "excellents" and "goods" were about equal.

His marks in the two years he spent in Hardwick High School were mostly "A" with some "B" grades. All marks had a "1" appended, which meant he received the highest mark for effort.

When Ernest's family moved to Boston he enrolled in Brighton High School, where he continued to do extremely well, receiving "A Plus" or "B Plus" in all subjects, making him a good candidate for entry into Massachusetts Institute of Technology.

In Brighton, he showed a talent for writing which was surprising in one so mechanically inclined. Ernest was on the staff of *The Imp*, the school's monthly literary magazine. He was *Imp* Room Editor for Room 13, responsible for acquiring stories from his fellow students, as well as, on occasion, providing an article he wrote himself. "Reddy, King of Foxes," was one of his stories, and it appeared in the May-June 1922 issue, when Ernest was a senior. It shows his love of hunting and his respect for wild animals and gives us an insight into his vivid imagination.

"To those who knew him," the story began, "Reddy, known as Bushytail, was the king of foxes. It was the ambition of hunters from far and near to bag this veteran of the chase. For it was long ago that, inspired by his size, his glossy coat and superb carriage, they first matched wits in a losing battle against him...

"And now, near the close of his career, Reddy would lie in his den or travel his beaten hunting paths, while before glowing fireplaces, circles of enchanted listeners would hear tales of his clever and crafty daring."

But Reddy was growing old and slowing down. Now, he only raided hen-houses for food as a last resort— he no longer enjoyed the thrill of being chased, which left him exhausted. But in a severe winter, with no wild prey to be found, he tried one last henhouse raid. The snow was deep. His favorite farm, guarded by an old dog, was locked up tight.

Desperate for food, he was forced to try the farm of Mr. Goodfield (Here Ernest harks back to the farm on which his father worked), who had a young dog, Rover. Rover had killed many of Reddy's friends. "Often he had heard the voice of this hound on the trail and was struck by the clear, confi-dent note. In a vague way, he had a presentiment that associated death with this dog."

Reddy goes to Goodfield's farm and the farmer almost catches him leaving the henhouse. "There was the flash of a gun but the light was bad and the shot went wild. Only the dog to fear now!" The chase lasts for hours. "Reddy sighed as he sped onward, for during the last rest he had grown stiff. Every leap through the snow now cost him more and more effort. A numbness was creeping on him and he had to shake off the blur that swept over his eyes."

Finally, he hears the jingling bells of an approaching sleigh and "he thought of a last, his last, desperate plan." As the sleigh passes his roadside hiding place, Reddy jumps into the back of the sleigh and "drags his aching body under the driver's seat." He hears Rover's confident baying change to yips of frustration as he tracks Reddy's scent to the road and loses it in the scent of the farmer and the sleigh. "The driver, Farmer Goodfield, turned to look back... he saw Rover running to and fro, excited and confused.

"The farmer shook his head, muttering, 'Bushytail, King of Foxes. He'll never be cornered by any dog.' Only too well did he speak the truth, for to the gentle tinkling of the bells and soft murmuring of the wind in the pine-tops above, the soul of Reddy departed."

At Brighton High School, Ernest first began to exhibit an interest in the military. He was a member of Drill Company A, which in his senior year won first place in the annual Hathaway Prize Drill competition. Company A defeated three other companies in the Brighton High School drill hall, observed by so large an audience that many spectators "failed to gain admis-sion to the hall, owing to lack of space," according to one local paper.

He also displayed a thespian talent, appearing as one of the characters in "Under Cover," an original play put on by the Class of 1922, with ticket sales of $492.85. This was "the largest amount ever made in the history of the school," according to a story in the June 16, 1922, issue of *The Recorder*, a weekly newspaper covering events in the Boston suburbs of Allston, Brighton, Faneuil and Aberdeen.

Ernest was featured on the front page of *The Recorder* , which published in full his Senior Class Oration of 1922, delivered at Brighton High School's annu-al Class Day. "Friends, teachers and classmates," he began. "A few short days

will see the close of the career of the Class of 1922 at Brighton High School...
Brighton High School has seriously attempted to give us an education...

"Never before did the world so need genuine manhood and woman-
hood... The World War has left society in a demoralized state, as our daily
papers clearly indicate... Boston, New York, Chicago all have records of
increasing crime...Only the triumph of character over all low, selfish motives
can bring this country back to normal and stabilized conditions."

In an eloquent half hour speech, Ernest implored his classmates to
imbue themselves with the "spirit that prompted Washington's men to make
the sacrifices and undergo the suffering of that Winter at Valley Forge, and
the spirit that made patriots offer their lives for the preservation of the
Union—Are we marching onward to a greater, grander, and more glorious
nation? Are we to be rated as a people of character, of honesty, of fair deal-
ing, as a people faithful to the splendid principles and ideals that have been
our heritage?"

He said they must not use their education as an excuse to look for
employment that does not require hard work. "It is only by work that man can
be happy. By the sweat of their brows, our forefathers have handed us down
the fruit of their labors... Classmates, let us be worthy of our alma mater and
our parents, and following in the footsteps of our noble forefathers, let us
inscribe on the tablet of memory our class motto: 'By Labor and Honor.'"

Ernest had great mechanical ability, which he inherited from his father.
When he was 17, he paid $13 for a Chevrolet "Baby Grande" chassis and
some parts of two other cars. He and his father cobbled them together with
a handmade wooden body to make his first car. He used it at least twice to
bring his mother and father from Boston to visit relatives in Gilbertville.

On one trip, Ernest left his car at his uncle's house, where his father was
spending the night. He then walked the few blocks across town to spend the
night with Charlie. At 7 A.M., the two teenagers were awakened by the sound
of a deafening crash. Joseph, who had never learned to drive, had decided to
drive his brother over to the Angell household for breakfast.

"I heard a hell of a crash," Charlie says. "I jumped out of bed and looked,
and here's Ernie's car with his father and his uncle, and the front end is up
against a big maple tree, and one of the front wheels is back to about three
feet from the rear wheel." Joseph had misjudged the turn and hit the tree.
Ernest "bawled his father out for trying to drive the car when he had never
been behind the wheel before. Ernie was mad!"

The car needed a new front axle. "I knew Walt Mundel, who lived way
up to the top of Ragged Hill, had an old junked Chevrolet up there. So we
got into my Model T and started up the hill. Well, the Model T's gas tank
was under the driver's seat, and the gas flowed by gravity down to the carburetor. There was no fuel pump. I didn't have much gas in it, so we had to turn
the car around and back up the hill so the level of the gas in the tank would
be higher than the carburetor. We laughed at that."

Once they had made it up the hill, it took a couple of hours to take the junked car's front end apart. Joseph paid $5.00 for the steering apparatus and the front axle. The trio drove back down the hill and spent the rest of the day repairing Ernest's Baby Grande and installing the new front end. The next day, Ernest drove his mother, father and himself back to Boston.

CHAPTER SIX

Ernest did well at Massachusetts Institute of Technology. The yearbook for the class of 1926 shows a photo of a very serious, unsmiling Ernest Keeling Warburton.

But though his photo was serious, Ernest himself was a happy, outgoing young man who took part in the fun of undergraduate life. For example, the April 20, 1924, *Boston Globe* carried a headline: "Tennis Ball Floating on Compressed Air Gives E. K. Warburton First Free Yearbook." The accompanying photo shows a human pile of 100 struggling M.I.T. students, Ernest among them (although not identifiable in the photo), each one attempting to climb on top of a low wooden hut while trying to keep other students from climbing up. The sloping red roof of the hut was coated with black motor oil, and before the scramble was over, the students were coated as well, and their clothing was torn to shreds.

This was "The Rush," the M.I.T. students' traditional way of announcing the publication of the yearbook, *Technique.* Inside the yellow and black hut, members of the *Technique* staff were pushing square wooden blocks called paddles, twenty in all, through a slot in the roof. The paddles were blown upward by a stream of compressed air. Paddles numbered one, two, three, four and twenty could be exchanged later for a free copy of the yearbook.

The newspaper describes the scene: "With the oil on the roof, and everyone keyed to a pitch of excitement, silence reigned. Then, a hissing was heard, and a yard or more above the hut, appeared a little ball, miraculously suspended.

"Immediately from every side the hut was charged. The little ball stayed up until a passing gust of wind blew it over. A mad scramble for possession followed. Each man was fresh and each was intent on gaining possession of that little ball. The movie cameras ground on. Kodaks were snapped. The girls danced in excitement.

"And from under it all crawled a grinning E. K. Warburton, class of '26, holding the first 'paddle'."

Each year, a "unique object" was used to start the M.I.T. melee. The tennis ball Ernest captured was the unique object for 1924 and it qualified as a winning paddle (in 1923, the *Globe* reported, the unique object had been a live beaver dropped from an airplane into the Charles River).

21

Ernest performed well academically. He majored in Mechanical Engineering. He and another student, Robert A. Nisbet, collaborated on their senior thesis "Test on Physical Properties of Formica," which was accepted by the faculty and qualified them for graduation.

Ernest was a good athlete and was on the wrestling team in Freshman, Junior and Senior Years. Of his first varsity wrestling match, against Stevens College, the M.I.T. student newspaper, *The Tech*, wrote, "Warburton, a prospect discovered in the interclass meet, represented Technology for the first time in the 135-pound division. Although losing the bout by referee's decision, his work indicated that he will be a valuable man with a little more practice."

He pursued his nascent interest in aviation while at M.I.T., as shown by his membership in both the Mechanical Engineering Society and the Aeronautical Engineering Society. Perhaps his imagination was stirred by the Army's 1925 feat of circumnavigating the globe by airplane, a journey that took 175 days. Jimmy Doolittle, already world famous as a daring aviator, attended M.I.T. for two years, 1924 and 1925, garnering both a Master's degree and a PhD in aeronautical engineering, but there is no record that Ernest and Doolittle knew each other then. Later, when he himself was an airman of note, Ernest would meet Doolittle professionally.

Ernest had joined the Reserve Officers Training Corps (ROTC) when he entered M.I.T. As an ROTC cadet, he was required to wear an Army uniform on drill days, usually twice a week, when the cadets would practice marching in formation for an hour. As a part of his curriculum, in class he studied military subjects for which he received academic credits. In Junior and Senior year he was in advanced ROTC and received a stipend from the Army, about eight cents a day, when school was in session, for "subsistence."

In the summer of 1924, Ernest and six other M.I.T cadets sailed on the coastal steamer "Berkshire" from Boston to ROTC summer camp at Langley Field, Va. Langley is near Newport News, where the James River meets the Chesapeake Bay and forms Hampton Roads.

It was a three-day trip. En route, he wrote one letter home, with the dateline "Wed., 4:10, Somewhere." He explained he didn't know the location of the ship because it had entered an area of fog the previous evening "and we are still in it. Can just see about 20 ft. in front of the boat. " No one had been able to sleep, he related, because the boat's fog horn sounded every two minutes. Nevertheless, he wrote, he was "having a fine time" and expected to sleep that night.

He reported he had inspected the engine room. Presumably, it passed the inspection. The dining room certainly passed—the rest of his letter concerned shipboard cuisine. "Have your pick of a whole menu. Had chicken with dressing, tomato sauce, buttered beets, peas, fish, ice cream, short cake, malted milk, potatoes, pickles, iced water, fancy beans with cream, etc. for dinner. You ought to be here, Dad. Lovingly, Ernest." (Text of letter at Appendix 3).

The "Berkshire" sailed down the mid-Atlantic coast, and, rounding Cape Charles, entered Chesapeake Bay, steamed across the bay into Hampton Roads, and tied up at Newport News. The cadets traveled by military bus from the dock to Langley Field.

Forty-six cadets from M.I.T. and one each from Harvard and Yale spent five weeks (June 18th to July 23, 1924) of summer camp at the field. While undergoing an intensive flying and ground training course, they lived in a camp made up of twelve four-man tents which they erected themselves. Mosquito netting hung over each cot. Ernest's tent happened to be white, while the other tents in the camp were khaki-colored. Under an aerial photo of the place, he wrote "the white tent sheltered the angels of the camp." In the hot, humid climate of Tidewater Virginia, the cadets wore standard wool olive drab Army uniforms, complete with tie, riding breeches, and flat-brimmed campaign hat.

It was during ROTC summer camp that Ernest first got "hands on" aviation experience. On the ground, he studied map reading, air navigation, principles of air observation, engine repair and maintenance, general airplane repair and maintenance. He demonstrated his marksmanship, firing the .45 caliber semiautomatic pistol and .50 calibre machine gun on a ground range. Under a photo of himself and another cadet, smiling as they aim their .45s, he wrote "We never miss." He took part in theoretical war gaming, with scenarios based on actual World War One battles. He was introduced to radio communication, although the aircraft radio was only in its developmental stage.

He also participated in daily marching and drilling sessions, and learned first aid and personal hygiene, Army style. Ernest took his turn on guard duty, patrolling a post with a heavy Springfield rifle on his shoulder.

The flying part of the curriculum was divided in three branches: pilot, observer and engineer. The pilot course had the highest mental and physical requirements, especially those concerned with eyesight and coordination. Aspirants who could not pass those requirements, or did not wish to be pilots, took the observer course. Those who did not wish to fly or were otherwise disqualified, took the engineering course, which was primarily concerned with aircraft maintenance.

Ernest was selected for the pilot course, and made a few short dual orientation flights with an instructor. In one photo, he poses next to a DeHavilland DH-4 in a slightly oversized helmet and goggles. With him is a leathery-faced pilot, also with helmet and goggles, identified as "Sgt. Johnson." He also appears in the front cockpit of a DH-4, engine running and propeller turning, with a "Lt. Foster" in the rear cockpit.

Langley was also the test and development site of the government's National Advisory Committee for Aeronautics, and the cadets observed many types of experimental aircraft during their encampment. At nearby Norfolk Navy Yard, across Hampton Roads, they saw submarines under construction and visited the U.S. S. "Langley," the nation's first aircraft carrier.

On weekends, they were free of duties and Ernest visited Fort Monroe, Norfolk, Yorktown, Richmond, and Washington, D.C., and swam in the ocean at Virginia Beach.

On July 9, all 46 cadets climbed into the cockpits of DeHavilland two-seater trainers and Martin three-seater bombers for a massed formation flight from Langley to Bolling Field, in Washington, D.C., and return. It was a warm, sunny day, with low, fleecy clouds, and excellent visibility, perfect for flying in open cockpit aircraft. After taking off, the planes formed up in a tight V-formation. According to the *Newport News Daily Press*: "it was an excellent example of perfect control on the part of the pilots, and all the students were given a flying performance they will not soon forget."

From 5,000 feet, flying above scattered clouds, the cadets saw the green terrain and blue streams of Northern Virginia, and then Maryland, displayed below. To the east stretched the gray expanse of the Chesapeake Bay. Just to the west, burgeoning cloud masses over the Blue Ridge Mountains pushed upwards into the sky. They flew over historic Yorktown, and near Fredericksburg, crossing the York, Rappahannock and Potomac Rivers. Before landing at Bolling Field, the cadets and their instructors flew up the Potomac, past Mount Vernon, and around the city of Washington. Ernest, flying in one of the twin-engine Martin bombers, photographed the white stone facades of the National Capitol, the White House and other Government buildings.

After lunch, they returned to Langley, capping off a perfect flying day. For Ernest, these short flight experiences at ROTC summer camp fanned the flames of his desire to be an Army pilot.

Ernest was commissioned a Second Lieutenant in the Air Service of the U.S. Army Reserve Corps the same day he graduated, Tuesday, June 8, 1926.

CHAPTER SEVEN

Before graduation from M.I.T., he had submitted his application for Army flying training. He was called to temporary active duty as a second lieutenant in the U.S. Army Air Corps Reserve on September 11, 1926. He reported in to the Air Corps Primary Flying School, Brooks Field, Texas, on September 15, 1926 and immediately began an intensive course of ground school instruction dovetailed with flight training.

He underwent a total of 279 hours of academic instruction. Academics covered theory of flight, instruments, personal equipment of the pilot, airplane motors, airplanes, meteorology, aerial navigation, military sketching and map reading, use of Federal troops in emergencies, training methods and principles of teaching, and Army organization. Interestingly, theory of radio, which he had studied in ROTC summer camp, was not required. Ernest scored highest in instruments (98%), airplanes (93%), army organization (93%), airplane motors (91%), and military sketching and map reading (90%). His lowest score was in theory of flight (73%). His general average was 84%.

Ernest made his first official student flight on October 4, 1926 in a Consolidated PT-1 trainer. The PT-1, a tandem-seat biplane, was the standard Air Corps entry-level trainer. He soloed on October 29. He had logged a total of nine hours and 40 minutes of dual flying time. His solo flight, which included three uneventful landings and takeoffs, lasted twenty minutes.

Shortly after his first solo, Ernest, while flying alone, experienced his first in-flight emergency and exhibited the cool self-control that would stand him in good stead throughout his test flying career. Without warning, a vertical shaft sheared inside his engine. The engine failed and he had to execute a power-off forced landing. He was in the vicinity of Brooks Field, and landed there without difficulty, except for sweating out the "deadstick" approach. He executed a perfect landing. He had logged a total of 15 hours and 45 minutes flying time, of which two hours and 30 minutes were solo.

Ernest graduated from Primary Flying School as a Junior Aviator September 16, 1927. At this point in his flying career, he had logged a grand total of 87 hours and 45 minutes, including one fifteen minute night flight, three hours and 40 minutes of formation flying, and four hours of cross country flying. He had one 30-minute dual transition flight in a DeHavilland DH-4. The DH-4, which he had first seen in ROTC summer camp, was a

British design, thousands of which had been built under license in the United States during World War I. In 1927, it was an aging mainstay of the U.S. Army Air Corps Basic Flying Training Course.

Ernest's training log was certified by Nathan F. Twining, 1st Lieutenant, A.C., Assistant Operations Officer. Twining became U.S. Air Force Chief of Staff in 1953, and was the first Air Force General to become Chairman of the Joint Chiefs of Staff, in 1957.

As was customary in that era, Ernest then was released from active duty and entered the Air Corps Reserve March 5, 1927. A little over two months later, he was thrilled, as were all Americans, by Charles A. Lindbergh's astounding feat of flying alone, nonstop, from New York to Paris, a journey of 3,600 miles, in a single-seat, single-engine Ryan monoplane. Lindbergh's feat raised the public's interest in flying to a fever pitch.

For the next five and a half months, Ernest flew as a reservist in the Air Service reserve unit at East Boston Airport. His aircraft was the venerable Curtiss JN "Jenny" two-place biplane. Ninety-five per cent of the pilots trained in the United States and Canada during World War I had been trained in the Jenny. It was reliable and easy to fly, with a maximum speed in level flight of 75 miles per hour. It was ubiquitous at "air circuses" around the country; in fact, Lindbergh had barnstormed in a Jenny before he became an airmail pilot.

Reliable or not, the Jenny gave Ernest his first real test as a pilot. While he was flying low over Boston July 28, 1927, his engine sputtered, caught again, and died. The slipstream whistling through the plane's guywires became the only sound to reach Ernest's ears, except the occasional toot of a horn from an auto on the streets below. There was no landing field in sight. He went through the emergency procedures but could not revive the engine. He was barely 1,500 feet above the rooftops of M.I.T. and the old Jenny was not noted for its gliding ability. The altimeter was unwinding rapidly when Ernest spotted the only open spot in which he could land, described in the *Boston Globe* as a "field between Memorial Drive and Vassar Street, near the Cambridge Armory."

It turned out to be the Cambridge city dump. He set the Jenny down among the trash heaps as gently as he could, the *Globe* story continued, "avoiding large piles of loam and curbstones which covered most of the terrain... The propeller, landing gear and left lower wing ...were smashed. Warburton, a '26 Technology graduate, escaped injury." Ernest had logged ten hours and 15 minutes of flying time since winning his Junior Aviator's wings. With a total of less than 100 hours in the air, he had already experienced two forced landings. This was a portent of the exciting—and sometimes dangerous—kind of flying he would pursue during his military career.

Ernest's log entry for that day reads "Washed out Jenny—forced landing—dump in Cambridge—Ran out of gas—mechanic failed to gas ship—no gas gage(sic) on this ship."

As luck would have it, Charlie Angell and Russell Parker were visiting Boston that day and saw the story in the *Globe*. "While we were there," Charlie remembers, "we heard a newsboy shouting 'Flyer Lands in the Dump!' And we looked in the paper, and it was Ernie! My cousin, in the paper because he's down in the dump! It was quite a coincidence we were there, because in those days, we didn't get to Boston very often. I was glad Ernie wasn't hurt."

It was at this time that Ernest began his custom of giving low flying demonstrations. On July 2, 1927 a Boston area newspaper reported: "Ernest Warburton of the flying squadron at the East Boston airport has been recently circling Faneuil and dropped down almost to the roof of his home on Newton Street for a surprise visit to his mother."

Following standard military procedure, immediately after being transferred to the Reserves, Ernest had sent in a request to be recalled to active duty in the Air Corps. In true military fashion, the Air Corps eventually replied that he couldn't be recalled unless he applied and was accepted for further flying training. Since that is exactly what he had in mind, Ernest complied and on November 10, 1927, he was once again a Flying Cadet at Brooks Field. This time, however, the course would last a full year, and when he graduated, he would wear the wings of a full-fledged Army Airplane Pilot.

CHAPTER EIGHT

Ernest was delighted to discover that a good friend he had met during his previous tour at Brooks Field, Homer L. "Tex" Sanders, also had requested active duty and was again in his class. Tex was a mechanical engineer out of Rice, a well-known Texas university. He was in the Texas National Guard. He said he decided to become a pilot one hot, humid day when he was surveying some land in the Louisiana swamps and an airplane began circling high overhead. "I knew he wasn't sweating to death and being eaten alive by mosquitoes like I was," he said, "so I decided that flying was what I wanted to do." That was a story he liked to tell for amusement. Actually, like Ernest, Tex had been smitten with the flying bug early on, and yearned to become an Army pilot.

Ernest and Tex argued frequently about who had the best engineering alma mater—Rice or M.I.T. Tex claimed he won the argument because one of the textbooks used at M.I.T. was written by a Rice professor, thus proving the author was a recognized authority at M.I.T. On the other hand, he could find no textbook at Rice written by anyone from M.I.T. Ernest said that just showed how backward they were at Rice. The argument was never settled.

As before, there was a full menu of academic training. In 225 hours of classroom work, Ernest studied training methods and principles of teaching, duties of squadron officers, anti-aircraft defense, balloons and airships, use of federal troops, aerial photography, gunnery, theory of flight, military organizations and employment, signal communications, and a number of other subjects too numerous to list here. The grading system ranged from 67% to 75%. A passing grade average was 70%, and Ernest averaged 73%.

Ernest started primary training on Nov. 22, 1927, flying the PJ-1, a venerable Air Corps primary trainer. He compiled 62 hours and 35 minutes of Primary flying training. Most of it was elementary flying—take offs, landings, joining up and flying in formation—with some basic instrument training and two night flights.

He then moved up to the larger, more powerful DeHavilland DH-4 for Basic training. Here, the emphasis was on the basics of maneuvering in formation, instrument flying, and cross country trips to hone navigational skills. There were few radio navigational aids to help pilots cruise the skies; the emphasis was on "contact" flying, which means keeping a close watch on the terrain below and tracking flight progress on a good map.

Another form of aerial navigation—"dead reckoning," which stood for "deduced reckoning"—was coming into use. It involved calculating aircraft heading and course by factoring in the aircraft's speed and the effects of wind velocity and direction. Unfortunately, meteorology was an art, not a science, and often the winds, as well as weather conditions, were not as predicted by the weather man on the ground. For this reason, great emphasis still was placed on contact flying.

The theory of flying "blind" by reference to instruments in the cockpit was being taught, and pilots like Ernest learned without a doubt that trying to fly in weather the old fashioned way, "by the seat of your pants," was a certain invitation to spin, crash and burn. But the blind flying instruments were rudimentary and often unreliable. They consisted of a "needle" which indicated the direction in which the airplane was turning, a ball in a race to indicate when the plane was sideslipping, and an airspeed indicator. This was called the "needle-ball-airspeed" system.

Using these basic instruments, pilots had to develop and maintain a very high degree of proficiency to fly with a minimum degree of safety. Instrument flying, without any visual reference to the ground, was still a theory, not a reality, except for very short periods of time. In fact, it was not until September 24, 1929 that Jimmy Doolittle, then an Army lieutenant, made the first completely "blind" flight at Mitchell Field, New York. In addition to the basic needle, ball and airspeed, his aircraft had three instruments that other Army planes did not: the first version of the Sperry Gyroscope Company's artificial horizon, a sensitive Kollsman altimeter, and a radio direction finder. Years later, when the Army was suddenly ordered by President Roosevelt to carry the airmail in weather and at night, and there never had been funding to buy these instruments, flying the mail had tragic results for many Army pilots.

Ultimately, Ernest learned, it is the pilot, and the pilot alone, who controls the aircraft. He is solely responsible for his plane and must make the right decisions as he reacts to conditions beyond his control, be they weather, darkness, mechanical failure or enemy action, or he will perish.

Ernie and Tex also found time to relax with other cadets in off-duty hours. Cadets were paid little more than a subsistence wage, certainly not enough to buy and run an automobile. But one of them was Felix DuPont, of the wealthy DuPont industrial family, who had a private income. Felix owned a Buick in which the three cadets often made forays into town. Sometimes, these trips were made on evenings during the week, when cadets were not supposed to leave the base. According to a letter written by Tex, these ventures were made "to have an ice cream and talk to the girls at the drive-in."

"One night," he continued, "a young man came over to us and asked, 'You men are Brooks Field cadets, aren't you?' Being careful never to tell a lie, we answered, 'Yes, sir, but who are you?' He replied, 'I'll tell you who I am—I am Lt. Weyland, an instructor at Kelly Field. I will give you fifteen minutes to get yourselves back to Brooks before I call Sam Ellis, your Commandant of Cadets!'

"We left at that instant, and set a new speed record for Buicks. We had just jumped into our bunks and gotten under the covers fully clothed, when Lt. Ellis came storming through the barracks, shining his flashlight on every bunk. We played possum and Sam never found out we were the culprits that night." The lieutenant was Otto P. Weyland, who eventually was promoted to four star General and was Commander of Tactical Air Command, with Ernest as is his one-star Chief of Staff, in the 1950s.

In March and April, Ernest practiced basic skills, either with an instructor or when flying solo, and in May and June, he concentrated on more instruments, cross country and night flying, covering most of the sky over Texas. Finally, at the end of June, 1928, with 143 hours and 40 minutes of primary and basic flying in his log book, he was transferred to Kelly Field, on the other side of San Antonio, for Advanced training.

Two courses were offered at Kelly—bombardment or pursuit flying (today, pursuit planes are called fighters). Both Ernest and Tex requested the pursuit flying course and were accepted.

Now, they knew, they were in the Big Time. At Brooks, Ernest and Tex had mastered the basics of flying the airplane. At Kelly, they learned to employ the airplane as a weapons platform. They learned to fly in both small and large formations, sometimes "attacking" other formations. There was risk involved, which they recognized. Death in the air was not unknown. Just a few years earlier over Kelly, Lindbergh himself had been forced to bail out of his trainer at low altitude after a midair collision during a large formation exercise.

The cadets learned to fire machine guns at simulated enemy aircraft in the air and targets on the ground, and to drop bombs in all kinds of situations, from high altitudes or while skimming the hilltops. They practiced a variety of employment tactics. This was as close as they could get to the real thing, short of actually being in a war.

They began flying at Kelly in the A-3, AT-4 and AT-5, which were two seater advanced trainers. Precision was emphasized. They flew in tight formations virtually every day, honing their battle skills. They practiced some night formation flying, which in those days, with inadequate aircraft lighting and landing systems, was a tense, dangerous, and exceptionally demanding operation. They learned the finer points of single-ship acrobatic flying.

Ernest and Tex successfully met the challenge of advanced training. On Oct. 16, 1928, they flew over Kelly in a formation aerial review as part of the graduation ceremonies. Ernest led the second V of nine DH-4s in the review. Each cadet was certified an "Airplane Pilot" in the U.S. Army Air Corps. Ernest had built up 342 hours and ten minutes of flying time.

They were delighted to learn their next assignment was to the famous 1st Pursuit Group at Selfridge Field. Selfridge is at Mt. Clemens, Michigan, on the shore of Lake Ste. Clair, not far from Detroit. Lake Ste. Clair, which measures about thirty miles at its longest point, forms part of the water link between Lake Erie and Lake Huron.

Before reporting in to Selfridge, Ernie, Tex and two other cadets went on leave and drove in Tex's automobile to New York and Boston. After visiting Ernie's parents in Boston, Ernie and Tex drove to Gilbertville for a short visit. The automobile was a Wills Sainte Clair, manufactured in Michigan by a company started by Harry Wills, a former Ford executive. It was a "prestige" car, perfectly suited to the needs of a young pursuit pilot. In the company's ads, it was called the "Gray Ghost" and was touted as a machine that could travel all day at 50 miles an hour.

Unfortunately, according to Charlie Angell, the car almost gave up the ghost. Ernie and Tex, squeaking along on a burned out rear wheel bearing, barely made it into Charlie's front yard in Gilbertville. After a few hours' sleep, they hopped into Charlie's Model T Ford to look for a bearing. They found one in a parts shop, but Tex thought it was too expensive, so they went to a junk yard and found a used axle with the right kind of bearing on it. Then, Ernie and Charlie used Charlie's kitchen to chill the axle with cold water and warm the bearing with hot water, so the two could be separated. "We finally got the bearing off and changed it," says Charlie, "but there's another day gone. Then, they were off to Boston." Once again, Ernest's mechanical talent saved the day.

Ernest wore his uniform home on that trip, the only time he did so. "He looked fine," Charlie recalls, "I remember especially his shiny boots."

CHAPTER NINE

By being assigned to the 1st Pursuit Group at Selfridge, Ernest and Tex realized the dream of every young pursuit pilot in the Air Corps. The group had distinguished itself during the First World War and now contained the Air Corps' three most famous pursuit squadrons. They were the 17th "Great Snowy Owls," the 27th "Black Falcons," and the 94th "Hat-in-the-Ring" squadrons.

Eddie Rickenbacker, the American "Ace of Aces, " had been in the 94th during the war. Ernest and Tex were assigned to the 17th Squadron, which was nicknamed after one of the fiercest hunters in the skies. The new young pilots had a lot of tradition to live up to.

At the time Ernest was assigned to the group, it was equipped with several different types of aircraft, ranging from some old World War One models to the newest types in the Air Corps inventory. Among them was the Thomas Morse MB-3, designed as a U.S.-manufactured pursuit plane for the war. It did not get into production in time, and was utilized as an advanced trainer. There were several versions of the Curtiss Hawk, and the Boeing P-12, both superb pursuit planes; and the Berliner-Joyce PB-1 two-seater pursuit plane (The Berliner-Joyce Company was soon absorbed by the Consolidated Aircraft Company).

Ernest made his first flight as a full fledged U.S. Army Air Corps Airplane Pilot on November 20, 1928, flying for thirty minutes in a Curtiss P-1 Hawk. At Selfridge, he would also fly the Curtiss A-3 ground attack plane, the PB-1 mentioned above and the Curtiss O-2 dive bomber, and in the mid-Thirties, more modern aircraft as they came into the inventory.

For the first time, Ernest lived in Bachelor Officers Quarters (BOQ) . Like all the young unmarried officers at Selfridge, he had a small, two-room suite with bath. Although these young pilots were underpaid, they were after all, officers and gentlemen, and they lived accordingly. He joined the Officers Club, which provided a dining room, bar, library and game room.

When not flying, he wore the standard U.S. Army uniform: olive green twill jacket ornamented with insignia of rank on the shoulders and Air Corps winged propeller insignia on the lapels. He wore a leather "Sam Browne" belt around his waist with a strap extending diagonally across his upper torso, and olive, gray or tan trousers. He wore a lighter weight khaki uniform during the warm months of the year.

On dressy but not formal occasions, he wore riding breeches and boots, especially if, weather and temperature permitting, he flew in duty uniform. Usually he flew in a heavy, one-piece fleece-lined leather flying suit or, in temperate weather, lighter weight cloth coveralls.

For flying headgear, he wore the usual leather-covered helmet and goggles. On the ground, he chose among an olive green garrison cap with Army insignia and leather visor (which the pilots called a "wheel hat"), the soft, peaked overseas cap (also called, in the Air Corps, the flight cap), or the flat-brimmed Stetson campaign hat. At the age of 24, with his firm chin, wavy hair, direct gaze, confident grin and muscular build, he was a dashing, handsome, young pursuit pilot who had the world by the tail. Photos taken in those days show he was enjoying every minute of his exciting young life.

Until the end of 1928, Ernest practiced the basics of flying: takeoffs and landings, formation flying, with some short cross country flights mixed in for navigation training. Most of these flights lasted twenty or thirty minutes, with a few as long as an hour and a half. Cross country flights to places like Buffalo, New York, or Dayton, Ohio, might last from two to four hours.

Because he had his mechanical engineering degree from M.I.T., he was placed on orders as an assistant engineering officer in January 1929. This was an additional duty and did not relieve him of any of his normal pursuit pilot duties. In this capacity, he began flying routine test flights on aircraft that had undergone maintenance and repair and needed to be tested before being turned over to pilots for operational flying.

With a total of only 380 hours flying time, Ernest had embarked on the career path that would lead him to test fly the most advanced combat aircraft in the Air Corps and Air Force inventory, as well as aircraft of the other armed services and other nations, both friendly and enemy.

At Selfridge, as his experience level rose and his flying capabilities were recognized, he soon was ordered to carry out experimental testing of new equipment and aircraft as well as basic maintenance testing. As home of the premier pursuit group in the Army, Selfridge was regularly assigned experimental and new aircraft for operational testing after the equipment had been initially tested at Wright Field, the Army's experimental field, near Dayton, Ohio. Many of these were "one of a kind" aircraft that eventually were not accepted by the Air Corps because of shortcomings revealed in the testing process. Ernest was one of the most prominent of the Selfridge pilots who tested these aircraft.

In 1929, Ernest had another accident, this one so mild it was classified as an incident. While taxiing his Hawk out for a practice mission, his aircraft's wheels sank into a mudhole, and the aircraft pitched up on its nose. His flight log for that day reads "Put P1C 29-140 up on nose in mud taxiing out to take off April 2. Only prop." But Ernest was not the only pilot to damage a prop at Selfridge in the spring.

The large, roughly rectangular- shaped field, like all military fields in those days, was sod-covered. There were no paved runways. On a given day, the direction of takeoffs and landings depended solely on which way the wind blew (Pilots always took off and landed into the wind). Selfridge was constructed on low, level ground between a river and the shore of Lake Ste. Clair. It was often partially inundated during heavy rainstorms, and after the waters receded there were many soft spots that remained undetected until someone taxied into them.

Major Ralph Royce, 1st Pursuit Group Commander, commented in his memoirs: "The winter of 1928-29 at Selfridge Field was pretty bad. There was a lot of rain and the wet surface would freeze, then there would be a snowfall, which would blow up into drifts, and then would come relatively warm days and certain spots would thaw out. So the field would become bumpy and there were soft spots, mud holes, and even small ponds. Minor accidents became quite common due to running into those bad spots. So that winter there were frequent good-natured references to 'Lake (pilot's name),' or 'so and so's Pond' in memory of the pilots who had come to grief in those spots. The doubtful honor of having a spot so named was earned by some of the best pilots."

In 1930, a system of "French drains," which consisted of a network of gravel-filled trenches crisscrossing the field, was installed. Later, a dike was constructed, which helped to keep the field reasonably dry. Even so, sometimes a plane would nose over at the lip of a trench. In the late Thirties, Selfridge was equipped with paved runways and taxiways, and the problem was solved.

The April 2 flight was Ernest's last for more than two months, because he contracted typhoid fever. Typhoid was still a killer disease in the early 1930s; it was terribly debilitating and survivors required a long convalescence. In a letter designed to reassure his mother, the Selfridge Field flight surgeon, Captain (Dr.) L.W. Ballantyne, wrote:

"I wish to allay your fears as to the condition of your son Ernest: he has apparently contracted an infection resembling Typhoid fever, undoubtedly from drinking water while visiting a relative, Mrs. Metcalf of Roseville, Mich. " (The Army required all pilots to have annual vaccinations for typhoid. Ernest had been vaccinated, so the diagnosis was conjectural).

"He is not critically ill, but is of course as uncomfortable as one is who is suffering with typhoid. I don't think there is anything to cause you untold alarm. At present we have day and night special nurses for him and have given him every aid and comfort obtainable… . Do not worry unduly about Ernest…" (*Letter from Dr. Ballantyne at Appendix 4*)

As one notes that the good doctor states Ernest requires round-the-clock special nurses, but that he is not critically ill, one wonders what condition, short of impending death, would inspire Dr. Ballantyne to give a diagnosis of "seriously ill."

Critical or not, Ernest was physically unfit to fly for the remainder of April, the entire month of May and most of June. For the month of April and part of May, he recuperated in the hospital. From his window, he could see daily flight operations, in which he longed to participate. Then, as he grew stronger, Dr. Ballantyne permitted him to convalesce in his quarters, with limited time out of bed. Finally, in late June, he was declared fit for flying.

CHAPTER TEN

His first post-convalescent flight was a one hour and fifteen minute refamiliarization hop during which he made ten take offs and landings on June 27, 1929. His notation in his flight log on that day reads: "Right hand sure weak. Using two hands on stick."

In a very short time, however, he was strong enough to perform normal duties in the air again. In July, among other things, he logged fifteen flights during which he practiced firing machine guns on ground targets, tested a new gun sight developed by the U.S. Navy, made three flights towing banner targets for the pilots of other pursuit planes to shoot at, and tested a new type of .50 calibre machine gun.

More importantly, during that month, Ernest carried out the first operational tests in which small "gliders," instead of banners, were towed as targets for air-to-air gunnery. The Army made several glider tests over the next couple of decades, but banners, since they were cheaper and less complicated, remained in use for a long time. With the introduction of lead computing gunsights and radar ranging in the 1950s, however, glider-like "darts" covered with reflective aluminum foil came into vogue and are used today for air-to-air target practice.

Tellingly, Ernest's log for July, 1929, contains the first recorded evidence that he had a life outside the cockpit. A notation for July 12, 1929, a day on which he performed two target towing missions, reads "Met Mary Hanson." This is the second "Mary" in Ernest's life. The first "Mary" appears in a photograph taken on a Texas ranch, perhaps Tex's family's ranch, in 1928. The photo was taken, apparently, when Ernest, Tex, and some other pilots were on a day or weekend jaunt away from the base. Mary is pictured on horseback wearing slacks, tomboy shirt and short hairdo with a headband. She was pretty, and is identified in several photos only as "Mary," no last name given. The first Mary never made it into Ernest's flight log, but Mary Hanson did.

Target towing missions were flown over Lake Huron, with flights originating at Camp Creel, near Oscoda, Michigan (Camp Creel today is Wurtsmith Air Force Base, named after one of Ernest's fellow pursuit pilots who was killed). Pilots would fly from Selfridge to Oscoda, a little over an hour's flight away, and stay there for several days at a time while they practiced gunnery. It may be assumed that Mary Hanson was a resident of

Oscoda, and that Ernest met her on a visit to town, as Tex Sanders had put it while they were in flying school, "to have an ice cream and talk to the girls at the drive-in." Perhaps they were introduced by a mutual friend. We will never know, because there is no further mention of Mary Hanson in Ernest's records.

It would not be unusual for Ernest to meet and date young women. In the early years of flying, military pilots were romanticized on the radio, as well as in newspapers, magazines and Hollywood movies. Like Ernest, most of them were bachelors. Whenever they flew into a town or city for an official visit, they were feted and lionized by the townspeople. There were always plenty of local young ladies in attendance, eager to meet and socialize with the dashing young "knights of the air" who cheated death in the sky every day.

Often, weather was the potential instrument of death. In August 3, 1929, Ernest led a flight of three P-1 Hawks on a cross-country navigation training mission to Cleveland, Ohio, Randolph AFB, Tex., and return to Selfridge. On the return leg, Ernest found himself and his flight over a seemingly endless expanse of ground fog. There were, as yet, no navigation aids for flying over weather. Flying in clear air above the fog, Ernest flew "heading and time" to a position he calculated to be over Selfridge. He led the flight down to the top of the fog bank. It was too thick to see any landmarks, much less the ground. Fuel was running low. He flew a series of two-minute legs, turning 90 degrees at the end of each leg.

Finally, flying over a break in the fog, he spotted a landmark he recognized. He turned the flight in the direction of Selfridge and rocked his wings, signalling his wingmen to move in tight. They started to descend, but only 500 feet above the terrain, entered thick fog which reduced visibility to zero. Ernest "gave it the needle," and, with his wingmen, climbed steeply up into clear air. A half hour later, the three fighters were "flying on the fumes," and Ernest considered climbing up to a safe altitude to bail out. Just then, he found another hole in the fog, this one almost directly over Selfridge. They spiraled down and landed. Ernest's log notation was "Ran into fog on ground. Nellie Morgan and Grover along. Pulled up, but finally found hole and got back down. No fun."

The next day, Ernest flew to Hornell, N.Y. for an overnight visit with an equipment manufacturing company. His log for that flight reads "Met Eleanor Whiting at Hornell."

Later in the same month, on August 25th, Ernest flew with his squadron to the Cleveland Air Races where they put on demonstrations for the crowd of over 100,000 people. The Navy and Marines also flew demonstrations at the show. The Air Corps pilots flew massed simulated attack formations against ground targets and performed "tactical drills," which demonstrated how they changed formations in midair to meet simulated aerial threats.

In those early years, Brigadier General "Billy" Mitchell, the famous airpower advocate, sponsored an annual race exclusively for Army Air Corps pilots called the Mitchell Trophy Race. It was named for his brother, John B. Mitchell, who had been killed in World War I. The race was always held in conjunction with one of the prestigious national air races of the day. It differed from other air races in that all the pilots flew the same type of aircraft, making the race a real test of skill alone. Ernest was one of the "Great Snowy Owls" pilots entered in the race.

Eighteen Army pilots, each flying a Curtiss Hawk, took part. AVIATION magazine emphasized the importance of the race: "This event has been competed for since 1921 and is the goal of every Air Corps pilot. An Army pilot wants his name on the Mitchell Trophy as badly as the old commercial racers wanted their names on the famous vest of 'Casey' Jones."

One newspaper account said the 1929 Mitchell Trophy race was the most exciting race ever seen at Cleveland. Although all the Army pilots flew the Curtiss Hawk, they used different techniques to negotiate the course. There was disagreement among pilots on how to execute turns in a race. One school of thought advocated going into the turn pulling g's until the aircraft was on the verge of stalling. This made for a tight turn, covering minimum distance, but it caused the aircraft to slow down considerably. The pilot using this technique had to build his airspeed back up on the straightaways. Another school of thought advocated using a smoother pull, not as tight. This kept the speed up, but made for a larger radius of turn. Covering more distance, a pilot using this technique might fall behind in the turns.

"Considering the amazing proficiency of the group in formation flying, there was a remarkable lack of agreement about the best manner of making a turn," an AVIATION reporter wrote. "Some were exceedingly good, others distinctly slow, and the time for completing the turn around the home pylon ranged from 2.4 to 11 seconds. Angles of bank were from 60 degrees to beyond the vertical. It would be impossible to pick out any one pilot as doing the best work, but the turns made by Lieuts. A.L. Moore, Morgan, Warburton, Pringle, and Schoenlin were particularly impressive."

Ernest used the "smoother pull, not as tight" technique, which had been validated by Jimmy Doolittle as part of his thesis research for a Ph.D. in Aeronautial Engineering at M.I.T.

Many of the pilots, including Ernest, thrilled the crowd as they stayed close to the ground, their wingtips almost touching the sod on the turns. A few stayed higher, avoiding the moving aerial traffic jam down below. One pilot dove down into each turn, climbing higher on the straightaways: "Lieut. Cobb gave the crowd incipient heart failure on each lap by doing near-wingovers and coming out at from ten to thirty above the ground." The crowd gasped each time he pulled up and leveled out just before crashing into the ground.

But it soon became apparent that four pilots in the race were better than all the rest, and Ernest Warburton was one of them.

Around and around the course, ten times, the quartet pulled farther and farther ahead of the rest of the pack, trading the lead back and forth among themselves. The spectators were on their feet, waving their hats in the air and shouting themselves hoarse as they cheered the racers on. Finally, only twenty feet above the ground, the quartet swept across the finish line almost as one plane. The winner was Lieut. P.B. Wurtsmith. Lieuts. Moore and Rogers tied for second, and Ernest came in third, only 3.2 seconds behind the leader. The *Cleveland Plain Dealer* reported "It was an exceedingly close race, the fastest and by far the most thrilling of the race meet."

After the race, Ernest's mechanic discovered one of the two magnetos on his engine had failed during the race. This resulted in a degradation of engine power because at some point, half the spark plugs stopped firing. Obviously, superior piloting technique enabled him to keep up with the winner. His laconic log entry about the race was "Came in third. Engine running on only one switch. 148+ mi/hr." (His official speed was 151.816 mi/hr.). As a general overall comment he wrote: "Air Races at Cleveland. Sure had a good time. Tex and I stayed at the Hollenden Hotel. Met Ted Riekers and Peg Anton."

CHAPTER ELEVEN

At the end of the return flight from Cleveland to Selfridge, Ernest had another close call. Landing into a stiff wind, the pilots had to approach the field over the hangars. This required a steep approach to provide a short touchdown point and and sufficient rollout distance. So, on short final, each sideslipped his aircraft. Ernest's log tells what happened to him next: "Engine cut out in sideslip when landing—almost pancaked in over hangars." Apparently, the second magneto had failed at the last minute, meaning the engine lost power completely. Another Warburton close call.

Five days later, on Sept. 6, 1929, Ernest flew in a two-seater to Wright Field, Dayton, Ohio, to bring Tex back to Selfridge after Tex had ferried a C-7 there. On a four hour flight back, they dodged thunderstorms and skirted frontal weather all the way. Another "no fun" comment in Ernest's logbook.

In October 1929, Ernest continued his maintenance test work at Selfridge, but still flew other, more interesting missions. On Oct. 4, he participated in a tactical demonstration for the U.S. Army War College, which at that time was located in Washington, D.C. The planes participating in the demonstration operated out of Bolling Field, across the Anacostia River from the War College. Ernest must have had some nostalgic thoughts about Bolling, which was the destination for his first Air Service cross-country flight, back when he was in ROTC summer camp at Langley Field.

He made two trips home to Boston that month, landing at Mansfield, Mass. on one of the flights to see a friend, Bud Robertson. On Oct. 11, he gave rides in his plane to his father and his brother, Frank. A local newspaper reported "Lieut. E. K. Warburton took his father, Joseph J. Warburton, for his first airplane ride from Boston airport yesterday in an Army PT-1, and looped and stunted above their home in Brighton." Each visit home was duly recorded in local newspapers and Ernest's name was becoming well known in Massachusetts.

About a month later, Ernest was again over Hardwick, Gilbertville and Ware. A local newspaper reported: "In an Army plane he arrived over Gilbertville about 12:40 yesterday noon when everyone was returning to work. High in the air, he put on a show that was a knockout. He flew upside down, he did barrel rolls and loops and a dozen other stunts that nobody in the crowd could even name.... He is getting to be known as one of the great stars of the Army aviation service, and at the big Cleveland meet recently he took third prize."

In addition to his assigned duties, Ernest frequently volunteered to fly missions that were purely humanitarian. One such flight took place on Oct. 28, 1929, when he flew over Lake St. Claire for two hours, searching for a boat with three men in it. Unfortunately, when he found the boat, it was empty—the boat had capsized and the three men had drowned. He would, throughout his career, fly many similar volunteer missions.

And he continued his off-duty passion, hunting, going out in the woods within reasonable driving range of Selfridge whenever possible. One hunting trip was particularly notable. A local Michigan newspaper stated "One of the neatest pieces of marksmanship reported thus far is the feat of Lieut. Ernest K. Warburton, of Selfridge Field, in bagging a deer going at a dead run at a distance of 150 yards. Lt. Warburton and a party of fellow officers had been hunting near Greenbush, Mich. The deer, weighing 200 pounds and carrying an eight-point rack of horns, was shot yesterday, and Lt. Warburton returned to Selfridge Field today."

Ernest continued to carry out operational and test flights on an almost daily basis, often two or more flights a day. But as the winter closed in, with marginal and bad weather restricting flying opportunities, his monthly flying hours dropped from 50 or 60 hours a month down to 27 hours for November, 1929, and finally, only five hours and 55 minutes for December. On December 10, 1929, flying at Selfridge closed down completely, as was the custom there, to be resumed after the holidays.

During the rest of the month, Ernest and the other pilots and ground crews prepared themselves and their planes for what would turn out to be one of the most notable aviation exploits of that era—the great Arctic Patrol Flight of 1930.

CHAPTER TWELVE

The Arctic Flight was not a flight in the Arctic regions of the earth, but rather, a flight across the northern tier of the United States in the dead of winter. It was intended to demonstrate to the American public and Congress the ability of the U.S. Army Air Corps to carry out tactical operations under arctic conditions. "Not a great deal was known about winter flying in those days," Major Ralph Royce, the 1st Pursuit Group commander later wrote, "especially when it came to servicing large formations."

He noted that while airmail planes of the day routinely flew in freezing temperatures and marginal weather, there was a huge difference between pushing one plane out of a warm hangar for an airmail flight, on the one hand, and on the other, getting eighteen planes which have been sitting frozen outside overnight in a field started up and launched on a mass flight.

In the end, the Arctic Flight did fulfill Air Corps objectives, although the flight took longer than planned and presented many problems its planners had not anticipated. Nevertheless, the flight was a success, due to the efforts of young airmen like Ernest. As a pilot and an assistant engineering officer, he would meet and surmount many unexpected challenges, both in the air and on the ground. In fact, at one point near the end of the Arctic Flight, he would almost lose his life.

The *New York Herald* summed it up: "Maj. Ralph Royce, commanding the 1st Pursuit Group of the United States Air Corps stationed at Selfridge Field, Mt. Clemens, Mich., related here today the story of the 3,700-mile flight of his command to Spokane, Wash., and return during January. Flying much of the time in temperatures well below zero in stormy skies and (with the pilots) suffering from frozen faces, hands and feet, seventeen of the eighteen little Curtiss Hawk pursuit planes made the tour and came through in good shape.

"They flew at altitudes ranging from ten feet above the ground to 18,000 feet. They suffered from frozen engines and the failure of heating apparatus.... .

"Every pilot in the group except Major Royce himself has been out of flying school less than eighteen months and the oldest man under his command is 27 years old." Ernest was 25, and he had logged 615 flying hours up to Jan. 10, 1930, the day the Great Arctic Flight began. Royce, on the other hand, was referred to as "at 34, ... the oldest pursuit pilot in the Air Corps." Older pursuit pilots were either assigned to desk jobs, or were dead.

Nineteen single seater P-1 Curtiss Hawks were to make the test, supported by two Ford Trimotor C-9 transports and a single-engine Douglas C-1 transport. The transports carried spare parts, including a couple of engines, new experimental radios and twenty mechanics. Because it was to be an "arctic" test, the aircraft were equipped with skis.

The original departure date was to have been Jan. 7. The itinerary called for four days of flying to reach Spokane, Wash., a day in Spokane for crew rest and maintenance work, and four days for the return trip, for a total of nine days. But, from the outset, the weather did not cooperate.

By the afternoon of January 6, there was no snow on the ground at Selfridge. The weather, however, had been consistently cold, with subfreezing temperatures that coated adjacent Lake Ste. Claire with ice. Royce ordered his planes, still equipped with wheels, to fly out of Selfridge and land on the ice. Ernest's log lists a twenty-minute flight (mostly in the traffic pattern) from "SFM to lake." The wheels were then removed from the pursuit planes and replaced with skis. By the time darkness fell, everything was in readiness for the fighters to takeoff the following morning. Skis were to be installed on the transports in the morning.

"Then," Royce wrote, "our troubles began." About nine P.M., one of the maintenance people heard a resounding "cra-a-ack!". He quickly discovered that one of the heavily loaded Ford transports had cracked the ice, and had sunk the newly created floe it was resting on to the bottom of the lake. Fortunately, the lake was not very deep near the shore, but the transport's wheels were in water over their axles. It would have to be moved onto the land. All hands were rousted out of their barracks to cope with the emergency. They all charged out onto the ice.

"That only made things worse," Royce remembered. "The added weight of the men only served to make the other Ford and the C-1 do the same thing. Then, lest the fighters sink also, all the men were ordered to return to shore." Men, four at a time, returned to the ice and attached ropes to the landing gear of the transport aircraft. Then they dragged the other ends of the ropes onto the shore to the waiting enlisted men, who ganghauled the heavily loaded transports, one at a time, onto dry land. The little fighters remained on the ice. By 3 A.M., the work was done.

Dawn brought another obstacle—in the early morning hours, a freezing drizzle had fallen, and each plane now was covered with an inch or more of ice. The pilots, from prior experience in the Michigan winter, knew that ice-covered planes can't fly. Ice is not only very heavy, but by coating the wings, it changes their cambered shape and destroys the ability to create lift.

"Now we were in a fine mess," wrote Royce. "We could not fly the planes back to the field and thaw them out in the hangars. We could not

43

build large bonfires on the ice lest we might weaken the surface and lose the planes."

The solution they found was simple but time-consuming. The men spent the day tapping the wings and fuselages with light wooden "switches" much like the ones used in those days by schoolteachers for disciplining unruly students. The wings and fuselages of the fighters were covered with taut linen. The linen gave and rebounded as it was tapped, causing the brittle ice to shatter and fall off without damaging the planes' surfaces. Only a small area could be fragmented at a time. "Even the metal-covered Fords responded to that treatment," Royce said. The job was finished by evening and the transports were turned around and repositioned so that they could be taxied onto the ice for the installation of skis. With the extra day of freezing weather, Royce was confident the ice would hold up long enough for the transports to take off.

But the next morning, before dawn, snow began to fall, and it fell heavily all day, cutting visibility to near zero. The flight was delayed another day.

Finally, on January 10, in the intermittent morning sunlight, the Arctic Patrol Flight was underway at 9:05 A.M. Led by Major Royce, the Hawks took off in flights of three, about twenty minutes apart. Ernest led the second flight. They pressed on, threading their way through light snow showers, which gave way to thick haze as they approached the Mackinac Straits. The temperature at altitude was near zero.

Looking down through the haze, Ernest guided his flight along the route, occasionally glimpsing a flight ahead or behind him. The route took them north over the snow-covered west shore of Lake Huron, along the Lower Michigan peninsula, and across the Mackinac Strait. Then they turned west along the Upper Michigan peninsula and flew along the south shore of Lake Superior to Duluth, Minnesota, where they landed and spent the first night.

Unfortunately, the transport planes with the mechanics and spare parts did not fare as well as the fighters. Back at Selfridge, they had trouble getting their engines started and got off late. A combination of weather and a couple of engine failures prevented them from catching up with the fighters on the entire outbound leg to Spokane. "For the next eight days," Royce said, "all the work on the fighters was done by the pilots." The onus was now on Ernest and another engineering officer to keep the little pursuit planes flying.

New problems began to crop up immediately. Tex Sanders later reported on an important one: "the skis, designed at Air Materiel Command, worked fine except for one flaw. The elastic shock cords which were supposed to pull the nose of the skis up after takeoff froze solid and lost their elasticity, so the ski noses stayed down, creating a terrible drag on the airplane. Just a minor AMC mistake." For the rest of the trip, the pilots removed the shock cords after landing, kept them warm overnight in their hotel rooms, and then reinstalled them just before takeoff. It took three pilots, two of them pulling to stretch the shock cord and one to handle the fastening nuts, to remove or reinstall a shock cord. Skinned knuckles and frostbitten fingers became daily hazards.

On the way to Duluth, they made a stop for fuel at St. Ignace, Michigan, landing there at noon. "The field at St. Ignace had been hacked out of a second growth forest by a Mr. Wing, an air enthusiast," Royce wrote. "It was rather short and, as we had no brakes on the skis, we landed as short as we could, using all of the field, and then had to slide around in a big ground loop at the end." Everyone got on the ground safely. The pilots refueled their planes, had lunch, and took off for Duluth.

Arriving at Duluth three hours later, they landed on frozen Lake Superior near the Yacht Club, where several dozen automobiles had been parked to mark the landing area.

Ernest's log shows two flights for Jan. 10, 1930, to St. Ignace and Duluth, for a total of six hours flying time.

The temperature aloft and at Duluth was much colder than it had been at Selfridge. There were no heaters in the open cockpits. "We had the best winter clothing the Army could buy in those days," Royce later said. "Our heavy leather one-piece suits were lined with layers of cloth or fur. We wore heavy gloves and boots, and heavy socks. Under our helmets, most of us wore a woman's silk stocking pulled down across the face, with the loose end wound around the neck. This, it was hoped, would reduce the chance of windburn and frostbite." Nevertheless, the pilots were thoroughly cold and walked with stiffened joints at the end of each leg of the flight.

Each pilot also donned a leather face shield with eye holes. "Some were of newfangled design that covered the neck and even fitted under the helmet." One of the pilots, Royce remembered, thought that putting grease on his face would reduce the chance of frostbite. The grease he used was camphor ice. "The idea may have been a good one, but nobody ever tried it out again after seeing the results. The camphor ice made his nose run and when he landed after three hours in freezing weather, he had a very long, slimy looking icicle hanging from the end of his face mask!"

Some pilots had experimental "heat packs" to which a couple of teaspoons of water were added just before takeoff. Placed inside their flying suits, "they did give out heat for about a half hour, then they froze solid. We learned to put on all of our clothing before leaving our hotels and not to take it off until we got into a warm room after the flights." The pilots were amused to discover that most of the small town hotels they stayed in had no fire escapes. Instead, each room was equipped with a coil of rope tied to the radiator. In case of fire, the occupant would throw the rope out the window and then slide down to the ground. Fortunately, there were no hotel fires during the trip.

But there were other hazards. Special cold weather goggles, designed by Air Materiel Command, were a disappointment. They fogged up and then frosted over, so that the pilots had to take them off in order to see where they were going.

They expected trouble starting the engines because the extreme cold—at or below zero— could cause the engine oil to congeal overnight into an almost solid mass. This made it very hard to turn them over, so all the engines were drained of oil at the end of the first day. The radiators were left filled with antifreeze. Then, after storing the oil in a warm place and filling the fuel tanks by hand pump, the pilots, cold and tired, departed for their hotel in Duluth.

The next morning, the pilots used funnels to pour the oil back into their engines. They turned them over, pulling the propellers through by hand, to get some of the oil circulating. Then they went through the laborious job of getting them started. To start an engine, they inserted a long-handled crank through the side of the engine cowling into the inertia starter, which was mounted on the back of the engine. Two men rotated the crank faster and faster to get a heavy flywheel inside the starter turning at thousands of revolutions per minute. When the sound of the spinning wheel reached a high pitch that sounded "right," the pilot in the cockpit would engage a clutch and the torque generated by the heavy flywheel would be transmitted to the engine, which would begin to turn. The pilot switched on the magnetos, which sent electrical power to the sparkplugs in each cylinder, and then opened the throttle to provide fuel. Theoretically, the engine would then rev up and the pilot would be on his way.

Unfortunately, the cold lubricating oil inside the starters had congealed into a gluelike substance which made it tough to get the inertia flywheel turning up to speed. Then, too, the cold affected the operation of the engines themselves, diminishing the strength of the spark and hindering the gasoline from vaporizing normally. This made it difficult for the engine to "catch." "So, that morning," Royce wrote, "we had to work up quite a sweat getting all the engines running okay. One, in particular, gave us a lot of trouble and we took turns on that crank, two at a time, until we were almost played out. Finally, it started okay and we were ready to go."

Only Tex Sanders had foreseen the problem. "Before leaving Selfridge," he wrote, "I had instructed my crew chief to remove the starter from the engine, drain it of oil, wash it out with gasoline, and put it back without a vestige of oil in it. Thus, I had the only engine which would start without too much effort." Unfortunately, the other pilots could not implement Tex's idea in the field, with no maintenance stands or proper tools.

And the starting procedure led to another problem, Major Royce said. "The work always got us sweaty in our flying togs, which made us very cold because we would still be wet when the icy slipstream hit us in the air."

Throughout the trip, upon arriving at a destination, pilots were feted at luncheons and dinners and treated as celebrities. Royce used these occasions to promote the Army Air Corps."I usually made at least one speech a day," Royce reported, "and usually two—one at lunch and one at dinner. One day, I made five, talking at three schools in addition to the usual lunch and dinner audiences."

CHAPTER THIRTEEN

On January 11, all the fighters took off from Duluth in good weather. On their westerly route, they looked down upon the huge open pit iron mines of the Mesabi Range and then flew over Lake Itasca, the source of the Mississippi River. The terrain below became more and more rolling as they traversed the northern Great Plains. They then angled northwestward and flew to Grand Forks, North Dakota, "where we found a nice little airport, landed and were met by quite a group of local people and taken into the hotel for lunch." There, Royce made another speech and all pilots returned to their planes and all got off without difficulty.

As they flew westward, the air became progressively colder and the rising terrain of the high plains below them was covered with deep snow. Their route generally followed the railroad that led to their next destination, which was Minot, North Dakota.

Major Royce's aircraft was very sluggish on takeoff from Grand Forks. He had to make three tries before finally getting airborne just before hitting the airport fence. Once Royce was in the air, his wingman flew under his aircraft and observed the thin aluminum covering on the bottom of Royce's skis had been caved in. Only the steel framework remained, and it had acted as a brake on the snow. Upon landing at Minot, an inspection of all the aircraft revealed that the skis on several of the other pursuit planes had deteriorated. Spare skis were in the transport aircraft, which had been left far behind by Royce's armada.

"It fell to Capt. Marion L. Elliott, who I pressed into service as acting Engineering Officer, and Lieut. Ernest K. Warburton, Assistant Engineering Officer, to somehow effect repairs. The two of them hopped around and discovered some steel sewer pipe in town that had grooves similar to the ski bottoms that had worn away. They had the pipes opened up and laid out flat. They then cut them into sections to fit the skis and had them bolted on. While it added about sixty pounds to each aircraft, it worked. So, again, we had surmounted in the field, under the severest conditions, a difficulty presented by a deficiency in our equipment."

Unfortunately, Ernest's ski frames were badly damaged while this work was going on, and had to be replaced by wheels.

On the morning of January 12th, the pilots were transported by school bus to the Minot airfield. "Brother," wrote Royce, "it had really turned cold!"

The engines were so cold that, even with warmed oil inside them, it took two men to pull a propeller through one revolution. Lieut. Theo Bolen, whose home town was Minot, was the first to try a start. With two men cranking, he waited until the sound of the inertia starter had reached the right pitch. Then, he yelled "Contact!" and engaged the clutch on the engine. The propeller moved about six inches and stopped.

"Come on," Royce shouted, "Let's get this starter whining 'way up in High C and that will start it!" A fresh two-man team began cranking the starter. At the proper time, Bolen shouted "Contact!" again and moved the clutch lever. "The prop turned a half revolution and we heard a loud 'Thud'," Royce said. They removed the rear engine cowling and discovered the starter had snapped off the back of the engine, taking a chunk of the crankcase with it. In the extreme cold, the crankcase metal became brittle and the lubricating oil in the starters and the engines had congealed into a nearly solid mass. "That meant getting a new engine for Bolen, who got to spend a week in his hometown," Royce said. "It also meant we had to find some way to preheat the engines. Warburton suggested borrowing plumber's blow torches, called plumber's pots, for preheating. In plumbing, they were used to heat solder and melt lead.

"He and Elliott showed us how to place a pot on the ground under an engine, with a stove pipe directing the heat up to the engine, which they covered with a canvas tarpaulin, right down to the ground. It worked! Working with three aircraft at a time, we found we could get an engine started in about half an hour."

Ernest's common sense had saved the day again. But refitting the skis and finding a way to heat the engines took a whole day, so the group stayed two days at Minot.

They took off on the morning of January 13th and, still following the railroad, flew to Glasgow, Montana, where they stopped to refuel and have lunch. At Glasgow, according to *The Service News*, "Handicapped by his wheel landing gear, Lieut. Warburton nevertheless made a nice landing on the snow."

The frigid air had grown even colder as the trip progressed. During the two-hour lunch break with its requisite speech by Royce, the pilots took turns starting the engines every half hour to keep them from freezing. They were able to take off with no additional problems, headed for Great Falls. They continued to fly in flights of three, with a half hour interval between flights.

But then the enroute weather turned bad. Solid clouds had moved above the route of flight and, in places, heavy snow showers cut visibility to zero. The frostbitten voyagers were now circumnavigating the Bears Paw Mountains, hoping to avoid the heavier snow showers. Ernest and his flight of three were last to get off and were forced to detour from the planned route by the fast-moving weather. They flew northward, away from the Bears Paws, and intercepted the Great Northern Railroad, which they followed to

Havre, Montana, instead of Great Falls, landing just ahead of a heavy snow-storm. The others had detoured to the south and made it safely to Great Falls.

By the the next day, the 14th, the temperature had plummeted to 45 degrees below zero. It stayed there for four days. Royce's group remained at Great Falls for the entire four day period. Ernest's group got off from Havre and by sheer grit and determination made it through the snow showers, along the railroad, to the Rocky Mountain Front and over the Continental Divide. Mountains in this, the "main range" of the Rockies, poked up above 10,000 feet into the clouds. At times, the intrepid young men flew as high as 18,000 feet attempting to stay above the clouds, but the tops were much higher. Descending, they threaded their way through Marias Pass and landed at Kalispell, Montana, in the Flathead Valley. The townspeople had learned by radio that the Hawks were coming, and the road leading to the airport was lined with cars waiting for them to arrive. After the three pilots landed, serviced and secured their aircraft, the local newspaper reported, they were guests at a luncheon given by the women of the Presbyterian Church.

By now, the pilots were not only draining and keeping their engine oil warm overnight, but the antifreeze as well. Even so, at Great Falls, Royce's group found that the plumber's pots did not provide enough heat at 45 below to start the engines.

Ernest's group of three Hawks, on the other hand, had to contend with relatively balmy air—The Daily Interlake, published in Kalispell, reported the temperature was a relatively warm seven below zero. The Kalispell group could have taken off the next day for Spokane, but Royce telephoned orders to remain in Kalispell until all aircraft could get off for the final leg.

To help Royce's group, the Great Falls city fathers mounted a steam boiler on a horse drawn wagon and pulled it out to the airfield, and steam was piped through the engines to warm them before the oil and antifreeze were poured back in. But it took until 5 P.M. to get all the engines started, so they called it off for another day because of impending darkness.

Then they discovered the hot steam, under pressure, had caused the radiators of three of the fighters to develop leaks, and they had to be repaired. On the 15th, six aircraft got off, but were turned back by weather in the high Rocky Mountain passes to the west. They returned to Great Falls. The next day, all the Hawks got off, but the passes were still cloud bound, so most returned to their field. Ernest's flight was joined at Kalispell by six of the pursuit planes and one transport while the rest remained with Royce at Great Falls.

Finally, on January 17th, the weather cleared somewhat and all planes got off safely for Spokane, Washington, the western terminus of the flight. But there was trouble in the air. One pilot, Capt. Elliott, Royce's acting engineering officer, experienced engine failure and made a forced landing in a farmer's field only 35 miles west of Great Falls. The farmer hooked up his two-horse sleigh and spent 23 hours transporting Elliott back to Great Falls.

Elliott telegraphed Selfridge for a new engine, which was delivered by rail in only three days. Then, with help from some people organized by the Great Falls Red Cross chapter, he installed the new engine himself, took off and caught up with the rest of the group in Spokane.

Since Ernest's group had started at Kalispell, which was closer to Spokane than Great Falls, they arrived over Spokane first. Now in a different, somewhat milder air mass west of the Continental Divide, they found no snow at the airfield. They were greeted in the air by a local National Guard plane which led them to frozen Newman Lake, where they landed. Noting that the temperature when they arrived was zero, compared to 40 below at Great Falls, Ernest's wingman Lieut. Paul W. Wolf commented to a local newspaperman: "Whew! It's hot here!"

It was at Spokane that the transport planes with their parts and mechanics finally caught up with all the fighters. Royce decided the group would spend a couple of extra days there so the mechanics could work on the airplanes.

For the first time during the expedition, the pilots had a few days off to rest in a city, and they decided to see what Spokane had to offer. They saw the sights, took in a movie, ate at some of the better restaurants and were feted at receptions and dances.

Ernest met another girl named Mary. On January 17th, after the entry showing two and a half hours of flying into Spokane, his log reads "Met Mary Gen." Her last name is not known, but he would later become engaged to Mary Gen. She was probably the first love in the dashing young fighter pilot's life, and until then perhaps the most important one.

But only in passing. Five years later he would meet Anna Miriam Ward of Hardwick, Massachusetts fall in love, and marry her.

CHAPTER FOURTEEN

By now, the Arctic Flight was getting nationwide newspaper and radio coverage. Headlines referred to the participants as "The Snow Birds." Ham radio operators kept the country informed of progress of the flight. Royce and his pilots found themselves inundated with requests for interviews, either by correspondents in Spokane or by reporters "Back East" who did their interviews by long distance telephone.

The pilots, including Ernest, took the attention in stride. Much attention was given to their physical condition. All had suffered some degree of frostbite on feet, hands or face. One had an infected foot, caused when frozen flesh had sloughed away, exposing lower layers of flesh. Royce had frozen a couple of fingers, but no amputation was required. Ernest had come through the first half of the journey virtually unscathed, but he would almost be killed on the return trip.

After five days of rest for the pilots and repairs for the fighters, the air armada took off for home on January 22, 1930. In clear, desperately cold weather, the pilots flew straight east across the Rockies, with spectacular snow-covered peaks thrusting up 10,000 feet and more into the blue. When they landed at Helena, Montana, in mid-afternoon, the temperature was twelve degrees below zero.

Anticipating trouble starting engines in the morning because of predicted extreme cold (the temperature dropped to twenty below during the night) Royce had asked the railroad for help. The pilots parked their planes on the edge of a field near a spur of the Union Pacific Railroad. In the morning, two locomotives pulled up alongside the field, and the railroad men, using hoses, piped live steam through the engines. This time, the steam pressure was kept relatively low to keep the radiators from being damaged. Aided as well by Ernest's plumber's pots, all the aircraft got started and took off without incident.

The next destination, for refueling and lunch, was Billings, Montana, which had no snow, so the pilots landed their planes on Rattlesnake Lake before a crowd of 800 spectators. The temperature was thirty below. Since the planes were shut down for a relatively short period of time and the engines remained relatively warm, all got started again and the group flew to Miles City, Montana, to spend the night. So far, the return trip looked like a cinch.

It was on the next leg, on the 24th, that things reverted to form. In the morning, Royce received a weather briefing from a man, "who," he wrote, "for the first time, impressed me with knowing what aviation weather was all about." Unfortunately the briefer didn't live up to his impression. He predicted a few light snow flurries under a solid overcast of about 1,000 feet all the way to their next destination, Bismarck, North Dakota. Since they were now back over the high plains, with no mountains to bar their way, the low ceiling did not shape up as anything to worry about.

They took off with light hearts. Before long, the light snow showers congealed into a raging blizzard. Royce led his group onward towards the east, following the Great Northern Railroad. The air was filled with white snowflakes, but the sky was black above and the airspace below became almost as dark as night. The little planes were buffeted by heavy gusts.

Heavy snow forms one of the worst hazards to visual flight. As the pilot looks ahead through his windscreen, the snow flakes going by on either side in his peripheral vision seem to be solid lines. The pilot experiences what is called "tunneling effect," which can be disorienting. If the pilot turns his head and looks directly to the side, the tunneling effect stops and he can see a short distance, but visibility ahead is virtually zero.

Royce described what happened. "The weather started to get bad. It was snowing hard and the snow was blowing thick through the air. Everything was white. Unless I kept my eyes on the railroad track and the telephone poles, I was apt to head in any direction" (They were experiencing what, today, is called a whiteout). "The light was bad and I could hardly see the instruments because it was so dark in the cockpit. The ceiling got lower. By the time we reached the North Dakota line, we were flying just above the telephone wires and crabbing badly because we had a strong wind from the northwest.

"Then, the wheat granaries and the water tower in what turned out to be Beach, North Dakota, loomed up. I pulled back on the stick to go over them and found myself flying blind in the low clouds! I pushed forward on the stick, throttled the engine back and eased down. All I could see ahead was a vast wall of white and as I got lower I saw what appeared to be wheat stubble so I decided on the spot to land and look the situation over." Landing very fast, practically at cruising speed, Royce's airplane tore through three barbed wire fences and he "ended up in a tangle of wires but right side up." To say Royce and his plane had incredible luck in surviving the landing is a monumental understatement.

With their leader gone, the other pilots were suddenly on their own. It was now every man for himself. They began to circle, looking for landing places. Buzzing overhead, in and out of the overcast, barely able to see because of the poor visibility, Royce wrote, they sounded "like a swarm of giant bees."

Tex Sanders tells a different version of what transpired. "We followed the railroad tracks. Major Royce had told us to form an echelon right if we

hit any snow. Recognizing the dangers of turning into an eighteen-ship echelon, he said if he made any turns, they would be to the left." The intrepid
young men formed up into a tight echelon right, moving closer and closer
together as the snow got heavier, severely restricting visibility. Finally, their
wingtips were almost touching.

The line of planes bounced up and down as the pilots strove to keep
position in the strong storm gusts. A movement up or down by the leader
meant the number two man had to follow suit, and he would overcompen-
sate slightly, which exaggerated the movement number three had to make,
and so on, each planes' movement growing larger as it progressed through
the echelon.

Ernest, out near the end of the echelon, was in a position akin to that of
a man on the end of a giant, vertical "crack-the-whip."

"The Great Northern made a mild turn to the left," Tex said, "and that was
just ducky, but unfortunately for us the tracks then turned immediately to the
right. Our leader turned right. All hell broke loose! The formation disinte-
grated and it was every man for himself!" When Royce turned right, everybody had to bank away from him (and from each other), and in so doing, suddenly everybody lost sight of everybody else.

Tex wrote, "I came over a snow-covered field with a red barn in it, which
made a fine reference point for landing. Visibility was much better to the side
than to the front. I found I had six of our planes in an echelon off my right
wing. I tried to set up a left-hand landing pattern. Then, I saw a P-1, flying
right at the barn. He couldn't have seen it until the last instant. When he did
see it, he pulled up sharply, to about a 60 degree angle, went into the overcast and almost immediately came back out, steeply nose down, and he
crashed on the other side of the barn, right wing first. There was no fire, but
I thought surely the pilot had been killed."

The pilot was Ernest. When the echelon formation broke up, he found
himself, like the other pilots, temporarily disoriented and because of the bad
visibility, apparently alone in the virtual whiteout. Knowing almost a score of
other unseen aircraft were flailing about in near proximity naturally made
him and all the other pilots apprehensive. "Best to get this baby on the
ground," they thought. Ernest began to make left turns as he scanned the
terrain below for a landing space. He learned later that everybody was making left turns, and this probably is the sole reason there were no midair col-
lisions as they all milled around, nearly blind in the roaring blizzard.

He soon realized he was over a good-sized field and set up a final
approach. Then, as he began to ease his plane onto the ground, a building
loomed up in front of him. Later, he had no recollection of the crash: "The
last thing I remember seeing was a barn." Instinctively, he pulled the stick
back to take his plane over the barn. The bottoms of the snowclouds were
virtually on top of the barn, so he immediately found himself flying blind,
with the engine throttled back. There was no chance to throttle up. The

Hawk stalled and then plummeted, nose first, right wing down, to earth. Ernest was thrown forward and his head struck the top of the instrument panel. The farmer who found him, dazed and sitting on top of the wreckage, said Ernest handed him the aircraft's Form One with the comment, "Here, sergeant, the airplane is fine!" Actually, the plane was virtually demolished, except for the tail surfaces and left wing. There was no fire because he had the presence of mind to "cut his switches" just before the crash.

Ernest, in shock, miserably cold and with deep cuts in his forehead and chin, was taken in the farmer's horse drawn sleigh to a small clinic in Beach, where a doctor sewed up his wounds.

The farmer then transported Ernest's almost frozen flight mates by sleigh into Beach, where they found warmth and food in the town's small hotel.

The next day, when the blizzard had abated, the pilots were able to salvage the machine gun, instruments, and one magneto from Ernest's wrecked ship. They removed the undamaged tail surfaces from Ernest's plane and bolted them onto Royce's plane. Royce had shredded his lower wings and tail surfaces on the barbed wire fences which brought him to a stop, and one fence post had slashed the bottom of his fuselage. Six pilots at a time, Royce included, took turns lying on their backs under the plane for most of the day, sewing up the gashes in the linen to make the Hawk airworthy again. They used curved surgical needles they had obtained from the doctor in Beach.

Meanwhile, Ernest, insisting he wanted to continue the flight even though he no longer had an aircraft, was transferred by rail, still on a stretcher, to a hospital at Fort Lincoln, near Bismarck, N.D. After a good night's sleep in the hospital, he had recovered well enough to climb into a sleeping compartment aboard a train for the trip back to Selfridge.

After Ernest left the group, Royce's armada took four days to fly back to Selfridge, twice being forced to turn back by snowstorms. They finished the trip by flying in review over the flight line.

The planned nine-day trip had taken nineteen. Yet, the airmen had proved that with typical American ingenuity they could keep their planes operational in the worst kind of Arctic-like conditions, with the loss of only one, on a 3,700-mile aerial odyssey. It was a triumph of gallant men and tough machines over truly terrible weather conditions.

It is interesting to note that Royce, in his after-action report, gave full credit to the lowly plumber's pots for the overall success of the Arctic Patrol. But he did not recommend the Air Corps procure them for future winter flying operations, because "they could be borrowed easily from the towns near which the planes would land."

A year later, an Assistant Secretary of War presented the Mackay Trophy to Major Royce. This trophy is awarded annually by the National Aeronautic Association to one airman for the most outstanding military aerial feat of the year. Royce accepted the award on behalf of all the 1930 Arctic Flight pilots, including Ernest.

Ernest received a commendation from the Commanding General of Headquarters, Sixth Corps Area, written in the stilted military prose style of the day:

"COMMENDATION FOR SECOND LIEUTENANT ERNEST K. WARBURTON:

1. For the excellent manner in which you performed, often under extremely adverse conditions, the duties assigned to you as a member of the flight of the First Pursuit Group from Selfridge Field, Michigan, to Spokane, Washington, and return, during the month of January, 1930.

2. I desire to sympathize with you in your accident at Beach, North Dakota, and desire to commend you upon the spirit you showed in desiring to work and continue on even when seriously injured.

(signed) Frank Parke
Major General, U.S. Army Commanding"

CHAPTER FIFTEEN

Ernest's injuries grounded him for the rest of January and all of February, 1930, but they did not keep him from moving on to the next phase of his flying career. He was very good at low level stunt flying, as shown by his frequent airborne visits to his home town, and he wanted to do more of it. He proposed reactivation of the First Pursuit Group's aerial demonstration team, which had operated for a time in the Twenties. His timing was right.

The Great Depression, heralded by the stock market crash of October 1929, had begun in earnest. Years before the crash, as the memory of World War One faded in the Congressional consciousness, the Army and Navy began to face steadily diminishing budgets. A planned 24,000-man Air Corps at the end of the war had been reduced to 12,000. The other services suffered as well. It was natural that the services turned up the heat on their public relations programs to increase citizen awareness of how important the military was to the health of the nation.

Since the end of World War I, the air arms of the Army, Navy and Marines had been staging public aerial demonstrations to spark recruiting and obtain favorable funding decisions in Congress. Usually, these had been mock air and ground battles which showed how the Services would act in war. Along with these massed flights, acrobatic demonstrations were put on by individual pilots.

The Services tried to outdo each other with their demonstrations, carried out before crowds of hundreds of thousands at the great civilian airshows in Cleveland, Chicago, New York, and other cities. A favorite, spectacular display put on by the First Pursuit Group at several airshows was the "Lufberry Circle." In this event, an entire squadron of eighteen fighters would circle in a kind of "follow the leader" snake dance, one closely behind the other, roaring around over the field at low altitude, climbing, diving, zooming and turning. The crowds loved it. The Navy's counter to this was the "squirrel cage"—six fighters simultaneously flying a loop, nose to tail. The Marines competed with an aerobatic trio in which the leader flew the entire show upside down.

These maneuvers emphasized the importance of precision flying, demonstrated how fighters interacted in the air and provided an exciting public relations tool to keep the services in the public eye.

As the Hoover Administration began a series of what proved to be ineffectual economic measures to stop the nation's downward economic slide, military public relations efforts intensified.

Now, to heighten the public's interest in the military, the Services established official aerial demonstration teams to perform low level aerobatics at the giant air meets and at local air shows, which drew thousands of spectators in their own right.

Ernest requested and received permission to reform the Selfridge Field aerial demonstration team that had performed informally in the Twenties. He was appointed leader in March, 1930. It is believed to be the first such official military stunt team and was the forerunner of today's U.S. Air Force "Thunderbirds." The little troupe became famous before airshow audiences across the nation. Journalists dubbed the team "The Three Musketeers." They flew the Boeing P-12, the hottest pursuit plane of the day.

Ernest's two wingmen in his "sensational stunting trio," as one newspaper labeled them, were Lieutenants Robert W. Burns and Hanlon VanAuken. In his flight log, Ernest refers to them as "Bobby" and "Van."

In addition to his regular flying, Ernest began frequent practice formation flights with his new team mates. The three young airmen practiced every conceivable formation—three-ship "V," echelon left, echelon right, in trail, line abreast, stacked up, stacked down, and others. At times, Ernest flew inverted with his two wingmen right side up, and sometimes they would fly inverted on his wing while he flew right side up.

During their air shows, they flew as one plane, looping, rolling, diving, zooming, with only three feet clearance between wingtips. To give the show variety, they would split up at times for individual maneuvers. One of Ernest's specialties was to climb to 3,000 feet above the crowd and enter a maneuver the public called a tailspin. He would spin down, turn after turn, lower and lower, while the spectators counted the turns aloud, their apprehension growing as he came nearer and nearer to earth. Then, at the last possible second, he would kick his plane out of the spin, seemingly grazing the ground on the pullout. This always elicited relieved gasps, delighted cheers and tumultuous applause from the spectators.

The spin demonstration was not as risky as it looked—recovery from spins was in every pilot's training syllabus—but it was not a perfected stunt. Many years after he retired, Ernest related to his son Frank a close call he had while practicing for one of the early shows. From experience, he knew how much altitude his plane lost for each revolution in a spin and how much was required to effect a safe recovery. He planned to start the spin at a certain altitude, fly the plane through a set number of turns, and then recover, pulling out three hundred feet above the airfield. In this particular practice session, he went through his procedure, but on the pullout, he came frighteningly close to smashing into the ground. So, on "show day," he added several hundred feet to the planned spin recovery altitude and was able to safely fly the event.

His calculations were not at fault. The problem was the rudimentary altimeter installed in military planes at that time. It simply wasn't calibrated precisely enough for stunt work, or for flying in instrument conditions, and could be off by more than a hundred feet. Pilots doing low level demonstrations found it was better to rely on their own depth perception and judgment rather than their instruments. Modern altimeters are far more precise.

Ernest developed one maneuver no other acrobatic team could do at that time— a formation slow roll, with the three aircraft line abreast. A slow roll looks simple, but in reality is complicated, even if performed by only one aircraft. The trio flew line abreast as if the three ships were one, with Ernest as the fuselage and the other two his wings. This required extremely smooth flying. Ernest led his trio in a shallow dive to pick up airspeed and then raised the nose of his plane to about ten degrees above the horizon, as his two wingmen emulated his maneuver exactly.

Next, Ernest slowly began to roll inverted, smoothly coordinating stick and rudder as the wingmen maintained their proper positions on each wing. As the three aircraft rolled towards ninety degrees of roll, when their wings would be perpendicular to the ground, Ernest gradually fed in "top rudder" to keep the nose up. Then, as the roll progressed to 180 degrees, when they would be upside down, he smoothly neutralized the rudder while at the same time moving the control stick forward to keep the nose pointing slightly above the horizon. If he allowed the nose to drop, the flight would descend and quickly crash into the ground, with tragic results for all three pilots. Without pausing upside down, he continued rolling, again using the rudder to keep the nose up as the three planes passed through the 270 degree point, gradually relaxing rudder pressure and feeding in back stick pressure as they returned to the normal upright position.

This maneuver had to be done smoothly, especially when the trio was rolling between the wings vertical positions of ninety and 270 degrees. Any jerky or sudden movement by Ernest could throw his wingmen out of position or cause them to stall out and crash. The lives of Burns and Van Auken were in his hands through all the maneuvers of every demonstration, but never more than while they were performing the line abreast slow roll.

The three Musketeers spent much of every show inverted, each man secured in his cockpit only by his safety belt. It was of standard design, with a "single point quick release" buckle. This buckle could be easily unlatched and allow the pilot to exit the cockpit quickly in case of fire other emergency. Ernest, Bobby and Van talked over the possibility of a belt somehow becoming unlatched while they were inverted, allowing one of them to tumble out at too low an altitude to deploy his parachute, with the obvious fatal result. As an added safety feature, the three stunters decided to fasten a large elastic band over their latches to keep them from snapping open. This band did its duty well, and a safety belt never came unlatched inadvertently while they practiced or performed in a show. It seemed to be the perfect safeguard against a potentially fatal event. Some months later, however, Ernest's elastic band would have the opposite effect and almost cost him his life as he tried to bail out of a flaming plane.

The three young airmen practiced intensively for each air show. Inevitably, they had close calls. While practicing for one show at Selfridge, they entered a maneuver with Bobby Burns directly under Ernest and Van Auken under Burns. Suddenly, Burns flew too close to Ernest and his whirling propeller ripped off one of Ernest's wheels, leaving him with only one wheel for landing. Bobby's propeller was shattered and the engine began to run rough. The midair collision took place directly over Selfridge, so Burns killed his engine and glided to a good landing on the field.

Van Auken flew close under Ernest's plane to assess the damage. He then joined up on his wing and signalled that Ernest would have to make a landing on only one wheel. The base fire station dispatched a fire engine and crew to stand by the edge of the runway in case Ernest nosed over or crashed and caught on fire. He skillfully brought his craft down, landed on the good wheel, and held the wing up on the no wheel side as long as possible. As his plane slowed, lift decreased and he allowed the wingtip to slowly drop until it touched the sod. The aircraft then swung around in a low speed ground loop and came to a stop with no further damage. Just another average day in the life of Ernest K. Warburton! The Three Musketeers' performance the next day was flawless.

Aerial demonstrations did not take place every day. Most of Ernest's work was "routine" military flying, which in itself was exciting and risky. He flew frequently with squadron mates to Aberdeen Proving Ground, Md., the Army's big artillery development and training base on Chesapeake Bay. There, they flew as simulated invader air forces, "attacking" Aberdeen from over the bay. At times, they towed targets on long cables for antiaircraft artillery units to shoot at and flew as targets themselves while the artillerymen practiced tracking (but not firing). The pilots also practiced intercepting "enemy" planes in the air.

As an assistant engineering officer, Ernest flew many times to Buffalo, N.Y., where he consulted on developmental matters with the Curtiss Aircraft Company. By now, with normal operational flying, maintenance test hops, cross country flights to perform demonstrations and administrative flights like the ones to Buffalo, Ernest was logging between 65 and 75 flying hours per month.

Considering the rigors of fighter flying this was (and would be today) a lot of flying time. Ernest loved it.

He was an expert shot in the air, just as he was while hunting on the ground, and was on the First Pursuit Group gunnery team. In August 1930, the team won the annual Army bombing and gunnery matches at Langley Field, Va. In individual competition, Ernest came in a close second. He fired machine guns at both ground and airborne targets and dropped small "hand bombs" during the competition. Under the rules of the competition, he could not simply fly over the targets to release his ordnance. For each pass, he was required to approach the target from a specific direction, then turn and roll out in a dive for the final attack phase of the approach. Ernests' score was 744.2 points out of a possible 1,000. The winner, his teammate Lieut. A.T. Johnson, scored 807.8 points.

Their victory was significant because another Air Corps pursuit group, stationed at France Field, Panama, had won the contest for several years running. Both groups were flying the same model Boeing pursuit plane, so the First Pursuit Group pilots felt their victory proved their skills were superior to those of the other group.

The Selfridge base newspaper reported, "Members of the Pursuit Group are showing their appreciation of the good work of these pilots in the form of a presentation of a saber and a musette bag to each of the ... pilots."

Ernest flew on missions to all parts of the United States. All were interesting and adventuresome, some more than others. On Sept. 19, 1930 he was dispatched along with his teammates to participate in a demonstration at Minneapolis, Minn. As they cruised along, the trio was overtaken and passed by a civilian Lockheed Vega. The Vega was the fastest civilian aircraft flying at that time.

It was equipped with a special "speed" engine cowling and streamlined wheel fairings developed by the National Advisory Committee for Aeronautics. Ernest and his team mates were flying their Boeing P-12Cs, touted as the hottest military planes in the air. When the Vega zipped by, Ernest related, "we quickly changed from cruising speed to nose down and wide open." They caught up with the Lockheed, which was moving at 185 miles per hour, and easily kept pace. When the Vega started to climb, the P-12s outclassed it easily, climbing faster and forging ahead.

This informal race was widely reported in newspapers across the country because it demonstrated the superiority of the P-12. At that time, because of the paucity of money for military weapons development, many aviation innovations took place in the civilian sector. On more than one occasion, a "homebuilt" airplane produced for the national air races was speedier than military aircraft, much to the embarrassment of the Army and Navy. As a result, there was public speculation about how well U.S. aircraft would perform in a war against foreign aircraft. The Boeings' victory in this well-publicized informal race provided a lift for people in military aviation and was proof to the American people that their tax dollars were being wisely spent.

At Minneapolis, the three airmen took part in aerial dedication ceremonies for a new airport building and flew in an Army Relief show. For this, Capt. Hoyt flew in the wingman slot usually occupied by Bobby Burns, who was on leave. A Minneapolis newspaper report described their demonstration as "thrilling."

Nine days later, the team did another show at Cincinnati, Ohio, this time with Burns in his accustomed spot. During the solo part of the show, Ernest's log shows, "Bobby turned it on, and almost whipstalled in doing a stadium special." Their work provided thrills aplenty, for spectators and pilots alike.

Many of the mass demonstrations put on by the military for the public in those days were called "Flying Circuses" by the newspapers. A typical "circus" took place at Selfridge on Nov. 22, 1930. Fifty- four aircraft took part in several different events, including the annual Mitchell trophy race over a 120-mile closed course. The previous year, Ernest had taken third place in this race at Cleveland. He did not enter in 1930 because he was leading the "Three Musketeers" during a different part of the flying program. This year, eighteen pilots raced, the largest number ever to compete for the Mitchell Trophy.

Besides the race, spectators saw what was described in the Detroit Evening News as "one of the most pretentious airshows ever held." One event was "balloon busting," in which helium-filled balloons were released from the ground and "speared" as they rose by First Pursuit Group fighters boring in at the astounding speed of 200 miles an hour. Another event was described as "squad maneuvers" involving all 54 aircraft, divided up into "friendly" and "enemy" forces wheeling overhead in simulated massed attacks. There were "one-on-one" and "two-on-two" dogfights.

Featured, of course, was "the triple airplane stunting of the famous team of Lieuts. E.K. Warburton, R.W. Burns and H.H. VanAuken… Flying at 200 miles an hour, these three pilots, with their planes only inches apart, bank, roll, dive and maneuver in a most perilous fashion…"

Among the thousands of spellbound spectators were some of the most important people connected with military aviation, including Billy Mitchell himself. There was also Maj. Gen. James E. Fechet, Chief of the Air Corps, and F. Trubee Davis, Assistant Secretary of War. Along with them in the stands were such prominent people as Edsel Ford of the Ford Motor Company, Detroit Mayor Frank Murphy, Michigan Governor Fred W. Green, and the famous jurist and National Baseball Commissioner Judge Kenesaw Landis.

While the newspapers liked to emphasize the danger inherent in Ernest's formation stunt flying, the fact is that normal pursuit flying always had an element of danger. This was graphically illustrated by a fatal accident involving Ernest's acting squadron commander, Lieut. Lawrence.W. Koons, and two other flyers. It happened just before Christmas, 1930.

In a carefully prebriefed scenario, six fighters were to simulate an attack on a two-seater observation plane flown by Lieut. Charles M. Wilson, with Sgt. Walter Lauver as observer in the back seat. The attack took place at 1,800 feet. Two planes flew above Wilson's plane, and four below. The plan was for the upper two planes to dive past Wilson's plane, simulating an attack, after which the other four planes, in pairs, would climb up and attack from below.

After the first pair dived past Wilson, Lieut. Koons led one of the pairs from below into their attack. Making a tragic mistake, he pulled up too sharply and crashed into Wilson's plane, clipping off a wing. The two aircraft spun down to earth locked together. Only Sgt. Lauver was able to get out of the falling wreckage, but at too low an altitude for his parachute to open. All three men were killed. Making the story all the more poignant was the fact that Sgt. Lauver's wife was shopping for his Christmas presents at the time of the crash, and Lieut. Wilson's mother, who had come to Selfridge to visit her son for Christmas, had sat in on the briefing for the flight. All flying "stood down" the next day, and all the men of the First Pursuit Group attended military memorial services for their three comrades.

By the end of December, 1930, Ernest had logged 1,031 flying hours, all of it in open cockpit biplanes. Most of his flying took place in daylight because the Army did not have a large enough budget to provide proper instrumentation for much flying at night nor in any kind of cloud. But he was a seasoned pilot, more qualified than most, ready for whatever challenges lay ahead.

Aside from the usual challenges of routine flying, he had only to wait until Feb. 15, 1931 for the next adventure. As reported by the Mt. Clemens, Mich. Daily Leader, he took part in what at that time was the longest Army night flight: "Marking the longest cross country flight ever staged by the U.S. Army Air Corps at night, eighteen pursuit ships and a transport carrying six enlisted men hopped off from Selfridge Field for Washington, D.C. at six o'clock last night."

The air fleet made the 500-mile trip in two hours, 45 minutes, landing at Bolling Field in the nation's capital. The pilots were led by Capt. Ross Hoyt, who occasionally flew as one of the wingmen in the 'Three Musketeers." They followed airway beacons from Selfridge to Cleveland, and then to Pittsburgh, and from there flew "dead reckoning" through the darkness over the mountains of Pennsylvania, West Virginia and Maryland to Washington.

For the first time, instrument panel lighting had been installed, and each ship was specially equipped with external navigation lights for the trip. Following the tradition of ships at sea, each aircraft had a green light on the right wingtip, a red one on the left and a white light on the tail. These enabled the pilots to keep track of each other in the darkness. With their lights twinkling, the Daily Leader reported, "the planes glided through the night in a kaleidoscopic array of color. The red, green and white lights made a thrilling spectacle as the ships roared over the aerial route to the nation's capital."

Each Boeing P-12 was also equipped with parachute flares which were to be ignited and dropped as aids in case of a night forced landing. The flares were clamped to the leading edge of the wing. They extended about six inches below the wing so that, when released, they would not foul it or set fire to the plane. A release cable led from each flare into the cockpit. The flares had been tested before the trip in flights between Dayton, Ohio, and Selfridge by

Ernest, assistant engineering officer of the 17th Squadron, and Lieut. A. T. Johnson, the assistant armaments officer of the 94th Squadron. Theoretically, the parachute flares would burn long enough to enable the pilot of a crippled plane to pick out a suitable landing place in the gloom below. If an engine failed over the mountains, the pilot was to deploy his flares, look for a suitable parachute landing area, and then bail out.

Ernest, Bobby Burns and Hanolin Van Auken were among the nineteen pilots on the aerial voyage. After landing, the young officers had a late supper at the Bolling Officers Club and spent the night in Visiting Officers Quarters. They did a little sightseeing around Washington the next day. They took off for the return trip the next night, circled the Capitol *en masse* with lights flashing and returned to Selfridge without incident. Hopefully, the flight demonstrated the flexibility of airpower to the Congress, which was still parsimonious in military appropriations.

Each pilot on the flight received a letter of commendation from Maj. Gen. Frank Parker, Commanding General of the Sixth Corps Area. This commendation was placed with the efficiency report on each man, which provided an extra boost for promotion.

Ernest had two more "interesting" flights among the routine ones that month. He was flying a single-engine C-14 with five passengers on board from Selfridge to Camp Skeel when the engine failed and he made a dead-stick landing in a field. A mechanic was flown in, repairs were made, and Ernest and his passengers went on their way.

Danger from the weather was always present. On March 9, 1931, Ernest and Bobby were on a cross country to Cleveland when they were caught in a blinding snow storm over Lake Erie. Things looked grim until, in Ernest's words, "we landed on Kelley's Island for a while in a cow pasture." When the snow lightened, they took off and continued the flight to Cleveland, returning without incident to Selfridge the next day.

During this period of his life, Ernest pursued his romance with Mary Gen, whom he had met in Spokane during the "Arctic Flight." According to his log, she traveled to Detroit to visit him during his convalescence after his Arctic Flight crash. Then, in September, 1930, he took the "Three Musketeers" to Cincinnati, Ohio, for a show, where Mary Gen met him. In October, he saw her in Detroit and again in St. Louis.

On Nov. 28, the Musketeers performed during the halftime break at the Army-Notre Dame football game in Chicago and afterwards he took Mary Gen for a hop in a two-seater. The romance apparently ended shortly thereafter, for reasons unknown. He does not mention Mary Gen again in his log. Then, in January 1931 during a trip to Pittsburgh, he noted "Bobby, Van and I got dates—terrible." Apparently, like the other young bachelor pilots of the day, he was back to playing the field.

CHAPTER SIXTEEN

Ernest, with a little over 1,200 flying hours, had now established himself as a first-rate pilot in the 1st Pursuit Group. This was demonstrated on April 6, 1931, when he was selected to lead a huge formation of 24 pursuit planes as part of a 53 pursuit plane Army Day flyover of Detroit. The feat garnered a page-wide photo in the Detroit Evening Times.

The Three Musketeers continued to fly demonstrations in 1931. On April 18, they flew to Scott Field, Illinois, near St. Louis, Missouri, to appear before an audience of several thousand on Boy Scout Day. Once again, Ernest noted in his flight log "We turned it on." They must have, because the commanding officer at Scott sent the following commendation to the commanding officer, Selfridge: "The Commanding Officer desires to express his appreciation for the assistance rendered by the airplanes from your station in connection with 'Boy Scout Day,' at this station. The demonstration of formation flying by the flight of the 17th Pursuit Squadron, led by 2nd Lieutenant Ernest K. Warburton, was the finest exhibition of its kind ever seen at this field and was greatly appreciated by the visiting scouts."

Later that same month, Ernest had another close call, and this one almost killed him. On April 29, 1931, the First Pursuit Group had another huge formation of 50 planes in the air, this time over Selfridge and the surrounding countryside. Divided into four squadrons, they were perfecting group assembly procedures in preparation for coastal defense exercises to be held over the Atlantic Ocean in May. Ernest was not part of the group, but happened to be flying nearby testing a new Pratt & Whitney Wasp engine on a Boeing P-12 fighter.

The practice exercise was being observed by a V.I.P. (whose name has been lost to history) flying with Major Royce in a large monoplane at the rear of the formation. As Ernest's flight path took him below and to the side of the monoplane, Royce saw him and made a horizontal twirling motion with his index finger, which Ernest interpreted to mean "Do a slow roll."

Ernest started the roll, but as soon as his ship became inverted, he was shocked to see and smell raw gasoline gush from under the engine cowling. Instantly, the hot engine exhaust ignited the stream of gasoline. Horrified spectators on the ground saw the little fighter burst into flames. In just a few seconds, the entire fuselage, the inner portion of the upper wing and the tail surfaces were engulfed in fire and blazing fiercely. Ernest knew his only chance for survival was to bail out. He rolled the plane upright. The cockpit filled with hot flames and choking smoke. His plane was becoming a fiery coffin. Instinctively, he kicked right rudder and applied left stick to put the plane into a sideslip so that the slipstream would carry the searing heat away from the cockpit. Trying to keep the ship under control, he grasped the stick with his left hand and attempted to release the safety belt buckle with his right. But to no avail—his heavy leather flying glove got in the way of his efforts to remove the elastic band he had placed over the belt release as an extra safety device. He would need both hands to remove the right glove. Still holding full right rudder, he had to let go of the stick. When he did, the aircraft entered a vicious snap roll.

Ernest could feel the roaring flames licking about his face. He concentrated on pulling his glove off so he could release the elastic band with his bare hand. With no hand at the controls and part of the control surfaces burned away, the ship continued a series of wild gyrations as it plunged earthward. Some spectators on the ground said they thought he was stunt flying. He succeeded in getting the right glove off. Now Ernest's bare hand was being singed. His helmet and flight suit were smoldering. The plane, out of control and burning fiercely, plummeted toward the hard ground below.

Finally, only about 300 feet above the ground, blinded by smoke and flames, Ernest was able to release the belt, stand up and dive out of the cockpit. The fighter's horizontal stabilizer smashed into his back, inflicting excruciating pain. Twisting around and kicking himself clear, he yanked the ripcord. Both parachute and flying suit were blazing. He swung once like a pendulum under the parachute canopy, and struck the ground with a thud, injuring his legs and further injuring his back. The parachute had not completely checked his descent. Because Ernest had gotten out at such a low altitude and was so close to the ground before his 'chute opened, Royce, who had circled to watch the crash, later stated he thought Ernest had gone in with the plane.

Ernest crunched to earth in a small field at the intersection of Six Mile and Southfield Roads in Detroit. His aircraft, now a charred hulk, crashed a few hundred feet away. One newspaper reported the plane had exploded scant seconds after Ernest bailed out. It was a total loss.

On the ground in excruciating pain, he released himself from the harness of his smoldering parachute and used his gloved left hand to beat out the flames on his flying suit. A passing motorist helped him to his feet, directed him to lie down on the rear seat of his car, and rushed him to the Detroit hospital. There, doctors treated him for burns of the hands and face and scratches and contusions on both legs. His heavy flying clothing, helmet and goggles had protected most of his body and face from the flames. His condition was listed as "serious" at first but then upgraded to "guarded."

The next day, he was moved by ambulance to the Selfridge hospital. Miraculously, his burns were not serious. His collision with the horizontal stabilizer had seriously injured his back, although the examining doctors thought it was just a bad muscle strain. For the rest of his life he would suffer periods of sometimes excruciating lower back pain. If a full medical examination had been carried out and his true medical condition determined, he probably would have had grounds for a medical retirement with full pay. But Ernest would never have thought of giving up flying. He remained on active duty.

Later, an accident investigating board determined the gasoline cap under the engine cowling had been improperly tightened (or not replaced) by the mechanic who fueled the plane. The cap was not visible to the pilot during his preflight inspection. When Ernest rolled inverted, it simply popped off, allowing the gasoline to gush out and burst into flame. Years later, in describing the event to his son, Frank, Ernest said "The V.I.P. couldn't understand why this harrowing stunt had been performed just for him."

Ernest noted laconically in his log "Jumped when P-12D 31-153 caught on fire in the air—sure almost got me—3,000 down to 500 feet before I could get out. Could not get elastic off belt. No more elastics for me. Sick on Post for a month, then put on another month's sick leave." He did not fly again until June 28, 1931, when he piloted a C-4A transport to Oscoda. Typically, he had another close call on this trip when he flew into a rare early summer snowstorm at high altitude, but he was able to land safely and wait until the storm passed.

CHAPTER SEVENTEEN

When he came back on flying duty, Royce offered Ernest the opportunity to attend the prestigious Air Corps Engineering School at Wright Field. He eagerly accepted the offer. As a full-time engineering officer, he would gratify his natural mechanical interest. Also, he would get to do a lot more test flying as well as his regular operational flying.

But the young officer could not foresee a serious drawback to becoming a full-time engineering officer and test pilot: while his new career offered many more interesting flying adventures, it placed Ernest on a slower promotion track than his comrades who stayed in operational flying. When promotions sped up in the military buildup for World War Two, he quickly moved up to full Colonel. But during World War Two, his career advancement slowed.

As the years passed, an astonishing number of the pilots in the 1st Pursuit Group were promoted to General Officer. For example, by the middle of World War Two, Tex Sanders had been promoted to two-star rank while Ernest was still a Colonel. Ernest was among the last to become a Brigadier.

Why? For reasons that can only be summed up as a "peculiarity of the Service," officers in the flight test business did not advance as fast nor as far as those in operational flying and related assignments.

Although there was not an official written policy, Air Corps leaders seemed to feel that an officer in test flying had a narrowly focused career, while the other flying officers acquired broader experience in operations, operational planning, intelligence and logistics, as well as staff experience, starting at a relatively early phase in their careers. This made them more likely candidates for promotion to general officer. This situation was not apparent to most young officers like Ernest, whose mind was more on flying than career advancement. Tex Sanders, in his retirement, wrote a letter to Anna Warburton in which he said he had considered applying for the engineering school at Wright Field early in his career, but that his wing commander had talked him out of it.

By June 29, 1931, the date on which he was transferred to the Air Corps Engineering School at Wright Field, Ohio, Ernest had accumulated a total of 1,263 hours of flying time, most of it in pursuit planes. He had flown the P-1C P-12C, P-12D, C-9, PT-3A, A-3, OA-1B, P-6, Y1C-14, and C-4A.

But flying was not central to the engineering course, although pilots had to accomplish enough flying to fulfill Air Corps flight pay requirements. The emphasis was on academic subjects learned in the classroom. The class of 1932 student handbook of the Air Corps Engineering School stated "The mission (of the school) may be defined as follows: to instruct and train officers in the fundamental principles and practices of aeronautical engineering, and to provide a general technical training with an understanding of the possibilities and limitations of Air Corps materiel and equipment."

Students spent their mornings in the classroom and afternoons in the laboratories, five days a week. They spent 300 hours learning shopwork production and processes, 405 hours on strength of materials and structures, 395 hours of thermodynamics and engine design, and 55 hours on optics, armament, meteorology, radio, and aircraft instruments.

Together, they spent the year on the class project, designing a theoretical new single-engine fighter.

"Flying and athletics may be left to the discretion of the individual," the handbook schedule said. Nevertheless, Ernest got his share of flying, mostly before and after duty hours and on weekends. By the time he had finished his year at Wright Field, he had accumulated 261 hours flying various training, observation, bombardment, cargo, attack and pursuit aircraft. This gave him a grand total of 1,524 flying hours. Only sixteen hours was flown at night. This paucity of night flying experience was typical for Air Corps pilots of that time and would be a deadly limiting factor in 1934 when President Franklin D. Roosevel ordered the Air Corps to take over flying the U.S. mail.

Ernest flew on a weekend to Coshocton, Ohio, to visit a cousin, and during the Christmas holidays he made one of his frequent flying trips home, landing at Westboro, where his parents lived, on December 29th. He also put on another one of his famous airshows over Ware, Gilbertville and Hardwick.

During his assignment at Wright Field, he was in a minor accident 20 miles southwest of Dayton. His log has this notation: "Forced landing 20 mi. s. Dayton. Hit fence on takeoff." No accident details are available today, but he was not injured and the plane apparently was not seriously damaged. Interestingly, Air Corps Form no. 11, "Transcript of Flying Records" had a space for "Aircraft accidents as pilot during the fiscal year," indicating that accidents were an almost normal part of operational flying back in those early days.

CHAPTER EIGHTEEN

During the same month Ernest left Selfridge for Wright Field, Anna M. Ward, the pretty sophomore coed who had watched several of Ernest's airshows over his hometown, graduated from Hardwick High School.

Anna was a bright, self-confident person who attended Hardwick kindergarten, elementary and high schools. Her classmates called her Ann. The 1931 Hardwick High School yearbook, "Memoriae," describes her: "A winning way, a pleasing smile, dressed so neat and right in style." Her photo, however, shows a serious young woman with short blond hair who is not smiling. The yearbook also says "Ann's character may be summed up in these few words: she is a good all round sport. But these words do not tell all, for her scholastic record, her athletic reputation and her social prominence have made her a very prominent member of her class."

Anna was on the staff of the school newspaper, *The Broadcaster* (successor to the *Melting Pot*), and she was business manager of the yearbook. Apparently, she was a very good business manager—the yearbook contained 40 pages, and sixteen of those pages were filled with paid advertisements. She was secretary of her Freshman and Junior classes, in Dramatics her third year, and on the track team and girls' basketball team in Freshman, Sophomore and Junior years. She was on the committee for the Junior Prom, and was a Prize Speaker in Sophomore, Junior and Senior years. Her grades were excellent.

She intended to go to LaSalle Business College in Boston after graduation, according to the yearbook. Actually, she attended Morse Business School in Hartford, Connecticut, and then returned to the Gilbertville area, where her parents lived. Anna and Ernest had still not met, and neither had an inkling that they would.

A matchmaker would have said Anna was well suited to be a mate for Ernest—she was adventuresome and brave. She had already flown twice by the time they met. "In 1929," she recalled, "airplanes were a novelty, and in rural Gilbertville, a rarity. I was excited to see a sign in a field between Gilbertville and Ware which read 'Ten minute flight for $5.00.' Whoopee, I had to do it! With my cousin, Florence, I drove from Gilbertville in my father's Packard. We were very excited—at least I was, but Florence wouldn't go up.

"The pilot" she remembers, "was a barnstormer, typical of the breed of the times. A self-confident, hardy young man who exuded the faint aroma of gasoline, oil, cheap cigars and possibly a little whiskey. The craft was a biplane, probably a Jennie like the ones Ernest had flown early in his career. We took off from a bumpy farmer's field that is now Ware Airport, where today my son, Frank, lands his Cessna."

Anna thrilled to the roar and vibration of the engine as they raced along the ground, picking up speed for the take off. She felt the wings gather lift as the speed increased, and then experienced the excitement of every flier as the plane left the ground, and they were flying, supported only by air. She then understood the freedom of being "up" in an open cockpit biplane, with the wind whipping around her. She knew that, like the birds, fliers were unfettered, detached from the earth below and able to go in any direction. She felt no anxiety or fear, only elation.

"We flew over my home, but no one waved because no one knew I was up there. Then we flew over the countryside, a beautiful sight to behold from the air. We landed without incident, but I didn't confess my daredevil ride to my family until some time later. The experience made me aware of the thrilling possibilities of air flight, so subsequently, I took a course in aerodynamics in high school offered at night by our principal, who was interested in aviation."

Anna's second flight took place during the summer of 1931. "We were at Falmouth on Cape Cod, where my family spent a vacation each year with a wealthy aunt. I took a young cousin, Charles, for a ride in my father's Packard. We came upon a small airport where sightseeing rides were advertised. The pilot was another barnstormer, much like the pilot on my first flight. the plane could accommodate two people in the front cockpit and the pilot sat in the rear cockpit. We decided to go up.

"We flew over Buzzard's Bay and the vicinity, and I was able to identify my Aunt's house, which I pointed out to the pilot. He started flying circles above the house. Immediately, all cousins, aunts, uncles and parents came running out, waving. One of them even waved a tablecloth!

"We landed and drove home. Everyone was still in a high state of excitement, telling us we had really missed it, this plane flying around *right up there*! Who could it be, they wondered? When I told them who it was up there waving back at them, the atmosphere changed dramatically. Charles's parents were aghast that I had taken their son for an airplane ride without permission. I found myself grounded for a few days.

"Later, in honor of the occasion, my Aunt gave me a beautiful large silver bowl presented to her husband when he retired from Gilbert Woolen Mills in Gilbertville. Her presentation words were 'Many happy landings in the future.' Prophetic words. Little did she—nor I—know that as an Air Force wife I would have many."

Chapter Nineteen

After successfully completing the engineering course at Wright Field, Ernest was transferred back to Selfridge, where he found to his delight that he was assigned as Squadron Engineering Officer of the fabled 94th Pursuit Squadron. He left Wright Field on June 30, and reported in to the 94th the next day, July 1, 1932. On July 3, he began operational duty by flying a P-6E Hawk to Chicago, where he spent two days participating in a Fourth of July "military tournament" at the National Air Races, returning to Selfridge on the sixth. On the eighth, he flew his first test flight in his new job, in an experimental Y1P-16, which was a new version of the Berliner-Joyce PB-1 two-seat fighter. On the 30th he made several flights between Selfridge and Oscoda "testing large tires on P-16."

He was back in the cockpit, enthusiastically flying a wide variety of missions, including test flights, formation, and cross-country flights to various destinations. He flew many aerial gunnery missions, both as an attacker and as one of the pilots pulling airborne targets for others to shoot at. He was selected to fly in a mass Air Corps demonstration at the National Air Races in August. He made many test flights in the new Y1P-16. He flew in a "military tournament" at the Cleveland Air Races in September. He compiled 43 hours of flying time in August, 64 hours in September and 67 hours in October.

On Sept. 16, 1932, Ernest was part of a group of pilots selected to take part in a "speed flight" from Selfridge to Rockwell Field, at Coronado, California, testing the new Y1P-16s. The planes represented a technological step forward. Among other innovations, they were equipped with three-bladed propellers and new, more powerful engines. For Ernest, the main purpose of the flight was to test the reliability of the new engines.

Led by Capt. A.B. Ballard, the six planes took off from Selfridge at 4 A.M. and made the 2,200 mile flight in just under 15 hours and 30 minutes. They made fuel stops at Scott Field, Ill., Fort Sill, Okla., El Paso, Tex., and Tucson, Ariz., and then touched down at Rockwell at 7:15 P.M.

"Our flying time would have been much less, " Capt. Ballard told the San Diego Union, "but we had strong headwinds all the way. Over the Imperial Valley, there was nothing but dust, and just before reaching the coast we hit a blanket of fog. This, however, did not last long and we popped out under a clear sky. It certainly felt good, after battling through that inland fog, to see the lights of San Diego sparkling and winking in the foreground."

Although the flight did not set a record because of the headwinds, it did prove the reliability of the new engine and demonstrated for the public how speedily military aircraft could be moved across the United States. The six pilots got a good night's sleep in the same Visiting Officers Quarters as two visitors from Washington, Col. H. H. "Hap" Arnold and Maj. Karl "Tooey" Spatz. Arnold eventually became the only five-star General of the Air Force, and Spatz the first U.S. Air Force Chief of Staff. Ernest's group began the return flight to Selfridge the next morning, making the return trip in a leisurely two days.

On Oct. 20, Ernest test flew the Air Corps' newest candidate fighter, the YP-26 "Peashooter." This stubby, speedy, low-wing aircraft was the Army's first all-metal monoplane. Equipped with a 600 horsepower Pratt & Whitney engine, it was believed to be the fastest thing in the sky in 1932. He, along with the test pilots at Wright Field, must have approved it, because on December 1, when he flew it again, the aircraft's designation had been changed to P-26, indicating it was now an operational, not developmental, plane (The P-26 did not enter the operational inventory in large numbers until 1934. Over 135 were bought by the Air Corps).

In November, Ernest flew a Y1P-16 to Mitchell Field, N.Y., and on the way back stopped at a small field in Pittsfield, Mass., near his hometown, to spend the Thanksgiving holiday. Charlie Angell remembers helping him get the plane started for the trip back to Selfridge. It had been tied down in the open for three days while Ernest enjoyed the holiday at home.

"Cripes," said Charlie, "it was cold when we got to the field. Down to zero the night before! Ernie had asked his father to bring along a plumber's pot." Ernest was putting to work lessons learned on the Arctic Flight. 'They put me underneath the nose of the plane to keep the plumber's pot going and threw a tarpaulin over the cowl to keep the heat in. After a while, Ernie says 'let's try it now.' He put me and his brother Frank up on one of the wings, and he stuck a long crank into the side of the engine cowling.

"Then he told Frank and me to turn the crank while he got into the cockpit. At first we could just barely move it, but then it started turning, slowly at first, and then faster and faster. We were turning a flywheel, I guess. We were up there a long time. Jesus, I'm going to tell you that was work! Then, all of a sudden, just when we thought we were going to collapse from exhaustion, Ernie calls out 'Contact!' and he did something in the cockpit, and 'Boom!', the engine started. As soon as it did, Frank and I pulled out the crank and jumped down so we'd be out of the way.

"While the propeller ticked over and the engine warmed up," Charlie continued, "Ernie got out of the cockpit and went into a house on the edge of the field where he'd left his flying suit to keep it warm. He put it on over the regular winter garb he was wearing, climbed into the cockpit and strapped in. He gave me a signal to pull the chocks away from the wheels. Then he gave us a wave, taxied to the end of the field, turned the plane around and took off. He buzzed the field twice and set course for Detroit. Man, it was cold! How he kept warm in the open cockpit of that plane all the way to Selfridge, I'll never know. I mean, it was cold!"

Actually, Ernest flew first to Mitchell Field, New York, landing there and then flying to Selfridge, spending more than five hours aloft in the freezing air that day.

During the first part of December, he flew solo acrobatics in the new P-26, performed some more tests on the Y1P-16, took part in an aerial review and checked out in a new observation plane, the Douglas BT-2B. Then, as was customary, flying was suspended at Selfridge for the last two weeks of December and Ernest drove home for the holidays.

CHAPTER TWENTY

Returning to Selfridge in January 1933, he kept up his intensive flying sched-ule in a number of different aircraft. At the same time he got his squadron ready for another cold weather test similar to the "Arctic Flight." This time, the detachment, under the command of Maj. A.H. Gilkerson, would deploy to Duluth, Minn., where a winter base would be set up. There would be no long flight to Seattle. Ernest was designated Engineering Officer for the force. Under his supervision, cold weather testing would take place for ten days. Although there were only seven aircraft in the test, newspaper reporters, remembering the drama of the 1930 flight, kept the public inter-ested in this new adventure. The force of planes consisted of two Keystone B-4A bombers, one Ford C-4 Trimotor transport, and four pursuit planes—two Berliner-Joyce P-16s and two Boeing P-12s.

Specifics of the tests to be carried out were given in a ten-page, single-spaced letter from Air Corps Materiel Division at Wright Field to the Commander, Selfridge. "The majority of the points covered above have pre-viously been taken up with Lieutenant Warburton, your station..." read the last paragraph of the letter.

The test force of eight officers and sixteen enlisted men arrived in Duluth on Feb. 24, 1933, and remained there for ten days. They used the municipal airport as a test base. Pilots were billeted in the Cascade Hotel in downtown Duluth.

Ernest was responsible for using and testing a broad range of new cold weather innovations. He kept track of the testing in a loose leaf notebook, penciling remarks in his strong, legible handwriting.

The group tested new equipment to cover the engines when the planes were tied down in the open at night. Also tested were electrically heated fly-ing gloves as well as twelve different types of unheated gloves for the pilots, four new types of winter flying suits, and two new winter helmets. Electrically heated goggles and air heated goggles were tested . The pilots flew in temperatures of 20 below zero at altitudes as high as 20,000 feet .

Also tested were oil heaters, wheel skis, a new variable spark control, special hydraulic fluids and machine gun lubricants, as well as a variety of engine priming fluids. Many new devices had to be installed in the field. This placed a heavy responsibility on Ernest, he wrote, since "all changes have to be personally supervised because no blueprints of previous installations are available."

Ernest, the reporters noted, was the only pilot in the group who had been on the famous "Arctic Flight." While overseeing installation and testing of the new equipment, he logged 20 hours of flying time during the ten days of testing, splitting time between the two types of fighters. He also logged a little over an hour in the Ford Trimotor. The pilots practiced air-to-air gunnery and ground attack, as well as formation flying.

Conditions were much better for the "Snowbirds," as the Duluth newspapers called them, than they had been for the Arctic Flight pioneers. Temperatures, while well below freezing, were not as cold as on the famous 1930 flight, and the pilots didn't have to fly through any blizzards.

Although there was no snow on the ground when the test group arrived, there was a snowstorm the second day of their visit and they had snow for the remainder of their stay. They tried two new types of skis for the fighters, both of which had to be reinforced. Temporarily, they performed satisfactorily, Ernest wrote in his notebook, "after their bottoms had been smoothed by a couple of landings."

For the transports, a new ski type could be fastened to the wheels in such a way that the tires extended out the bottom and could be used on a hard surface. They were acceptable, Ernest noted, landing on light snow, as was the norm at Selfridge, but not on a heavy snowfall. But overall, he wrote, "Skis are washouts—the wood breaks and the steel frames are altogether too weak. Even when reinforced with four braces they still fail." In addition, he concluded that for extended operations, "metal corrugated skis are impractical." This was a significant finding, because on the Arctic Flight, Ernest had helped to jury-rig skis from flattened corrugated piping, which seemed satisfactory. Those skis, however, were used for only a few landings before the cross country flight ended. At Duluth, one set of skis was subjected to 97 landings, requiring almost continual repairs.

The new cold weather engine covers proved relatively ineffective. The crews were forced to use Ernest's stand-by, plumber's pots (which the Air Materiel people had designated "firepots") to start the engines for the first time each day. An Air Corps innovation, "heated bricks," was unsatisfactory. Canvas covers for the transport engines had to be redesigned and reworked to fit.

The heated flying gloves were a success, but the air-heated goggles fogged up and became a hindrance to visibility. Electrically-heated goggles were barely satisfactory. After several flights the pilots decided to discard them and use conventional goggles. Machine guns performed perfectly in the cold air, Ernest reported. On the other hand, new Army carburetors were "all kinds of trouble" which was corrected by changing a restrictor.

Also tested were new gasoline driven external power units for providing electrical power while starting engines. They were successful.

The Duluth tests did not have the glamour of a cross-country flight from Selfridge to the West Coast and didn't produce much copy for the newspapers. One reason is that nobody crashed in a raging blizzard as Ernest had in 1930. Another is that the group was not on a cross country odyssey with constantly changing weather and terrain. But the tests were far more significant than the Arctic Flight in that they provided much empirical data on the worth of new equipment and the implementation of new techniques for cold weather flying. During the tests, Ernest made several demonstration flights for Fox Movietone News, which filmed the flights for newsreels shown in theaters across the United States.

The tests were a success. In due course, a citation for the Commander, Selfridge Field, "copy for 2nd Lt. Ernest K. Warburton, A.C. arrived:

> "1. It is desired to commend the Commanding Officer, Officers and Enlisted personnel of the Winter Test Detachment for the excellent work performed by them in testing cold weather operations and equipment of airplanes.

> "2. The results obtained by the hard work, energy and initiative displayed by the personnel of the detachment operating under very severe weather conditions are considered of material value in the future development of cold weather flying.

> (signed)
> B.D. Foulois
> Major General, Air Corps
> Chief of the Air Corps"

After completion of the tests, Ernest returned to Selfridge and threw himself into his job with zest. In May he flew a wide variety of different aircraft and logged 120 flying hours, an astounding total for that era.

During the year, he flew to both Wright and Patterson Fields in Dayton, as well as to Louisville, Kentucky, Chicago, Illinois, Columbus, Ohio, Fort Knox, Kentucky, Chanute Field outside Chicago, Scott Field, Illinois, Langley Field, near Newport News, Va., Bolling Field in Washington, Dallas, Texas, New Orleans, Louisiana, Cleveland, Ohio, Buffalo, New York, Cadillac, Michigan, Pensacola, Florida, Nashville, Tennessee and Edgewood, Maryland. And he managed to make several overnight stops near his parents' home in Massachusetts.

Then, he was grounded for the last two weeks of July because of an ear infection. His log notation: "Sick in quarters—bad ear from surfboarding spill."

Meanwhile, overseas, in both Europe and Asia, ominous portents of a world war were taking place—the Japanese were encroaching on China and Hitler suddenly announced Germany had pulled out of the Disarmament Conference in Geneva, Switzerland.

CHAPTER TWENTY-ONE

Then, Ernest was selected to participate in what would become the newly elected Roosevelt Administration's most successful social experiment - - the Civilian Conservation Corps. He was one of 5,500 officers of the Regular Army, the Army reserve, the Navy and Marines, along with 300 contract surgeons, who directed this huge program.

By now—1933—the United States was in the depths of the worst depression in the country's history. All government budgets, including the military, were cut to the bone. Big companies had collapsed. More than 12 million people were out of work. The national unemployment rate was estimated at 25 per cent. Vast numbers of citizens were forced into the streets, having lost their homes and farms because they couldn't make their mortgage payments. New jobs were almost nonexistent and hordes of citizens barely survived by eating at soup kitchens and waiting in long lines for government food handouts. Men who formerly had been gainfully employed were reduced to going from door to door begging for food and clothing for their families. Many sold apples on street corners at a penny apiece.

The Roosevelt Administration implemented many innovative programs to put people to work and give them rudimentary food and shelter. the Civilian Conservation Corps (CCC) was one of the most successful. Over nine years, three million young men were taken into the program (A small number of young women were taken into the program in Rhode Island). They enlisted for up to twelve months, during which each man was paid $30 a month, of which $25 was sent home to his family. In addition to construction duties, tens of thousands of these men attended classes to learn new occupations like carpenter, plumber, mechanic, and technician.

They were housed in a total of 4,500 large and small camps, mostly in rural areas all over the United States. The men built the camps themselves, living in tents until buildings could be erected. Military men like Ernest were placed in charge of these camps. They made sure assigned projects were carried out expeditiously and correctly, and they kept "good order and discipline" among the men.

Ernest was assigned to Camp Huron Hayes, along the Muskegon River, Michigan, in the First CCC Forestry District, in August 1933. There is no longer an existing record of exactly what Ernest's CCC troops accomplished, but it is certain they did their part in the overall program.

In Michigan, an average of 57 camps a year were in operation, housing 102,000 men. More than 485 million seedlings were transplanted there. Recreational and wildlife facilities were built in the state, many of which still exist. Millions of fish were stocked in lakes and streams.

When the program terminated just after the United States entered World War Two, CCC men across the nation had contributed more than six million man hours fighting forest fires, planted two billion trees, created 13,100 miles of foot trails and dirt roads, mostly in National Parks, and restored 3,980 historic buildings. Over $662,895,000 in allotments had been sent home to the impoverished families of CCC men.

Because his camp was not far in flying time from Selfridge, Ernest was able to log a not insignificant number of hours in a wide variety of aircraft. Many flights were logged as "CCC Administrative" flights. There was not much time for flying, however, because of his CCC ground duties. So in November, for example, he logged only ten hours and 30 minutes and in October, four hours and 35 minutes. By helping to run the CCC, he had made a significant contribution to getting America well on its way to economic and social recovery.

In December, just before being reassigned to Selfridge, he braved heavy snowstorms to take part in a fruitless search for a downed pilot near Lansing, Michigan. By the end of 1933, he had logged a total of 2,134 flying hours. He was reassigned to the 94th at Selfridge in January, 1934.

CHAPTER TWENTY-TWO

No sooner had Ernest gotten back into routine operational and test flying, however, than he volunteered for a dangerous new duty for Army pilots: flying the mail for the U.S. Post Office Department. This adventure turned out tragically for the Army Air Corps because pilots were not adequately trained nor were many of their planes properly equipped to fly in weather or at night. How did the Air Corps get into such an embarrassing, serious—and for several pilots fatal—predicament?

During President Hoover's Administration, it had been discovered that the airlines were in collusion with each other and had submitted astronomically high bids for contracts to fly the U.S. mail. The government contracts were let at these high prices. This illegality was discovered by a Senate investigating committee and reported to newly elected President Roosevelt. Since the contracts had been granted during a Republican administration, the situation made a good target for the incoming Democratic administration.

Back in 1918, when President Roosevelt was an undersecretary of the Navy, he had seen the Air Service arm of the U.S Signal Corps successfully demonstrate it could carry the mail between Washington, New York, and Philadelphia. It was done for a period of ninety days utilizing four JN-4 "Jennies" with front cockpits modified as baggage/mail compartments. By the time the experiment had been concluded, the Army had made 270 flights carrying 40,500 pounds of mail between the three cities. "Why not have the Army do it again," Roosevelt wondered. He did not seem to grasp the significant difference between carrying a few ceremonial bags of mail for a few months and flying three million bags a year on a fixed schedule, over a 25,000 mile airways network.

Operating secretly, the President told his new Postmaster General, James Farley, to draw up an executive order cancelling the airmail contracts. At the same time, an assistant postmaster general conferred secretly with Maj. Gen. Benjamin ("Benny") Foulois, Chief of Air Corps, and asked if the Army could carry the mail, as it had done briefly in 1918.

Foulois was in a spot because the Post Office Department had bypassed Army Chief of Staff Douglas MacArthur by talking to Foulois directly. Foulois also had been informed of the President's harsh fiscal 1934 proposed budget for the Army. The total proposal for all branches of the Army was a meager $615 million. This figure could be partially met, the proposal said, by the forced furlough of as many officers as the President deemed advisable. While on furlough, these officers would receive half their base pay, but no allowances except for travel expenses to their homes. All civilian employees of the Army with 30 or more years of service would be forcibly retired. Flying hours would be cut drastically to save money on maintenance and fuel costs. These were truly draconian measures.

During their secret conference, the assistant postmaster general mentioned that $800,000 in postal service funds might be made available for Army flying time if Foulois accepted the challenge.

Foulois was a good soldier, and wanted to comply with his Commander in Chief's requirements. Also, he saw the challenge as a way to obtain additional funding and modernized equipment for the Air Corps. Thinking the operation would start some months later, he said the Air Corps could fly the mail if ordered to do so, and it would take about ten days to get ready for the operation once the order was given. Foulois had no inkling of how speedily the pending executive order would be issued.

That afternoon, to the consternation of Foulois and MacArthur (and the nation's airline executives), Executive Order 6591 was announced by Roosevelt at his daily press briefing. It cancelled all commercial airmail contracts and directed Secretary of War George Dern to order the Air Corps to start flying the mail on Feb. 19, 1934. The starting date was only ten days away!

The nation's skies were still in the bitter grip of winter weather. Knowing the air mail planes had to operate at night and, if necessary, in weather, Major Carl ("Tooey") Spaatz, the Air Corps Operations Officer, was blunt: "We haven't got the equipment to take over this airmail job," he informed Foulois (Spaatz undoubtedly said some other things, but they are not recorded in writing). He wasn't the only one who objected. Lt Col. Frank M. Andrews, Ernest's First Pursuit Group commander at Selfridge, after being informed he was to provide 38 of the pilots who were going to fly the mail, wrote Foulois "They are not trained in instrument or blind flying. Furthermore, Selfridge has not a single directional gyro or artificial horizon." This was true throughout the Air Corps. Although Jimmy Doolittle had flown "blind" on Sept. 24, 1929, the Air Corps had never had the funding for proper instrumentation for its planes, nor flying training time for its pilots. Further, only a few Air Corps planes were equipped with landing, cockpit and navigation lights.

Ernest's instrument and night experience level was typical of Air Corps pilots. He had logged a career total of only 100 hours of night flying time, 20 hours of daytime radio beam navigation, and only three hours of practice instrument time.

Nevertheless, in ten days, the Air Corps was ordered to start flying the mail. Foulois was persuaded by his staff to operate only twelve of the nation's 26 commercial airline routes. This would serve cities in which Federal

Reserve banks were located, thus facilitating overnight transfers of funds. "One hundred twenty-two planes of all types—pursuit, attack, bombers and observation—were assigned to the effort," according to the book "Flights— American Aerospace - Beginning to Future." The small baggage compartments and second cockpits in the pursuit and attack planes were modified to provide cargo space. On the bombers, bomb bays became baggage compartments. Radios and instruments were installed in only a few of the Air Corps planes. There was not enough time for the Army pilots to learn instrument flying.

Two hundred officers and 324 enlisted men were assigned to fly and maintain the mail planes. Tragedy began to unfold almost immediately. Three days before the operation was to start, two pilots making practice runs in the western U.S. flew into weather, crashed, and were killed. During the first three days of flying the mail, another pilot crashed and was killed in heavy fog and rain over Maryland. Nationwide, there were twelve forced landings. A supervisor was killed flying out to oversee flights on the midwestern routes. Then, a plane carrying a group of pilots to their duty station at Mitchel Field ditched in the waters off New York and one of them drowned.

In March, there were crashes in Ohio, Florida, and Wyoming. Gen. Foulois was called to the White House to explain personally to the President what was going on. The newspapers made "flying the mail" the biggest story in the country, which pushed the depression, unemployment, the Oklahoma Dust Bowl, and even Adolph Hitler's depredations in Europe right off the front pages. Roosevelt was furious because the newspapers blamed the White House for the fatalities. "The continuation of deaths in the Air Corps must stop," he thundered. Foulois called a ten-day training stand down and reduced the number of routes.

Chapter Twenty-three

When flying resumed on March 19, the New York Times reported: "At noon, Lieutenant Ernest Warburton took off from Newark with three bags of mail for Cleveland and Chicago.... The route from Newark to Cleveland, Chicago and west to San Francisco is the backbone of the curtailed service." Ernest got through and delivered the mail. But before nightfall, another pilot crashed and was killed in Iowa.

There were big problems on the ground, too. At first, Army people were not paid for travel or per diem. Enlisted men lived beside the planes they serviced, in freezing makeshift hangars, which were usually no more than lean-to shacks and tents. These men, who earned only $17.00 a month, survived on handouts from pilots like Ernest or local townspeople. There was a shortage of parts. Ernest flew the mail out of bases at Nashville, Tennessee, Cleveland, Ohio, and Newark, New Jersey. Each flight took about four hours. These routes traversed mountainous territory. Civilian mail pilots called the route between Newark and Cleveland the "hell run." On that route, Ernest flew through gray daylight or the gloom of night over the Allegheny Mountains, with vicious storms above and fog-filled valleys and hollows below. Often, the airports at either end were "socked in" because of their location near large bodies of water, and he would have to make his way to an alternate airport, wait for the weather to clear, and then fly to his destination. He flew every kind of aircraft the Air Corps had on these routes, including the new YB-10 bomber, and never missed a delivery or lost a sack of mail.

Congress was in a frenzy over the crashes. Republican Rep. Edith Nourse Rogers of Massachusetts, Ernest's home state, according to the New York Times, declared on the floor of Congress "the record of the air mail will be written in blood across the record of the Roosevelt Administration." She called a proposed bill authorizing the Air Corps to fly the mail for another year "a stamp of approval on murder."

Through it all, Ernest and his cohorts remained steadfast and continued carrying the mail. With practice, they improved their ability to fly on instruments. Gradually, the pay situation got better. Parts began to arrive when needed. Better buildings were provided at the air mail bases. But in one day in March, there were crashes in Ohio, Florida and Wyoming. Finally, because of the bad publicity, Roosevelt decided to shut down the Air Corps airmail operation and put the mail on civilian airlines. The last bags of mail were carried by the Army between Chicago and Fargo, North Dakota on June 1, 1934. "Just when when our organization was beginning to operate properly," one young lieutenant said, "we found ourselves out of work!"

Overall, there were 66 crashes and twelve fatalities during the three spring months of 1934. Another six pilots died on training or ferrying flights. The Air Corps flew more than 1.5 million miles carrying more than 770,000 pounds of mail, with less than half the number of planes the civilian airlines had —no small accomplishment.

The Air Corps turned out to be more reliable than the civilian air lines— during 1933, the civilians had lost an average of 172 pounds of mail per month; while the Air Corps, despite the crashes, lost none. There was one good thing about the whole operation: everyone in the United States, from the President and Congress on down, now knew that the Air Corps was woefully underfunded and underequipped and obviously would come out second best in a conflict with any one of several potential enemies.

A twelve-member investigative board under Newton D. Baker, secretary of war in World War One, was formed to evaluate the Air Corps. Among other things, the board stated the Air Corps should have at least 2,320 aircraft for peacetime operations. Pilots should fly at least 300 hours a year, the board said, and should be trained in instrument, night, and cross country flying. Also recommended were improvements in aircraft equipment, armament, and communications. But it was a long time before the Baker Board's recommendations were implemented.

Postmaster General Farley wrote General Foulois a letter, stating, in part, "the country and the Congress will, without doubt, give a more adequate support to the Army, will see to it that it has the most modern equipment obtainable and that sufficient funds are provided for the flyers to have the additional hours of flying which they have so long needed."

During the operation, Ernest logged over 157 hours of daytime flying. He logged 44 hours of night time, almost half the total he had previously logged in his entire career, and his instrument time increased from three to 36 hours. He was now an all weather pilot.

He still found time for a flying visit to his hometown, showing off the new P-26. On April 18, 1934, the Ware River News reported "That was Lieut. Ernest Warburton, star flyer in the United States Army, in one of the newest and fastest of the army combat pursuit planes, who was making some maneuvers over Ware and Gilbertville Saturday and who flew over again on Sunday... That plane he had was a queer looking one, small in some respects, big in fuselage, and stubby, with single wings set on low. It is made for speed, high speed, and he showed some of that speed hereabouts."

Returning unscathed to the 94th in July 1934, Ernest continued test, maintenance and operational flying. He had already demonstrated his knack for engineering innovation many times, including the invention of the first manual control tab on P-12 ailerons, which gave much improved lateral stability in flight. He became something of a specialist in night weather flying, often carrying the commanding officer of the weather bureau as an observer.

Ernest, as usual, was one of the pilots selected to represent the 1st Pursuit Group at the National Air Races in 1934, where the group demonstrated air to air mass attack and dogfighting. On September 6, Chief of Air Corps Maj. Gen. "Benny" Foulois sent the following commendation to the Group: "I desire to extend my congratulations to the officers and men making up the personnel of the Pursuit Squadron from the First Pursuit Group who participated in the Air Corps Demonstration at the 1934 National Air Races. From the officials of the National Air Races and from spectators, nothing but the highest praise was heard. The conduct, flying and general performance of the participants were of the highest order and reflected the greatest credit upon the Army Air Corps as well as upon the participants themselves."

On September 7, he had another forced landing, this time because of engine failure in a C-14.

On September 12, 1934, Ernest, with Capt. William J. Kinnard, was recording high altitude weather data at 25,000 feet over Selfridge when the weather closed in beneath them. Low clouds and poor visibility blanketed the entire midwestern United States. They radioed Selfridge base operations that they could not locate the field. They circled overhead until their fuel was almost exhausted, in the hopes a hole might develop in the clouds below. No such luck—Selfridge remained socked in. They prepared to bail out when the fuel was exhausted. Then, Ernest picked up a radio transmission from the municipal airport operations office at Jackson, Mich., about 80 miles southwest of Selfridge. The radio operator informed him the weather there was opening up. Fortunately, Ernest knew the heading to fly from Selfridge to Jackson. He throttled back to conserve what fuel he had left, traded altitude for distance, flew to the field and landed with the gas gauge on "empty."

Ernest continued to fly acrobatic exhibitions, which were always well received. On Sept. 14, 1934, he received this letter from the President, Buffalo Air Races, in New York: "A note of appreciation for the fine flying exhibition you gave us Sunday during our air show. This was as fine a piece of flying as I have ever seen and, according to the comments of the spectators, was considered the hit of the show. We are greatly indebted to you for helping us out in this situation and want you to know that everyone genuinely appreciated it. Sincerely yours, Lawrence D. Bell, President."

CHAPTER TWENTY-FOUR

On October 1, 1934, Ernest was promoted to First Lieutenant. After pinning on the silver bars of his new rank, he decided to celebrate with a month's leave during which he spent November with family and friends back in Massachusetts. That would prove to be the most significant personal decision he would ever make in his life.

By then, Ernest's father had retired from the wool business. The Warburton family now lived in Westboro, Mass. Anna Miriam Ward's father had also retired and her parents owned a farm in Westboro, where they spent summers. Shortly after Ernest arrived home on leave, his mother asked him to drive her over to visit Anna's mother. They had become good friends back in the days when both families lived in the village of Gilbertville.

It was a bright, crisp November day—a good day for a drive in the country and a good day to start a romance. Warburton mother and son arrived unannounced at the farm, and were greeted by Anna, who informed them her mother was not at home. Anna was there only because a workman was rebuilding the chimney and someone from the family needed to be in the house.

She invited the couple in. She knew who Ernest was, of course—the dashing pilot she had seen "up there" in his gyrating pursuit planes. Mrs. Warburton formally introduced them. He was resplendent in his service uniform, and looked quite handsome. He had an easy manner, displayed a sense of humor, and had a hearty laugh. The scar over his right eye, which was inflicted in the Arctic Flight crash, gave him a rugged look. They chatted for a while. And then the Warburtons left.

That was it. There was no startling burst of heavenly light, no angel choir singing above, no bells ringing, no twanging of Cupid's bow, no realization of love at first sight.

But a flame had been lit. Two days later, Ernest telephoned to ask Anna for a date. She said yes. They had a good time. Then he asked her for another date, and they dated again, and then again. In fact, they were together more than they were apart throughout November. At the end of the month, Ernest's leave was up and he returned to Selfridge. "When he left." Anna remembers, "he told me he would be back at Christmastime."

He returned on December 21, 1934. By that time, Anna was back in her own home in Gilbertville. Ernest's Aunt and Uncle (Charlie Angell's parents) lived in Gilbertville, too, so when Ernest came back he stayed with them. He brought another officer, a Lieutenant Doubleday, with him, who had a girl friend in nearby Worcester. They double dated and went to a Christmas dance in Worcester. "We had a wonderful time," said Anna.

By now, the two young people knew they were in love. "We dated every day until he had to return to Selfridge," Anna remembers. "Before he left, he asked me to marry him. I said 'yes.' He said he would be back in January, with a ring."

Ernest temporarily was assigned to four days of flying at Mitchel Field, N.Y., starting January 10, 1935. He telephoned Anna he would be going there. Anna decided to stay with her sister in Hartford, Conn. while Ernest was at Mitchel because he could get there easily by train. "He came up to Hartford," she recalls, "and brought the engagement ring. Then he said, 'I also have a wedding ring. Why don't we get married right now?' "

Anna agreed. Two days later, on January 12, 1935, they were married by a Justice of the Peace in Windsor, Conn. The J.P.'s two children were witnesses. "We just took off for an afternoon and were married." They told no one before the wedding, not even Anna's sister. Afterwards, they telephoned the news to their parents.

2nd Lieutenant
Ernest K. Warburton,
U.S. Army Air Corps.

Ernest and his mother, Betty Whitehead Warburton, at Boston Airport, Mass., in September 1930 with his Boeing P-12B showing the insignia of the famous 94th Pursuit Squadron.

B/Gen. Ernest K. Warburton and wife Anna at a gala affair at Eglin AFB, Fla. in 1958.

The Warburton family, shown during the Christmas holidays at Pope AFB. N.C., just before General Warburton left for a year's unaccompanied assignment in the Korean war starting January 1952. The children are (from left) Keeling, Sally, Frank, Mark, Ward, Joanne and Darby.

Ernest in a Curtiss A-3B Falcon equipped for winter operation.

"The Three Musketeers": (l. to r.) Lieutenants Robert W. Burns, Ernest K. Warburton, (leader) and Hanlon Van Auken.

Keystone B-4A bomber—one of two supporting the Air Corps winter test group Ernest commanded in the winter of 1933.

Support crew and Ernest next to a Berliner-Joyce P-16 at Selfridge.

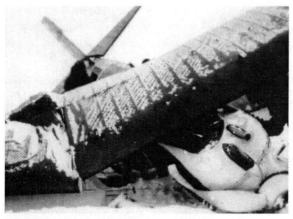

The wreck of Ernest's Curtiss "Hawk" near Beach, N.D., after he crashed in a blizzard during the "Arctic Patrol" flight.

Formation of Air Corps
Boeing P-12Es.

Spectators pick through the remains of Ernest's crashed Boeing P-12 in Detroit, April 29, 1931. (Photo printed with permission of *Detroit News*).

After breaking through the ice on Lake St. Clair, a Berliner-Joyce P-16 awaits the installation of skis.

A Barling—bomber relic of post World War I era.

Martin B-10.

Ernest leads a formation of Boeing B-26 "Peashooters."

Consolidated PBY "Catalina" was one of several seaplanes Ernest flew.

Ernest made dozens of flights in the Loening OA-18 "Duck."

Grumman OA-9 "Goose."

Ford C-9 Trimotor "Tin Goose."

During World War II, Col. Warburton, as a Support Group Commander, was assigned several personal transports which he named after his wife and daughters. This one is a C-47 named "Anna."

Ernest mans the controls of B-25 "Joanne."

He sits in the cockpit of Stinson L-5 "Sally II."

North American O-47 observation aircraft.

Seversky P-35 was speedy but heavy.

The Curtiss P-40 "Warhawk" was basically a P-36 airframe with an Allison liquid-cooled engine.

The XP-40, flown here by Ernest, had the airscoop under the fuselage.

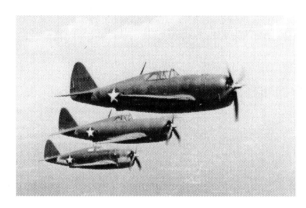

The Republic P-47 "Thunderbolt" was a well-liked workhorse in World War II.

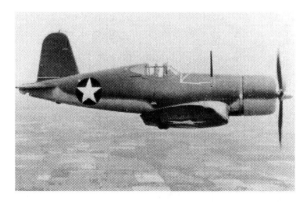

The Vought F4U Corsair was a U.S. Navy fighter.

The Bell P-39 "Airacobra" was a unique fighter with the engine behind the pilot and a 37 mm cannon firing through the nose.

The Curtiss XP-37 was a very early and underpowered version of the aircraft that became the P-40.

The North American P-51 "Mustang" was the most effective, most popular and best-looking fighter of WWII.

A portrait of U.S. airpower includes (from left) North American B-25 "Mitchell," Curtiss P-40 "Warhawk," Consolidated B-24 "Liberator," Bell P-39 "Airacobra," and Boeing B-17 "Flying Fortress."

The Lockheed P-38 "Lightning" was the only U.S. fighter to be built before WWII and still be in production at the end of the war.

The Grumman F4F-3 "Wildcat" was a Navy workhorse in the early days of WWII.

Ernest takes off in the on-of-a-kind Douglas C-47C, the only one to be put on floats.

Ernest logged considerable time testing the Sikorsky R-4 (at first, designated XR-4) helicopter, the first helicopter in the world to be put into production and the first widely used military helicopter.

The Army considered, but did not make operational, the Pitcairn PA-34 observation autogiro.

The Douglas B-26 evolved from the A-26 "Invader" of World War II and was still in use during the Vietnam war.

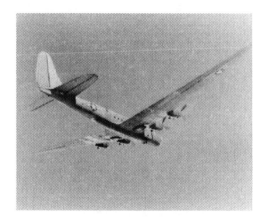

The XB-19 was another one-of-a-kind aircraft and when first flown was the largest aircraft in the world.

The Boeing B-17G, with chin turret, was the ultimate version of the famous WWII "Flying Fortress."

The Consolidated B-24 "Liberator" was produced in larger numbers than any other WWII bomber.

The Martin B-26 "Marauder" at first gained a reputation as a dangerous airplane, but after a wing extension and a better pilot training program, became one of the most effective bombers of WWII.

B-17C, the first version of the "Flying Fortress" to be purchased by the Army Air Force.

Ernest poses in front of captured and rebuilt Japanese "Nick," which he tested in the Philippines during WWII.

JACK II—TAIU—SWPA—APRIL 1945—RESTRICTED

Ernest rated this captured Japanese "Jack II" a first-line fighter.

Ernest flew the Junkers JU-88, a captured Nazi aircraft, at Wright Patterson.

The Fairchild XC-120 "Pack Plane" never became operational.

Only thirteen Bell YFM-1 "Aracudas" were bought. The aircraft was too heavy and underpowered to be effective. Ernest flew one to New York for display at the 1939 World's Fair.

Ernest first flew the Bell XP-59 in 1943. America's first jet fighter, it never proved to be successful.

The Lockheed P-80 "Shooting Star" was the U.S. Air Force's first operational jet fighter. It evolved into the two-seat T-33 and was in widespread Air Force use for more than 40 years.

The North American F-86 "Sabrejet" was the first swept-wing jet fighter to go into operational use. It is probably the most admired jet fighter ever built.

The Lockheed F-94 "Starfire," an interceptor, evolved rom the original F-80 "Shooting Star."

The Republic F-84G "Thunderjet" was a formidable fighter bomber, first used during the Korean war.

The Lockheed F-104 "Shooting Star" interceptor came into the inventory in 1957. Its top speed was over 1,200 mph.

The Martin B-57 was the U.S. version of the English Electric "Canberra." It evolved into a formidable attack aircraft.

The Fairchild C-123 "Provider" was first proposed by Chase Aircraft Co. as a glider transport.

The KB-50 Stratotanker, air refueling version of the B-50, is shown refueling a flight of F-100 Supersabres.

The Boeing B-52 Stratofortress, which was first delivered to the U.S. Air Force in 1956, is still in operational use today. This aircraft is older than the crew members who fly it.

This is an Armed Forces Day display of the huge variety of aircraft based at Eglin Air force Base while Brigadier General Warburton was deputy Commander, Development and Test, Air Proving Ground Center.

Brigadier General Ernest K. Warburton logged his 10,000th hour of flight time in the F-104 Starfighter, at that time the fastest aircraft in the world, just before his retirement in 1959. His career spanned the era from Jennies to jets.

CHAPTER TWENTY-FIVE

If Ernest's genes and family heritage had prepared him for a life in the sky, so had Anna's genes prepared her for the adventurous and many times demanding life of an Air Corps flyer's wife.

She was a member of one of America's founding families. The family patriarch, William Ward of Sudbury, Mass., had brought his wife and five children from England in the spring of 1638. They were passengers on one of the first ships to make the dangerous Atlantic crossing after the "Mayflower."

The Wards were tough and adventurous people. They had to be tough to withstand the voyage's rigors of foul weather, sometimes freezing temperatures, and mountainous waves. Along with 150 or so other immigrants, they shared space with cattle, goats, sheep and poultry. Only women and small children shared crude cabins. Men slept in hammocks, suspended in the open space below decks, like the crew. The passengers cooked their own meals in the ship's galley, mostly salt beef and pork, cheese, salt cod or smoked herring, with vegetables such as dried peas, turnips and cabbage. Occasionally, a fresh caught fish relieved the monotony of the menu. The voyage took almost two months.

Disembarking after dropping anchor in sight of the three hills of old Boston, the Wards came ashore with their belongings, farm implements and tools. They spent the spring, summer and fall of 1638, working with other Massachusetts Bay Colony settlers, clearing the land with teams of oxen and planting crops by hand. There were forty or fifty settlers who carved out farms and built cabins on a grant of land called "Sudbury Plantation." The cabins were grouped for mutual protection from the Indians, who had already begun to resent the invasion of their land by white people.

The settlers survived a typically harsh New England winter, and felt themselves well established in the new world. William Ward soon emerged as one of the leaders of the colonists. He was elected to a number of local offices and the Massachusetts General Court. He was repeatedly elected a deacon in the church and was a leader defending against the Indians, who began to attack farmhouses in 1645.

In 1661, Deacon Ward and his contemporaries founded a new plantation called Marlborough. There the settlers expanded their farming operations despite Indian attacks that became more and more frequent. Finally, in 1675,

the bloody conflict known as "King Philip's War" broke out. All the unforti-
fied houses in Marlborough were destroyed by King Philip's braves.
Atrocities were committed. One of Ward's sons was killed, and a son in law
as well, but Deacon Ward, 73, stayed to fight.   Finally, in 1675, the
Massachusetts Bay Colony raised an army of 600 men. They confronted the
Indians head on. In one major battle they wiped out virtually all the Indian
braves, women and children. King Philip himself died in 1676 and the fighting ceased for good. William Ward died in 1687 at the age of 84.

Ward's descendants carried the bloodline to other parts of the
Massachusetts Bay colony and to other colonies as well. They were justly
proud people—tough, forthright, honest, and idealistic. Tempered like steel
in the harsh fires of early colonial life, they contributed much to the development and progress of what is now the state of Massachusetts and other
parts of the United States as well.

The most famous Ward ancestor was Artemus Ward, who led the citizens of Massachusetts against the British after the battle of Lexington and
Concord became the powderkeg that touched off the Revolutionary War.
Before that battle, he had been a lawyer, judge and civic leader, and he had
fought with the British in the French and Indian War. He was elected a
colonel in the militia. Later, he became a vociferous opponent of England's
infamous Stamp Act. In retaliation, the English Governor revoked his
colonel's commission.

By then, Artemus Ward had become very vocal at Worcester County
Conventions. These conventions issued declarations stating that
Massachusetts no longer owed obedience to the English Parliament. He was
a delegate to both Provincial Congresses, during which he was named
Second General Officer to command the militia if war came. His old militia
regiment reelected him Colonel.

After the battle of Lexington and Concord, the British retreated into
Boston. General Ward assumed command of all colonial forces laying siege to
Boston because the man elected First General Officer did not respond to the
emergency. The ragtag colonial army, made up of men from other colonies as
well as Massachusetts, accepted Ward's authority. He became the *de facto*
Commander in Chief of Revolutionary Forces. He was in command during
the Battle of Bunker Hill, in which was uttered the famous line "Don't fire
until you see the whites of their eyes." The British won a Pyrrhic victory at
Bunker Hill and because of their battlefield losses retreated back into Boston.

On July 2, 1776, George Washington arrived on the scene and relieved
Ward of command, making him commander of the army's right wing. Eight
months later, Ward's men seized and fortified the Dorchester Peninsula,
forcing the British to evacuate Boston and the colony of Massachusetts.
They never returned. In 1779, Ward was elected to the Continental
Congress. He died October 28, 1800, having made an indelible mark in the
history books of Massachusetts and the United States.

In 1831, a descendant, William Ward of Belchertown, married Melinda Bassett of Hardwick. He was employed by the George H. Gilbert Woolen Company of Ware, Mass. In November, 1843, a son, Albert Bedford Ward, was born in Ware. He grew up and became superintendent of the woolen mill. His son, Charles Albert Ward, later became superintendent and vice president of the same mill. He and his wife, Fannie L. Richardson, produced two daughters, the second of whom was Anna Miriam Ward, born April 1, 1913. Destined to marry Ernest, Anna was, by bloodline and heritage, indeed well suited to face the challenges to be met by an Air Corps pilot's wife.

CHAPTER TWENTY-SIX

Ernest was scheduled to return to Selfridge on Jan, 13, 1935, the day after the wedding. The weather was marginal, but Ernest decided to attempt the flight. He had flown to Mitchell in formation with a Lieutenant Tyson, and the two took off on schedule for the return trip. They could always turn back, they had agreed before takeoff, if the weather got too bad. About an hour into the flight, they ran into a heavy snowstorm which cut visibility virtually to zero. Using hand signals, Tyson indicated he wanted to press on through the storm. "I've just gotten married. I have a bride," Ernest thought. He waved goodbye and turned back. Tyson continued on into the storm, crashed, and was killed. Getting married had saved Ernest's life.

His log for January 13 shows a two hour and twenty minute flight from Mitchel to Mitchel, with the notation "Returned account of weather." On the same page in his log, slanting in big letters across the page, he wrote "Married Jan. 12, 1935—Windsor, Conn."

On January 16, 1935, the following notice appeared in the Gilbertville newspaper: "GILBERTVILLE GIRL WEDS NOTED ARMY FLIER. Mr. and Mrs. A.C. Ward of Gilbertville have announced the marriage of their daughter, Anna, to Lieutenant Ernest Warburton of the United States Army Flying Corps (sic) stationed at Selfridge Field, Detroit. The marriage took place in Windsor, Conn., Saturday, January 12. The bride is a graduate of Hartford (sic) Business School. The groom is one of the outstanding aviators of the United States. He was born in Gilbertville and is a graduate of M.I.T."

"A week or so later," Anna remembers, "I got a trousseau together, and took the train to Selfridge." When she arrived, she found Ernest had moved out of Bachelor Officers Quarters and had arranged for them to live in a "nice little cottage" on the post, at the edge of the flying field.

Anna was something of a celebrity at Selfridge. Everyone wanted to meet this young woman who had finally captured Ernest's heart, since he had long been the most eligible young bachelor on the post. She entered into and enjoyed the social life and the friendship of the other wives. There were frequent dances and dinners at the Officers Club, and small parties in the officers' homes.

She was introduced to the formality of Army social customs. Formal calling cards, white gloves and afternoon teas, coffees and bridge parties were *de rigueur*. One designated night a week, the young couple stayed home, Ernest in dress uniform, in the event the squadron or group commander and his wife decided to call.

A local newspaper ran an article about women's life at Selfridge: "Life on the post is scheduled very much as life on the 'outside.' There are the usual private bridges and teas, with sleigh rides on the flying field and volley ball games twice a week in the men's gymnasium. Each month, Mrs. Ralph Royce, wife of the Commanding Officer, selects a host and hostess for the dance at the Officers Club, always a gay affair. Children, who average two to a family, ... assist at all these activities—except during school hours in Mt. Clemens where the youngsters are sent in the school bus."

Ernest showed signs of domestication and in their first spring together planted a vegetable garden next to their quarters. An Army officer's life in those days was one of "genteel poverty," in which his family had to subsist on a relatively low income. Growing their own vegetables was one way to save on expenses. Ernest continued to plant vegetable gardens throughout their career, wherever they were stationed, both for practical purposes and because he enjoyed working with plants.

At Selfridge, it didn't take long for Anna to realize there were certain risks involved in pursuit flying. Takeoff and landing accidents, while not frequent, took place on the field right outside her window. Pilots usually walked away from these. But the reality of the risk was forcibly brought home to her when the 1st Pursuit Group put on an aerial demonstration for Rudy Vallee, the famous band leader and singer (all the military units of the day put on demonstrations for visiting VIPs because the newspapers always gave them good coverage).

In the middle of the program, Anna, at home, watched in horror as two speeding pursuit planes crunched together in a head-on midair collision right over the landing field. The planes plummeted to earth and crashed on the field. Nobody walked away. The crash site was some distance away, and Anna could not tell who the pilots were. Was Ernest flying one of the downed craft? Was Ernest one of the still, slumped, helmeted bodies she could see in the wreckage? The emblem of his squadron, the 94th "Hat in the Ring," was plainly visible on the two aircraft. An ambulance roared out to the crash scene. The two limp bodies, unconscious or dead, were lifted from the downed aircraft, placed in the ambulance, and taken away. After ten tense minutes, the phone rang. It was Ernest. "I don't know if I told you this morning," he said, "but I did not fly today!" Anna was extremely relieved to get the news.

CHAPTER TWENTY-SEVEN

In December, 1934 , Ernest had been given more responsibility and transferred to the 57th Service Squadron. Service squadrons performed "upper level" aircraft maintenance that was beyond squadron capability. His responsibilities now included test flying for all the squadrons at Selfridge. He continued operational flying with the 94th Pursuit Squadron, including frequent acrobatic flights.

Two months later, in February 1935, his responsibilities were further broadened when he was appointed Base Engineering Officer. He now was responsible for the operational readiness of all planes and equipment at Selfridge. He flew operations and test missions in all the Selfridge aircraft, including the speedy all-metal, low-wing P-26 "Peashooter," which he had tested in 1932. It was now coming into the modernizing Air Corps inventory. Considered the hottest thing in the air, its landing speed was so high the plane was fitted with split wing flaps to slow its final approach speed. The Peashooter would later prove to be seriously lacking in fighting capabilities, however. In the early war days of 1941 and 1942, it was still on active duty with the Philippine Air Force.

Although the U.S. Army Air Corps was still woefully underfunded, underequipped and undermanned, the Army reluctantly agreed to the permanent establishment of General Headquarters Air Force at Langley Air Force Base, Va., in March 1935 (In the same month, Hitler revealed the existence of the Luftwaffe). Formation of GHQ Air Force provided a degree of autonomy to the nation's air arm, a major step toward making the Air Corps an independent service on equal terms with the Army and Navy (real autonomy would not come until the unification of the armed forces in 1947). Brigadier General Frank M. Andrews, who as a Lieutenant Colonel had been Ernest's Group Commander at Selfridge, was named GHQ Air Force commander. A month later, Ernest was promoted to Captain—promotions seemed to be speeding up.

The proponents of airpower, including Ernest, began to think things were improving. They were, marginally. They did not really improve, however, until 1939. That is when the United States began in earnest to gear up a defense industry to face the threat from Nazi Germany, Japan. and even then, from the Soviets, and begin rapid expansion and modernization of the armed services. But in the mid-thirties, manufacturers were turning out newer and more capable aircraft, a few at a time. These prototypes were sent to Wright Field, to Selfridge, and to other Army Air Forces bases to be evaluated by dedicated, steel-nerved pilots like Ernest.

Anna proved to be a very understanding wife, even when he decided to make a practice parachute jump with a new type of 'chute (it was a successful jump, of course). He conscientiously practiced instrument and night flying, and by July 1935 had logged just over 171 hours of night time. He flew everything the Air Forces had; in a typical month, he logged time in the PT-3A, P-26A, A-11, C-19, O-19, BT-2B1, and C-14, for a total of 50 hours and 55 minutes. By October 1935, he was leading formation acrobatic flights in the new P-26 and flying the P-26 most of the time. At the end of 1935, Ernest had accumulated 2,983 total flying hours.

Ernest and Anna celebrated their first Christmas together at Selfridge. They celebrated their first wedding anniversary there on Jan. 12, 1936, and their first child, Keeling, a boy, was born in a Detroit Hospital on Feb. 27, 1936. Now they were a family.

During the same month, Ernest underwent and passed his first flying Instrument Check. The institution of this semiannual test for all pilots was an indication of the growing capabilities of the Army Air Forces. There had been a lot of improvement in weather flying since the Air Corps flew the mail in early 1934.

His flight log shows almost all local flights at Selfridge during the month of March. Ernest was staying near home to lend support to the new mother. In April, he flew test hops almost daily, along with practice instrument flights, and made several trips to Boston and Buffalo. On April 6, 1936, the Springfield Daily News reported he made an unscheduled landing there because of weather. "Fog and 40 mile per hour winds covered most of the route between Boston and Detroit," the paper reported. All the local pilots at Springfield were on the ground, spinning tall tales in the coffee shop. "Suddenly, to the surprise of all, the roar of an engine was heard and through the haze at the north end of the field, emerged the blue and yellow colors of the United States Army on the wing.

"The ship, a Thomas Morse biplane, skimmed easily to earth and came to a halt on the taxiway in front of the administration building. The two Army aviators climbed out. They were Capt. Ernest K. Warburton and Sgt. Arnold Filiberti, ... bound from Boston to Detroit." They had run into fog and clouds in all directions and had decided not to land at Northampton, the first field they came to, because the torrential rains had softened it too much.

"The visit here was routine in the lives of the two aviators. They stopped only to listen for weather reports on the airport's short wave radio. Learning that the storm was still widespread ahead of them, with promised clearing skies later in the day, they decided to pause for lunch.

"'Yes,' Captain Warburton told a reporter, 'it was kind of bumpy. We had a hard time keeping our goggles on, the ship tossed so. The wind is terrible, but I think it will clear.' " It did, and Ernest was home with his family at Selfridge that night.

CHAPTER TWENTY-EIGHT

By early 1937, Japan was waging total war in China and Hitler had repudiated the Versailles Treaty, which had forbidden Germany to rearm after World War I. Germany had been rearming anyway, in defiance of the terms of the treaty. Young German males were being conscripted for the army. German troops were deploying into the Rhineland, a supposedly neutral area along the Rhine River. Germany and Italy were directly involved in the Spanish Civil War, using it as a testing ground for new weapons and tactics. On April 16, waves of German bombers proved the devastating effects of airpower by destroying the Basque village of Guernica, killing 1,654 civilians and wounding 889.

In May, almost as a response to war rumblings abroad, General Headquarters Air Force conducted "Hot Weather Tests" during what was described by the Selfridge News as "the greatest concentration of American aerial might since 1931," involving 2,300 men and 250 airplanes. Ernest, along with a full complement of First Pursuit Group people, was part of an organization of 600 officers and men and 90 airplanes operating out of Muroc Dry Lake in the Mohave Desert of lower California.

"From the frozen wastes of northern Michigan to the torrid heat bowl of lower California is proving a real efficiency test of men and equipment through which the First Pursuit Group of Selfridge Field is emerging with flying colors," the Selfridge News stated. "Muroc itself is merely a temporary military post office constructed of wood from bomb-boxes and a ramp for loading livestock."

"Besides the complete resources of General Headquarters Air Force, there are two airdromes on the West Coast and a regiment of anti-aircraft artillery working in collaboration to match wits with imaginary enemies in a mimic war. The pursuit ships are flying in shifts of three hours daily under actual wartime conditions… . All repairs must be made in the field with a minimum of equipment. The sand encountered in the desert provided a puzzling contrast to the snow and ice of the various trips to Oscoda, Mich. last winter. "

In the U.S., pursuit aviation progress was falling behind progress in other fields and in other countries. Ernest's P-26 was the fastest fighter in the U.S., but the newly developed Boeing YB-17 bomber could outrun it, as could the Mitsubishi and Heinkel bombers of Japan and Germany. Worse, several foreign countries were producing fighters that were much faster than the P-26.

Ernest and his squadron mates got a first-hand look at the new YB-17 on May 17, 1937, when one of the new bombers was flown into Selfridge for a short visit. Only twelve had been built (the Y designation meant the aircraft was in development and the Army had ordered only a small number—usually 12 or 13—for evaluation. When an aircraft had been tested, accepted and put into full production, the Y was dropped). The Selfridge News reported: "The engineering perfection, to say nothing of the size and beauty of this silver supership, inspired awe even to the aviation accustomed eyes here. The cruising speed of the ship is greater than that of the speedy little P-26, as it is powered by four twin-row 14 cylinder engines." Disappointingly, no one at Selfridge was offered a chance to fly the new bomber that day. After only a 45 minute stopover, it was flown on to Chanute Field, Illinois, and then to other bases.

Ernest continued flying all the fighters and observation planes of the day as well as the C-33, a military version of the Douglas DC-2 transport.

He also made many flights in the B-10, a twin-engine bomber the Army General Staff had decided would be the Army's primary bomber, even though GHQ Air Force wanted the B-17. (Eventually, the Air Force won out over the General Staff and the B-17 was bought in quantity and, along with the B-24, was the mainstay of the U.S. bombing force in World War Two).

On June 6, 1937, the Warburton's second child, Joanne, was born in the Mt. Clemens hospital. Now Ernest and Anna had a boy and a girl. Ernest had accumulated 3,549 hours of flying time.

Three weeks later, on July 1, 1937, Ernest flew another plane home to visit his father briefly in Westboro. "First Lieutenant (sic) Ernest K. Warburton, Engineering Officer at Selfridge Field, just outside Detroit, Michigan," the local newspaper reported, "piloted a large U.S. Army attack plane to Westboro from Detroit last Saturday afternoon, making the trip in three and a half hours.

"He landed at the Westboro Flying Field on Otis Street about four P.M. and returned to Selfridge Sunday evening. The attack plane which he flew to Westboro is equipped with six machine guns, weighs six tons and carries a 1,000 horsepower motor." The aircraft was a Northrop A-17, the Army's main attack plane of that era. While it was heavily armed compared to other planes of the day, it was relatively slow and cumbersome to fly. The A-17 did not see combat in World War Two.

But things in the fighter field were looking up for the Air Force. A month later, Selfridge received the first of the new breed of fighter planes, the Seversky P-35, which Ernest "wrung out" in the skies around Selfridge. In August, he also was testing another modern fighter, the Curtiss P-36. Both these single seat aircraft were modern in every respect, with radial air-cooled engine, retractable landing gear and enclosed cockpit. The struts and drag-inducing guywires of the P-26 were gone; the new planes had cantilever wings, and the result was higher airspeeds.

The P-35 and P-36 were a definite step up in capability for the Air Corps, but still not as good as some foreign pursuit planes. For one thing, they were armed with only two machine guns. The fact that the War Department grudgingly was now modernizing the Air Forces attests to U.S. government concerns about the war looming ever more ominously just over the horizon.

The P-35 was touted as attaining more than 300 miles per hour in level flight. A Detroit newspaper carried an article describing a test flight flown by Ernest: "Climbing up to 20,000 feet, the little ship is whipped over into a power dive. The airspeed indicator registers only up to 450 miles an hour. But Capt.ain Ernest K. Warburton swears he hit 500 miles an hour on the way down. At that speed, the flexible cockpit enclosure swelled and bulged under the pressure, but it held.

"You don't jerk out of a dive like that. As the hard earth seems to rush up toward you, you ease back, ever so slightly, on the stick and wait long seconds for the horizon to crawl down the windshield, while the terrifically accentuated pull of gravity jams you down in the seat. That, perhaps, is the most dramatic phase of the testing. That and the spins.

"The P-35 doesn't spin readily. But when it is once started, it spins fast— the fastest spinner Warburton's ever seen. But it comes out of it all right.

"It is axiomatic in the Air Corps, particularly in pursuit, that the airplane must be able to withstand more punishment than its pilot. And these Army test pilots are punishing themselves so that the three squadrons of Seversky pursuit planes that will soon fill the hangars at Selfridge Field may be flown in utter confidence by the officers of the First Pursuit Group."

CHAPTER TWENTY-NINE

A few weekends later, Ernest demonstrated his new plane for the hometown folks. The story read "'Here's Warburton,' everybody in Gilbertville and hundreds in Ware remarked, when that big, handsome fast army monoplane began circling over the towns, one after the other, Sunday afternoon.

"And it was Capt. Ernest Warburton, distinguished United States Army flier, stopping by to pay his respects to relatives and friends. Over Ware, he spiralled around not stunting but yet doing some highly thrilling flying. And in Gilbertville, he not only did the same, but he swooped down so low along the river that his plane could have skated, had it been properly equipped... .

"Captain Warburton's plane greetings are now so well known in Gilbertville that everybody in the community knows who it is and why, and they all came out Sunday and enjoyed it."

In November, 1937, his log shows, he had to make a forced landing in an A-17. The landing took place without incident, repairs were made, and Ernest went on his way. In July of the following year, bad weather compelled him to make a forced landing at Albany, N.Y. in a P-35.

Then, for almost a year starting in August, 1938, Ernest found himself back in the classroom, assigned to the Air Corps Tactical School at Maxwell Field, Montgomery, Alabama. This was a good career indicator, because only bright young officers with great potential were selected to attend the school. He moved Anna and the two children to Montgomery with him. There was no housing for student officers at Maxwell, so they lived in a Montgomery suburb. Anna missed the closely knit life on base, although there was plenty of socializing among the student wives. At the same time, she was very busy taking care of two small children.

Ernest had now compiled 4,007 hours of pilot time. He was disappointed to find his flying activities sharply curtailed at school. While attending class every day, all day, Ernest and the other pilots were able to get flying time only when they could work it into the academic schedule, at night, on weekends, or during brief academic breaks.. Four hours a month was required to qualify for flight pay, but Ernest consistently logged more than that. He usually flew "round robins," during which he would shoot landings at several southern airports, stopping if necessary to refuel, and end up back at Maxwell on the same day. His top month was October 1938, when he logged 20 hours and 45 minutes.

While Ernest was in the Tactical School, the war clouds had gathered ever more ominously in foreign lands. The Japanese were virtually overrunning China, and Generalissimo Chiang Kai Shek's troops were hard put to defend the northwestern part of the country. In Europe, on September 29, 1938, the infamous Munich Pact had been agreed to by the British, French, Nazis and Italians. The agreement turned over 10,000 square miles of Czech territory to Nazi Germany. Persecution of the Jews began in Czechoslovakia and was intensified in Germany.

In 1938 and1939, a flurry of new alliances had been consummated between Germany, Italy, and other European states. Japan and Soviet Russian signed a mutual defense pact. Japan announced the New Order for East Asia, which stated Japan would be supreme in that area. Recognizing the obviously growing threat to the United States, President Roosevelt in January 1939 asked Congress for a $525 million increase in defense funds, principally for air and naval forces. He submitted requests for more funding on March 4 and April 29. On April 3, 1939, he signed the National Defense Act of (fiscal) 1940, which included authorization of $300 million for 3,251 Army Air Corps aircraft and increased the number of Air Corps personnel to 3,230 officers and 45,000 enlisted troops.

Soon, the war became a reality. Early in the morning of September 1, 1939, German Stuka dive bombers attacked the Dirschau Bridge just inside Poland. Other border points were hit minutes later. Hitler's blitzkrieg juggernaut of tanks, planes and troops poured into the country at several border crossings and World War Two began. President Roosevelt pledged aid to European allies, against the desires of a strong neutralist bloc in Congress. He urged Congress to support a huge military buildup for defensive purposes. On October 30, 1940, during his campaign for reelection, he reassured the people with these words: "I have said it before and I shall say it again and again and again—your boys are not going to be sent into any foreign wars." This was campaign rhetoric. We know from memoirs and government records that he realized war was inevitable for the United States. His problem was how to convince Congress and the country to agree to get into it before the forces of Germany, Japan and their allies had taken over the whole world outside of the United States. That problem was solved when the Japanese attacked Pearl Harbor on December 7, 1941, and Americans were forced to go to war to defend themselves against the Axis Powers who had declared war on us. Once the U. S. was in the war, it was no longer a "foreign war."

With war underway, Roosevelt called for the production of 50,000 aircraft a year. When he made that announcement the goal seemed completely unrealistic, but before World War Two was over, U.S manufacturers were producing over 80,000 planes a year. Wright Field became busier than ever.

Chapter Thirty

Ernest graduated from the Tactical School in May 1939 and then moved to what would turn out to be the most satisfying job in his career. His new assignment to Wright Field would make him extremely happy and important. He was assigned to Air Materiel Command's Flight Test Branch at Wright Field, near Dayton, Ohio.

Ernest and Anna found a small home in Dayton for themselves and their two children. A third child, Sally, was born on August 1, 1939. After six months in Dayton, the Warburtons were given base housing, and they settled into "standard issue" family quarters with two bedrooms upstairs and a maid's room on the first floor. Nice, but rather cramped for a family with three children. Ernest, as usual, planted a vegetable garden in the side yard.

On 18 August, 1940, Anna gave birth again, this time to twin boys, Darby and Ward. Now they had five children and their quarters were bursting at the seams. In fact, Anna said, the twins' nursery was really a closet, and not a very large one at that. Ernest was away from home a lot, on testing assignments at manufacturers' factories.

Anna kept her ears open, and after a time, heard of a large house on the base, a former farm house. It was about to become available because the occupants were being transferred out. It had five bedrooms. She called the Base Housing Officer and was told it had already been assigned to another officer. She explained the Warburtons' plight—all those children in such a small house. "Anna," he said, "I can't do anything unless Ernest outranks the assigned occupant." Anna told him Ernest's date of rank. Fortunately, Ernest did outrank the other officer, so the house was assigned to the Warburtons instead. This would not have happened if Anna had not taken the initiative. The house is still in use today, as General Officers quarters, and is called "The Benjamin Foulois House" because Foulois lived in it before becoming Chief of the Air Corps

When Ernest returned from his trip, he found his family comfortably ensconced in a large, old converted farmhouse with a big fenced yard. The house overlooked Huffman Prairie, the hallowed land on which the Wright Brothers had done much of their experimental flying. Ernest wasted no time putting in a new garden, a big one.

125

It is in the big house at Wright Field that the older Warburton children have their first memories of their father. "One of the first thing I remember," Keeling told an interviewer, "is Dad cutting my hair in the bathroom. Dad always cut our hair, oh, gosh, until I went to college, I guess. When I got into high school, I felt he didn't do quite the best job, and I wanted a barber to do it, but he wouldn't hear of it. He loved us, but he was a strict disciplinarian. He was away a lot during the first ten years of my life, and my mother ran the family. Even so, he still wielded the stick and was the boss."

Joanne remembers falling out of a second story window. She and Keeling were chatting in a small dressing room off the master bedroom. Her mother was elsewhere in the house. "I leaned back against the screen," she said, "and it gave way and I fell onto a concrete step at ground level. I couldn't stand on one ankle, and I had cut my chin and lip and there was lots of blood. Mother drove me to the hospital. There was nothing broken because the screen, somehow, broke my fall. I always claimed that Keeling had pushed me. Dad came home and I was sitting up in bed, propped up by some pillows. I was all bandaged up. He sat down in a chair at the end of the bed and just looked at me. Finally, he said 'Now what have you done, young lady?'"

The younger children, Sally, Ward and Darby, were energetic and very mischievous. They loved to play Indian, painting each other with lipstick, rouge, eye shadow and nail polish.

Chapter Thirty-one

Wright was the center of all aircraft test activity for the Air Force. The book "Test Flying at Old Wright Field," published by the Wright Stuff Association, described it: "Wright was a well-established research center with facilities and laboratories to develop and test experimental airplanes, engines, propellers, communications, armament and a host of other flight equipment. By the time of Pearl Harbor, it was already the largest aeronautical research and development center in the world."

Yet, when Ernest arrived in 1939, there were no paved runways, just a huge sod field. There were three large hangars connected to a building called the head house, which contained a number of shops, instrumentation rooms and a single large room (20' x 20') with desks for test pilots and engineers. The office of the Chief of Flight Test measured 6' x 10'. There were two huge wind tunnels. Later, at least one additional wind tunnel was constructed at a cost of $2.5 million. The first paved runway was under construction as the U.S. entered World War Two. Paving was completed in 1942. But well before then, Wright was the world's premier flight test and development center.

Ernest was a full-fledged test pilot and, eventually, Chief of the Flight Test Section for the Air Force. His first boss was Major Stanley Umstead, who with his ever present cigar was famous Air Force wide as the Service's most noted test pilot. Umstead had been a test pilot at old McCook Field with Jimmy Doolittle and the other early test pilot pioneers. He passed on many "lessons learned" to Ernest, who would succeed him as Chief of Flight Test..

Although Ernest's assignments at Selfridge Field had included many test activities, he also had been required to fly operational missions and as Base Engineering Officer, he had many administrative duties. Now, Ernest's work was exclusively in testing

When he arrived, he found business booming in the Flight Test Branch. In the face of the looming war, millions of Government dollars were becoming available for new weapons systems and patriotic, money-hungry manufacturers were eager to develop new types of aircraft by the score. All had to be tested by the Army to be sure they were, first, practical and useful, and, second, up to specifications.

In June 1939, his first full month at Wright Field, Ernest logged 67 hours in 15 different types of aircraft, including two X-models (experimental). He flew every type of airplane. For example, in October he was in New York, testing the Grumman OA-9 amphibian. This was an Army version of the popular Grumman G-21A Goose amphibian, modified for reconnaissance and aerial photography work. He logged five water landings in it at the old Pan American flying basin next to La Guardia Field . Over the next several months he logged 161 water landings in the OA-9, flying out of both Wright and Selfridge.

In the months and years to come, like the other pilots in the unit, he would log over 100 hours a month on a regular basis. By the end of December 1940, Ernest had logged over 5,000 career flying hours.

Six pilots (later increased to eight) did all the testing. They flew long hours, usually seven days a week (On Sunday, December 7, 1941, the day the Japanese attacked Pearl Harbor, Ernest was at work, logging two hours and ten landings in a Martin B-26). All were experienced pilots with extensive backgrounds in both single and multi engine aircraft. All the pilots were expected to be able to fly all the aircraft assigned at any time. Several years later, with a further increase of assigned pilots and engineers, the Flight Section was reorganized for and categorized by type of aircraft—bombers, fighters, transports and miscellaneous aircraft such as helicopters. Even then, it was expected that, when time was available, all pilots get checked out on all available aircraft, and there were many.

There was a constantly changing inventory of new planes. When a new aircraft, called a prototype, was picked up at the factory by a Wright Field pilot, he would receive a briefing on it from the test pilot of the company producing the aircraft. He would read whatever technical information was available and familiarize himself with the cockpit. If it was a two seater or a larger aircraft, he might get a familiarization flight with the company test pilot. With or without the familiarization flight, he would then fly the plane, with the technical information, to Wright Field. He would brief his cohorts at Wright, including specifics he had learned about the aircraft on the flight. The other pilots would then go through the same process and fly the new aircraft. This, then, qualified them to fly any type of test on it.

Aircraft manufactured for the U.S. Government had to meet certain design specifications for speed, rate of climb, service ceiling, range, takeoff and landing distances, stall speeds in various configurations, stability and handling characteristics, and myriad other requirements. Wright Field pilots at first tested all prototypes at Wright, but later, as the tempo of the war picked up, to save time, they usually test flew them at the contractor's facility.

Gabe Vaca, a P-47 pilot sent temporarily to Wright Field for a specific test in 1943, described a typical single seat test flight. "After taking (my) position at the head of the runway, I ran the engine up to 30 inches of manifold pressure and after a final instrument check, released the brakes and went to full throttle, with the throttle interconnected to the turbosupercharger. I flipped on the water ejection switch as I started to roll. This became a very busy time because as I did these things, I had to write down all the instrument readings, as well as the airspeed, manifold pressure, rpms, etc. on takeoff and at each 1,000 foot interval during the climb. The specified climb speed changed at every 1,000 foot interval. I used a stop watch and record the elapsed time at each interval."

"The notepad was strapped to my knee and it took some doing to try to control the aircraft, hold torque rudder pressure, maintain a smoothly changing climb airspeed and still maintain air surveillance of what (other traffic might be around me... .)"

He was describing a check climb, which in a single seat fighter was the most difficult test for a pilot because it required great dexterity. Later, a flight engineer would use his data to calculate the actual rate of climb.

"Another segment of our test procedures was to go to altitude and fly inverted until (I) lost fuel pressure and the engine quit, but stay inverted until the oil pressure dropped, then flip right side up. The crux of this problem was that (I was) to write down all the instrument readings, plus the time the fuel pressure dropped and then how much the oil pressure dropped, while at the same time trying to keep my feet near the floor so I could hold the rudder, but the knee pad and the right knee would be up near my right ear while all the debris and dirt from the bottom of the aircraft were falling up into my eyes and face. I still had to check the stopwatch and write on the pad at the same time!" Presumably, pilots assigned full time to Wright Field became accustomed to doing this.

When an aircraft was ready to be tested at the factory, Ernest was notified and he would promptly dispatch a test crew, which consisted of a pilot, copilot (if required) and a flight test engineer. At the factory, the engineer installed special instruments designed by Wright Field's Flight Test Division Instrument Laboratory, and the tests began the next day.

A Wright test pilot, in flight, would record instrument readings at specific times during the test, compiling data points for postflight evaluation. When a second seat was provided in the aircraft, the flight test engineer went along to record instrument readings and make performance notes. the testing was extensive and extended over several days, dawn to dusk, Saturdays and Sundays included.

After the test, the engineer recalculated the instrument data to determine if the aircraft had performed successfully. An aircraft had to attain airspeeds, rates of climb, and so on, within 1 percent of the specified design levels. The Government imposed severe payment penalties if design specifications were not met. Some contracts were cancelled outright for failure to perform, which meant the contractor lost his considerable investment in developing the plane as well as income from production of the aircraft..

These decisions were made based directly on the reports of the test pilot and the flight test engineer.

The Wright Field pilots had to test many more than one version of each plane. There were many models of every aircraft produced. Even though a plane might be designated, for example, "B-25," each model could be a distinctly different aircraft. The B-25 was a medium bomber with a gun in the nose, tail, and a top turret. It gradually evolved through the B-25A, B-25B, etc., through B-25M. The B-25H, for example, was an attack aircraft with a 75 mm cannon in the nose, along with fourteen .50 cal. machine guns—four in the nose, four in fuselage "packages," two in waist "bulges" and two each in turrets on top of the fuselage and in the tail. It was heavier, with more powerful engines, and it flew differently than other B-25 models. Each new version of a plane had to be tested for attainment of performance parameters.

Almost all new planes, over a number of years, evolved through several models as improvements were made or new missions were developed for them. After a few years of flying at Wright Field, each test pilot, Ernest included, had flown hundreds of different aircraft models and types.

Chapter Thirty-two

The Wright test pilots and engineers learned to be skeptical of some manufacturers' claims for new aircraft capabilities. Sometimes these new planes were ready for testing, sometimes not. After he retired from the Air Force, during Ernest's acceptance speech when he was inducted into the Society of Experimental Test Pilots, he recalled one airplane, an extreme case, that definitely wasn't ready for testing. "A test pilot needs both skill and luck to survive, and an understanding wife," he said. He then related how he was ordered to St. Louis to test the ill-fated Curtiss C-76 Caravan, a newly designed twin engine all wooden transport (The British had developed more than one all wood aircraft, most notably the DeHavilland Mosquito, and Washington bureaucrats, anticipating a wartime shortage of aluminum, thought the U.S. should have some wooden aircraft, too. Several different companies produced prototypes of wooden planes, all unsuccessful).

While taxiing out on a blustery day for the ship's first flight, he turned crosswind and heard a crashing sound behind him. Looking back, he realized the wind had snapped the vertical stabilizer off the fuselage! If that had happened in flight there could have been fatal results for Ernest. In strong language, he recommended further development and testing by the company before it was presented again for testing by the Wright test pilots.

What happened next was described in an article written by Walter J. Boyne in Wings magazine.

Some months later, Boyne wrote, Ernest flew the "improved" version of the aircraft. While it did meet design specifications for speed, range and single-engine ceiling, he pronounced it ponderous to fly, heavy on the controls, and at the design gross weight and c.g., almost uncontrollable with gear and flaps down. He also noted "a vibration throughout the whole structure in rated power climb." Back to the factory for more reworking.

Two months later, on May 10, 1943, the C-76 crashed with a three man Curtiss test crew on board. Eyewitnesses said the tail section appeared to blow off in level flight, after which the aircraft pitched straight down, the nose section collapsed inward, the outer wing panels snapped off and the aircraft crashed vertically into the ground. There were no survivors. Investigation revealed the horizontal stabilizer had been glued onto the fuselage, but no attaching bolts had been used, nor had any holes been drilled for attaching bolts (Curtiss had hired some workers from a piano factory who were experienced in wood working). The C-76 project was cancelled. In his "Wings" article, Boyne nominated it as "a candidate for the worst aircraft of World War Two."

The C-76 was almost an anomaly—most new aircraft measured up pretty closely to design specifications. Many, however, did not and deficiencies would be discovered during the test flights. While testing for shortcomings, the Wright test pilots also faced a plethora of in-flight emergencies such as engine and electrical fires, engine failures, runaway propellers, controllablity problems, structural failures and any number of unexpected emergencies.

They would then face the daunting task of getting the airplanes safely back on the ground. Sometimes, this was impossible, and a pilot would have to "hit the silk" to save his own life. Sometimes, he could not get out and would go down with the plane. Most of the streets at old Wright Field and at Edwards Air Force Base are named for test pilots who died while doing their job. It was challenging and often dangerous work which Ernest loved.

There was an urgency to the test work because it was carried out against a background of the spreading conflicts in Europe and Asia, which, of course, eventually included the United States.

In the days before World War Two, there was a need to let the American people know, generally, what was going on at Wright Field and what the Army was doing with their tax dollars. Accordingly, Ernest periodically arranged for mass formations of Wright Field aircraft to be flown over Dayton and other Ohio cities and towns on appropriate a holidays. Usually, Ernest led these formations, which contained fighters, trainers, transports and bombers.

The flights garnered excellent publicity for the Air Corps. For example, on August 2, 1939, the Dayton Herald headlined "Army Parades Aerial Might Over Dayton." Two huge photos filled the top half of the front page. A caption read "Dayton had a preview of what the next war might look like—from the air—when the Army Air Corps turned 60 of its newest planes loose in celebration of the Corps' 30th Birthday. Slim Gregory, of Mayfield-Gregory Aerial Surveys, in an army basic combat plane piloted by Capt. E.K. Warburton of Wright Field, flew with the massed air fleet as it circled over Dayton shortly before noon Wednesday so that Daytonians might see the Air Corps' strength." Wright Field also hosted open houses for the public, with all the field's aircraft on display on the big ramp.

CHAPTER THIRTY-THREE

With mobilization and then entry into World War Two, promotions came rapidly and by March 1942, Ernest had been promoted to Colonel. So had Umstead, who went on to another assignment. Not long after Ernest arrived at Wright Field, Umstead had turned over responsibility for test assignments to Ernest. By the time Colonel Umstead left, Ernest was made Chief of the section, but he had been the *de facto* Chief for a long time. Early each morning, he would chair an informal pilots meeting and give out the assignments for the day. These were marked on a large scheduling board at the front of the room. Usually each pilot flew more than one test a day, and Ernest assigned himself as many tests as any of his pilots. As Chief, he also was able to assign himself some of the more interesting projects. One was the XB-19, the world's largest airplane. Colonel Umstead had been the original Wright test pilot for the big bomber.

The Douglas B-19 was a one-of-a-kind aircraft designed specifically to be a "flying laboratory." It was flown to Wright Field in mid-1942. Huge for its day, much was made of its 212-foot wingspan, which was almost twice the distance of the Wright Brothers' first flight at Kitty Hawk.

Everything about the aircraft was enormous—the main landing gear had wheels eight feet in diameter and the propellers measured 17 feet. Each of the four engines produced 2,000 horsepower. There was provision for a crew of ten, with sleeping accommodations for eight. Although it was never used as a bomber, the B-19 could carry 18 tons of bombs. Its range was 7,750 miles. Colonel Umstead did most of the initial performance testing on it. Ernest tested it after larger engines were installed and the fuselage was lengthened. He had no problems flying the B-19—it was a good design, well constructed—but he must have marveled at the contrast between this behemoth and his little Curtiss Hawk pursuit plane. For example, when landing the B-19, the pilot was still twelve feet above the runway when the main wheels touched down!

Ernest did some of the early testing on the Bell XFM-1 Airacuda. The Airacuda was a misguided attempt to satisfy a misperceived need by the Army General Staff for pursuit planes to be multiplace flying tanks, with a bombing capability as well. It was propelled by two pusher engines. Two gunners, each manning a 37 m.m. cannon, were mounted in glass enclosures on the front of each engine nacelle. The Airacuda also mounted two .30 cal. and two .50 cal. machine guns and could carry twenty 30 pound bombs. It had a crew of five, including the pilot. Ernest found it slow and ungainly as a fighter. The aircraft was a design ahead of its time, with electronics that were too rudimentary to be reliable. It received a Y designation, thirteen were built, but it never saw operational service.

Ernest was a good boss who knew how to keep problems under control and the morale of his pilots high. Nathan R. (Rosie) Rosengarten, Flight Test Engineer, joined the outfit in June 1941. He remembers "All the pilots had very extensive flying experience, many hours in all kinds of aircraft. In one day, a single pilot at Wright Field might test a fighter, a trainer, a cargo plane and a bomber. The day started with Major Warburton directing his pointer at a schedule board in that small room: 'Ozzie, you fly that B-17, Estes, you fly the B-24,' and so on down the line. I never observed an expression of displeasure on an assignment; all did what had to be done."

But as the war expanded, some test pilots moved to staff and project officer assignments while the workload increased. The first new pilots to join Flight Test were fresh out of flying school—no operational experience at all. Ernest took it in stride. He decided to give the new pilots intense on the job training, guided by the more experienced test pilots. Lieutenants Ralph C. Hoewing and Emil Sorensen were among the first neophytes to report in. Hoewing said "The first person I met was Colonel Warburton. He said, 'Welcome. We really need you. I want you to get checked out in all the airplanes we have. Start in on primary trainers. After you have flown those, move up to basic trainers and then to the advanced trainers. When you're proficient in those, we will be ready to check you out in fighters.'

"I had to get at least an hour of flying time and five landings in each aircraft I flew, then demonstrate an ability to fly the airplane and be familiar with the operating limitations, take a blindfold cockpit check, and I was considered qualified in the airplane. Nobody told me the proper speeds for take-off, landing, stall, or anything else. I had to find those things out for myself. Of course, back then, a typical Tech Order was only ten or twelve pages long.

"Well, that went on for about month. Then Colonel Warburton gave me a shot at my first operational airplane. It was a British fighter, a Hawker Hurricane. I took the blindfold check, answered some questions on the technical data, and took off. It was easier to fly than the AT-6 I'd flown in flight school! Got my five landings, and I was on my way to becoming a real test pilot."

Actually, it was a little more complicated than that. The training of new test pilots was conducted by both experienced test pilots and flight test engineers, who acted as mentors. A flight test engineer, usually Rosengarten, would prepare the instruction card for each flight and check the results. Two aircraft were used for training: an AT-6 advanced trainer and the Hurricane.

The Hurricane had been equipped with testing instrumentation, so Hoewing consulted one of the test engineers about the specifics of flying performance tests. The engineer explained there were several tests. Hoewing was expected to maintain exact airspeeds, rates of climb, altitudes, turn rates and power settings for each one of the many tests. The information then had to be entered on the test card on the young pilot's kneeboard. Performance tests had already been flown on the Hurricane by one of the experienced test pilots and Hoewing's results were then checked against the experienced pilot's numbers. Apparently, he performed well because he was then assigned performance testing work on the Curtiss P-40.

Hoewing soon learned about the risks of test flying. The Hurricane crashed and burned while being flown by his roommate. The engine quit on take off and the young pilot was killed trying to make a 180 degree turn back to the field. Hoewing had flown it just before the crash and was scheduled to fly it again after it returned from what turned out to be its final flight.

The test pilots did more than just fly. There was much technical information to be gotten on the ground. During periods of bad weather—and there were many bad weather days at Wright Field—Ernest would conduct meetings at which the pilots were briefed by flight test engineers, scientists and project engineers in the Wright laboratories. Details of new engines, aerodynamic developments, aircraft types, fuels and experiments underway in the laboratories would be discussed. On non-flying days, some of the pilots might be used in experiments in Wright's altitude chambers, testing new oxygen masks and high altitude survival equipment. There was always intense activity in the Flight Test Division.

Hoewing and, in fact, all the pilots were encouraged to get as much flying time as possible. Flying time translates into experience, and experience is what enables pilots to stay cool and successfully survive inflight emergencies. If a pilot found time between tests, he was encouraged to fly any ship on the flight line that was in commission and not being tested. "Sometimes," Hoewing said, "I would take off in a fighter and spend an hour or so doing acrobatics, shooting landings, or practicing instrument flying, building flying time."

Soon after the flying school graduates like Hoewing came a number of pilots who had been instructors in Air Force flying schools. Most notable among them was First Lieutenant Gus Lundquist (more about him later). By mid-1942 the cadre of test pilots was further reinforced by a number of pilots with combat experience. Ernest's group had grown to more than three dozen.

CHAPTER THIRTY-FOUR

There was plenty of camaraderie among Ernest's pilots. On Saturday night, there was always a party at the Wright Officers Club near the flight line. The Patterson Officers Club was subdued, formal and quiet. The Wright club, on the other hand, was lively. Located not far from the flight line, it consisted of one large, high-ceilinged room with tables for dining, a bar and a dance floor. About half way up the wall, a balcony edged the room. Married officers, mostly pilots, brought their wives there, as did single officers who could get dates, and stags who didn't have dates. The atmosphere was very informal. Music was provided by records on a juke box..

Although the club was open to all officers, on Saturday nights it was monopolized by the pilots and flight engineers in Flight Test, on a "bring your own bottle" basis. Ernest and Anna would appear at these Saturday night soirees about once a month. On many occasions they invited several young couples to their home for a nightcap and conversation.

Ernest was all military. When reporting to his office, pilots who were not flying that day were expected to be in regulation Class A uniform, complete with tie. The only place for a flight suit, he believed, was in an airplane or on the way to fly one. He followed these rules even when his pilots were at Muroc Air Base. Once, Ralph Hoewing accompanied him to Muroc and as they were leaving the flight line, suddenly realized he had forgotten to bring his cap. When he admitted this to Ernest, Ernest thought for a moment, smiled, and said "Well, you'll just have to walk one pace behind me."

Fresh from combat, Lieutenant Dick Muehlberg and another pilot reported in to Ernest at the same time. The other lieutenant was a fighter pilot. His regulation garrison cap with leather visor had been shaped into the customary "50 mission crush" but it was dirty and squashed down until it was almost unrecognizable as military headgear. The two men stood at attention before Ernest's desk. Ernest asked the fighter pilot to hand him his cap. When he complied, Ernest slammed it into the wastebasket by the side of his desk. Without comment on the cap, he launched into his standard introductory speech, telling the two new pilots what was expected of them at Wright Field. When he had finished, he told the fighter pilot to retrieve his cap and throw it into his own wastebasket. That cap was never again seen around Wright Field.

Rosie Rosengarten noticed that Ernest always carried a pair of tennis shoes out to the flight line and usually wore them while flying. He never wore them except in an aircraft, however.

There was plenty of friendly competition among the pilots, both for the most flying time and for being checked out in the greatest number of airplanes. Ernest sometimes would use this competitiveness to get a little laugh. Rosie Rosengarten remembers he frequently baited two of the pilots, Lieutenants Gus Lundquist and Perry Ritchie. At the beginning of a month, Ernest would ask Lundquist "How many hours did you get last month?" If Gus said "100," Ernest would say "Hmm. Ritchie got 120." Then, when Ritchie came into the office, Ernest would ask the same question. If Ritchie said "110," Ernest would say, "Hmm. Gus got 120." When the two pilots got together later in the day, one would say "I'm going to build up a little time and fly tonight." Of course, the other would say, "Me, too." Ernest got a kick out of this, and the two pilots got a lot of flying time. Nobody ever told them what Ernest was doing, according to Rosengarten.

Ernest frequently was away from Wright Field. For example, he spent all of June 1943 in Alaska, logging a total of 37 hours in the AT-10B, C-54, C-47, P-51B, and B-17E.

All the test pilots, Ernest included, wanted to go overseas and fly in combat but were deemed by the Air Force to be more valuable as test pilots. Lundquist and Ritchie bantered often over who would be the better in combat. One day, the argument got rather heated and Ritchie said "Let's settle this today. I'll get a P-38 and you get an A-20 and I'll wax your butt." "You're on," replied Lundquist. The dogfight, which of course was unauthorized, took place directly over Wright Field. With engines roaring, the two gyrated all over the sky trying to simulate shooting each other down. "Everyone stopped work to watch the display," said Rosengarten.

The fight was a draw. When the two warriors landed, they were greeted on the flight line by Ernest, who chewed them out royally for being irresponsible and stupid. His final remark devastated both of them: "You're both grounded until further notice!" No pilot wants to be on the ground. Sheepish and dejected, the two pilots left for the day and spent a sleepless night in their respective quarters. At Ernest's meeting the next morning, without comment, he gave each a flying assignment for the day. Without a word being said, they were "ungrounded." Undoubtedly, he remembered his own acrobatic demonstrations over Hardwick, Ware and Gilbertville.

Other pilots felt Colonel Warburton's wrath. On July 16, 1943, Captain (Dr.) Hilliard D. Estes was descending from 43,000 feet in a B-17E equipped with special engines and superchargers when the propeller on the Number One engine "ran away, " surging to over 3,000 r.p.m. Estes shut down the engine but the propeller kept spinning violently, emitting a high-pitched scream. Almost immediately, the Number One turbosupercharger oversped and began to tear apart, slinging steel blades all the way through the fuselage behind the bomb bay. Shortly, the cowling on the front of the engine was torn off and the engine itself began to twist rhythmically. Suddenly, one of the upper engine mounts broke loose and the engine sagged down at about a 20 degree angle, and it canted toward the cockpit. The rest of the engine cowling was torn loose by the vibrations and soon the engine assumed a rotational rhythm that caused the wing to flex and shudder. Oil streamed back along the wing and then black smoke gushed from the engine. By now, Estes and his crew members had put on their quick-don parachutes and were discussing bailout procedures. All this time, the propeller emitted a nerve-wracking constant shriek that sounded like a huge, tortured soprano singing at the very top of her range.

Finally, the propeller tore loose and, howling crazily, spun down and away from the aircraft. The horrendous noise stopped. So did the shuddering. There was no fire. Everything became comparatively serene, so Estes flew back to Wright Field and made a three-engine landing. As he taxied in, the tower commented on the missing propeller and the sagging engine with dripping fluids and asked if there was an emergency. No, said Estes, there had been an emergency, but it was over now. He stopped the B-17 in front of the repair hangar. Just before shutting down, the tower radioed that Estes's commanding officer wanted to see him immediately.

Estes relates what happened next in "Test Flying at Old Wright Field." "When I walked in the front door of the Ops Building, THERE HE WAS. I mean Col. Ernest K. Warburton, Chief of Flight Test and my commanding officer. It was perfectly clear to me where the real EMERGENCY was going to be - - right here, and NOW! He was red in the face and his pointed devil's eyebrows were dancing a malevolent jig. I even think I saw a pointed tail switch once, maybe twice. He was not mad about the propeller, which had concerned ME a lot. He explained in short, blunt Anglo-Saxon terms that our recent landing had been AN EMERGENCY, in capital letters. He had wanted to see fire trucks, crash vehicles, meat wagons, MPs, (you name it), all over Wright Field. Maybe it had been a slow day for Ernie. But I GOT THE MESSAGE!"

Ernest was liked and respected by all of his pilots. Dick Muehlberg was assigned to Wright Field in 1944 after flying B-24s in Africa and Europe. "Col. Warburton was the Chief of Flight Test and a wonderful person and pilot," he wrote. "He continually kept his finger on the pulse of the organization and really pushed those of us who demonstrated a real interest. Our primary job was to run tests on aircraft assigned to the Flight Test Division. Secondly, he wanted us to learn aeronautics and obtain flying experience on as many aircraft as possible."

Ernest proved to be something of an early pioneer on the subject of Women in the Workplace Doing Men's Jobs. Ann Baumgartner, a WASP (Women Air Force Service Pilot) had, at her own request, been assigned to Wright Field. Initially, her assignment was to test high altitude clothing and equipment in B-17s flying at high altitudes. The job required sitting in the nose of a bomber, wearing a variety of cold weather equipment. Sensors attached to different parts of her body recorded temperatures as the plane flew at altitudes up to 35,000 feet.

She also tested different kinds of boots, socks, even underwear, for comfort as well as for protection. She often participated in these tests in smaller aircraft like the AT-6 trainer and the A-24 and A-26 dive bombers, with canopies open, exposing her to the effects of wind and cold at altitude.

Important as the job was, it wasn't the same as piloting airplanes, which is what Ms Baumgartner was qualified to do. She had well over 200 hours of flying time before becoming a WASP and had subsequently completed regular Air Force Primary, Basic and Advanced flying training. Previously, she had been assigned to a tow-target squadron in North Carolina. "To train artillerymen," she said, "we flew small cubs, old B-34 bombers, ancient SBD dive bombers, C-45s, tired old fabric covered C-78s and heavy SB2C dive bombers." She considered herself to be, and was, *an experienced pilot.* and was determined to fly airplanes, not just sit in them. She asked her fellow pilots how she could change her status.

She was directed to see the chief of the Flight Test Division, Col. Ernest Warburton. She asked Ernest if she could be a test pilot. At that time, the paperwork in the testing business was getting very heavy, and he saw in her a chance to get some administrative help. He hired her as an assistant operations officer, assisting Captain Darrell Sims. He said she couldn't fly until she had proved she could be an efficient assistant operations officer. Over a couple of weeks she proved she could work hard and be a worthwhile assistant to Captain Sims. Major Chris Petri, who was temporarily in charge of fighters, asked her to take him up in an AT-6, in which she demonstrated her proficiency. She then flew administrative missions in a variety of single and twin engine aircraft, on flights which ranged from flying General Officers to and from Bolling Field in Washington, to picking up aircraft at outlying fields and flying them to Wright Field, to demonstration rides for school children. Soon, Petri assigned Major Gus Lundquist to give her a check ride. "She actually did O.K.," Gus reported.

Finally, Major Petri said she could fly a P-47, "but no acrobatics." Captain Ken Chilstrom crouched on the wing and gave her the cockpit familiarization checkout before she took off. Other fighter flights followed. On these flights, she tested many new warfighting devices. Among other things, she tested an electronic navigational device that was a forerunner to LORAN, and evaluated a new gunsight on a P-51, firing at a target on an island in Lake Erie. At about that time, Major Harney Estes (not to be confused with the aforementioned Hilliard Estes), the "real' head of fighter flying, returned from a long tour of temporary duty in England. He called her to his desk and explained he didn't want any women flying his fighters.

139

With Ernest's concurrence, Ms. Baumgartner was transferred to the bomber branch. There, she checked out in the B-25, B-26, C-47, B-17 and flew as copilot on the B-24 and the B-29.

Later, she was transferred back to fighters, where she was one of the pilots to fly the XP-55 canard (dubbed the Ass-ender) the Bell XP-77, and an XP-47 with a pressurized cockpit. During her tenure at Wright Field, she met Orville Wright many times, and because they were both single, was often paired with him at Flight Test luncheons and dinners. Finally, Ann Baumgartner became the first woman to fly a U.S. jet, the Bell YP-59A. Thanks to Col. Ernest K.Warburton.

She later married. Mrs. Ann Baumgartner Carl's flying experiences are detailed in her book "A Wasp Among Eagles."

CHAPTER THIRTY-FIVE

Ernest flew his share of flight tests, and always flew the riskier ones himself. In fact, he flew at least one of each of the hundreds of types of aircraft tested at Wright Field during his tenure, from small liaison birds like the fabric-covered L-5 right up to the B-29 and the aforementioned XB-19. At Wright and at Muroc, California, he flew jet fighters, including the Bell XP-59 and the Lockheed P-80. The number of different types he flew in any given month was amazing, ranging from old aircraft like the 1930s era Loening amphibian, through fighters, observation planes, cargo carriers, and twin engine and four engine bombers. He also flew light aircraft like the Piper Cub, different models of the Stinson, Ballanca and other planes produced by small plane manufacturers.

Each pilot carried a small yellow "Pilot's Aircraft Qualification Card" which listed all the aircraft he was currently qualified to fly. One of Ernest's cards listed 88 different types and models of aircraft, including trainers, attack planes, transports, bombers, foreign planes and experimental models.

Emergencies were part of many flights. Once, while Ernest was testing a B-25, the propeller on one engine began to change from high pitch to low pitch continually, without regard to the pitch control setting on the cockpit pedestal. This caused the airplane to violently oscillate back and forth, first skidding left and then right in a seemingly endless cycle. He tried shutting down the engine with the uncontrollable propeller, but the prop would not feather. The windmilling prop produced so much drag the remaining engine did not have enough power to enable him to fly to a landing field. The aircraft kept descending. The copilot suggested bailing out, but Ernest convinced him they had enough altitude to solve the problem. He shutdown and restarted the engine several times and finally succeeded in feathering the propeller. After that, he executed an emergency single engine landing at Wright.

On another occasion, Ernest was testing a glider retrieval system. He was the glider pilot. It was poised on the runway hooked onto a long, elasticized cable that ran from the glider's nose to a harness that was suspended from the tops of two poles, about twenty feet in the air. A multiengine aircraft trailing a hook flew down the runway, engaged the cable and pulled the glider into the air. The elasticized cable was designed to stretch and absorb the initial g loading of the hookup so that the cable fastening mechanism was not jerked out of the glider and the glider came up to flying speed rapidly and smoothly, as if propelled from a slingshot.

After being towed around the flight pattern, Ernest released the cable and flew the glider to a deadstick landing back on the runway. Ground crewman then repositioned it for another pickup. Several successful retrievals and landings were accomplished. But then, something went wrong. On the next retrieval, the cable stretched, Ernest came off the runway, and the cable snapped. The section of cable hooked onto the glider whipped back and wrapped around the tail section, immobilizing the stabilizer and rudder. Already a hundred feet or more in the air, Ernest found himself at the controls of a wildly gyrating aircraft with practically no pitch control. Somehow, he wrestled the glider to a safe landing. The ground crewmen, wild eyed with apprehension, ran up alongside. "Well," said Ernest, "let's get this thing fixed and we'll try again."

Gus Lundqist carried the tow procedure one step further when, flying a P-39, he successfully hooked up by cable to another aircraft in midair, feathered his propeller, and then was towed. The experiment was to determine the feasibility of towing fighters over long distances with bombers, and releasing them in the target area to start their engines and protect the bombers from enemy fighters. At that time, fighters could not carry enough fuel to accompany U.S. bombers all the way to their targets and return to their bases. But towed fighters would not use any fuel on the way to the target area and thus have enough to fend off enemy fighters and then fly home.

Ernest also carried out this test. Ralph Hoewing was in the rear of the B-17 that was used for Ernest's first hookup. "It was a pretty sporty operation," he said. The cable from Ernest's P-39 ran from a harness on top of the cockpit and was taped along the leading edge of a wing out to a wingtip. "At the wingtip," Hoewing remembers, "the cable was connected to a hook intended to latch onto another cable trailed back from the tail of the B-17 towship when the P-39 was maneuvered into the proper position. The plan was for Ernest to fly up to the end of the trailing cable and engage the hook. When the hookup was made, he was to fly off to the side and above the towship, cut his engine and feather his propeller. As he lost airspeed and started to fall back from the tow ship, Ernest's cable would be stripped from his wingtip and be pulled straight out ahead of the fighter.

"The problem" Hoewing said, "was getting hooked to the cable. It wasn't very stable. About 150 feet of it was reeled out, and then it was whipping around in the air. And there's Warburton, trying to latch onto it. A couple of times, the tow cable almost got tangled in Ernie's propeller. But, finally, he made the hookup and we towed him around for about 30 minutes." Subsequently, Gus Lundquist made several plane to plane midair hookups. One tow flight, with Lundquist flying the P-39, lasted ten hours. Lundqist demonstrated the procedure for General Hap Arnold, Chief of the Army Air Forces, but when he was cut loose from the tow plane, he had considerable trouble starting his engine.

This system was never used in World War Two because of the anticipated difficulty of starting fighter engines that were cold soaked after hours of flying in the thin, frigid air at high altitude. Ernest, in a P-39, also made a hookup to a cable towed by another P-39. He attempted a rope retrieval of a dead engine fighter by using a B-17 as the tow aircraft, but the fighter was too heavy for the rope, which simply parted.

In September 1941, he successfully carried out water take off and landing tests of the first and only C-47 transport to be equipped with floats, the Douglas XC-47C-DL (His prior experience flying the Grumman OA-9 amphibian was helpful here). The aircraft was not put into production.

He did the performance testing on the Bell XFM-1 twin engine pusher fighter and made more than one forced landing in the YFM-1 because of engine failure. He carried out performance testing on the Lockheed P-38, Douglas C-54 and Curtiss C-46. He flew the initial spin tests on the Curtiss P-40D. He flew many, many other tests.

At the same time he was testing aircraft himself, Ernest was providing leadership to the pilots under him. "When I arrived at the old Flying Branch in 1941," Rosie Rosengarten wrote, " ... I quickly learned that then Major Warburton ran a tight ship. A test pilot and flight test engineer team would be dispatched the same day or no later than the next day to a contractor facility when the contractor called his aircraft was ready for evaluation." At times, Ernest would call the team and tell them that at the completion of the testing they were doing, they should accomplish more testing at another contractor's facility in a different locality instead of returning to Wright Field. "We always carried a lot of socks and underwear on our trips because we never knew how long we'd be gone," Rosie recalled.

"In no small measure, his leadership brought out the best in the young pilots under his command," Rosengarten wrote. "He was very demanding. He insisted that all young pilots check out in all types of aircraft. He required that all pilots get lots of flying time—night, day, and instrument flying.

"He was responsible for the making of some of the most outstanding test pilots of the World War Two era. He was a modest man, he did what he thought was his job and he never sought publicity, although those who served under him received a fair amount of it. "

"At first, at least to a young person," Rosengarten wrote, "Ernie Warburton didn't appear friendly. In time, we learned that he had a very bad back that kept him perpetually in pain." (This was the result of injuries sustained in his crash during the Arctic Flight and his emergency low altitude, flaming, bailout over Detroit back in the Thirties).

"He was all business but he could be humorous and he laughed at practical jokes played on him as well as those he played in return." Ernest exchanged practical jokes with a Major Shanahan, who headed up the Armament Laboratory. Apparently, they had been stationed together in the past. "These two," Rosengarten wrote, "when they could, would head up to North Dakota to shoot wild ducks and geese."

Rosie was a bachelor and lived with several other Test Division bachelors in the Dayton YMCA. They formed an unofficial group called "The Gravy Club," and they ate their meals together at restaurants and hotels in the city. "One evening, we Gravy Club members were invited to his home for dinner, and we feasted on wild duck and pheasants that he had personally laid to rest. Mrs. Warburton was a superb cook. He was a fortunate man." The Gravy Club members were also invited from time to time to eat at the homes of other married officers. They, in turn, reciprocated by inviting married couples to dine with them in Dayton's finer restaurants.

Ernest also exercised his authority at Muroc, where much Wright Field testing was done because of the good flying weather. Rosie spent a lot of temporary duty time at North Muroc, billeted in a barracks aptly nicknamed "The Desert Rat Hotel." One room served as both bedroom and office. On more than one occasion when Ernest visited Muroc, he would discuss operations while lying down on Rosie's bed to ease his back.

In July 1942, a new type of airplane, the helicopter, arrived at Wright Field. It was the Sikorsky XR-4, prototype of the first production military helicopter. Helicopters were more difficult to fly than conventional aircraft. They could move forward, backward, sideways and could hover in one place. Unlike today's "choppers," they did not have a stability augmentation system. Flying a helicopter, one pilot reported, was like balancing the machine on the point of a pin.

Ernest's first flight in the XR-4 was on July 17, 1942, when he logged 15 minutes of training time and two landings. He logged a total of 11:35 hours and 124 landings in the YR-4, which became the first operational Air Force helicopter. He became quite good at helicopter flying—one day, Anna was working in the garden, heard the roar of an approaching aircraft and looked up to see Ernest in the YR-4, hovering right over the front yard! He gave her a smile and a wave.

In May 1943, Ernest was awarded the Distinguished Flying Cross. The citation read, "for extraordinary achievement while participating in aerial flights at Wright Field, Ohio, during 1941 and 1942. While on duty at the Materiel Center, Colonel Warburton served as test pilot involving thousands of hours of hazardous experimental flights with new types of aircraft the performance of which under various conditions have been untried. These flights were made in scores of bombing, fighter, observation, training and cargo airplanes, and called for the most expert flying technique.

"Although engaged in a type of flying where danger is seldom absent, Colonel Warburton never resorted to an emergency parachute jump, despite the fact that numerous models being tested experienced mechanical or structural failure while in flight. In each instance, he managed to make an emergency landing so that the airplane would be available intact for engineering inspection. By refusing to abandon these airplanes, Colonel Warburton frequently endangered his life, and his extreme devotion to duty in the face of threatened fatal landing accidents is in the finest traditions of the Army Air Forces." At that time, Ernest had flown over 2,000 test hours in more than 250 different aircraft.

CHAPTER THIRTY-SIX

In September, 1943, Ernest was temporarily ordered to England, Italy and North Africa to fly Royal Air Force aircraft and captured German aircraft and observe performance of U.S. tactical aircraft in the war zone. He was accompanied by Capt. Emil Sorenson, one of the pilots sent to Flight Test Branch directly from flying school. By now, Sorenson was a full-fledged test pilot. Their mission was to observe British flight test establishments, study their test procedures, fly the latest type of British equipment and gather information on operational performance of tactical aircraft in the European Theater of Operations. At Wright Field, Ernest had flown early versions of the British Hawker Hurricane, Supermarine Spitfire, Fairey Battle, Bristol Beaufighter, and Boulton-Paul Defiant fighters, the Avro Anson trainer and the Mosquito and Wellington bombers. He had also flown a captured German Messerschmitt Bf109. Sorenson had flown some of the British planes also.

It was a whirlwind two-month trip. The duo spent nine days at the RAF Aircraft and Experimental Establishment at Boscomb Down. There they observed organization of the Performance Squadron, flight test procedures and data reduction methodology. Between them, they flew sixteen different aircraft. Six were bombers: Halifax II four engine bomber with Merlin XX engines, Halifax III four engine bomber with Hercules engines, Stirling I four engine bomber with Hercules engines, Lancaster II four engine bomber at 57,000 pounds gross weight with Hercules engines, Lancaster III four engine bomber at 45,000 pounds gross weight with Merlin engines, and a Warwick twin engine bomber with (U.S.) Pratt & Whitney 2800 engines.

They flew eleven British fighters: the newest fighter version of the DeHavilland Mosquito, then, Mosquito with an aft c.g. load condition, Westland Welkin, which was a new experimental high altitude twin engine airplane, Spitfire VIII standard production aircraft with Merlin 66 engine, Spitfire IX with bubble canopy, Spitfire IX with counter-rotating propellers, Spitfire XIV test bed for the Griffin engine, Spitfire XXI production model with the Griffin engine, Typhoon fighter-bomber with Sabre engine, Tempest V fighter-bomber and the new Firebrand air arm shipboard fighter.

They also flew the Focke-Wulf 190 German fighter. Ernest flew the Gloster 9/40 "Meteor" twin engine turbojet fighter, the first British jet, which he found to be slower than many propeller-driven fighters (later versions of this plane were much improved, with more powerful engines, and they were used near the end of the war for shooting down V-1 flying bombs. the Meteor was the only Allied jet to fly in combat over Europe).

They visited ten aircraft and engine factories. Nine U.S Army Air Force units at wing, group or headquarters level were visited in England, as well as one at Foggia, Italy and another at Gerbini, Sicily. The two briefly visited bases in North Africa and were flown up to Foggia by none other than General Jimmy Doolittle,who at that time was Vice Commander of 12th Air Force. Doolittle piloted a B-25 on the trip to Foggia, and Ernest was his copilot.

At the time of their trip, the US Army Air Force was testing a Canadian built Mosquito to see if it could be adapted for reconnaissance missions. The British employed it as a light bomber and as a pathfinder for British night heavy bombing raids over Europe. The Mosquito was a two seat, single pilot aircraft. Ernest tested one, with Sorenson in the right hand seat acting as flight engineer, when they encountered an emergency.

The British had just begun installing armor plating under the engines to improve survivability in combat. While they were in a shallow dive at 400 knots, the large sheet of armor under the left cooling radiator was torn off by the slipstream. "It let go with a loud bang," Sorenson said. It hit the exhaust for the left engine and just missed the tail. "That closed up the exhaust quite a bit, and caused fire and sparks to shoot out, and of course that doesn't give you too good a feeling when you're flying a wooden airplane." Ernest immediately throttled back the left engine and turned back towards the base, about 20 miles away. "He did a masterful job of getting us down on terra firma," Sorenson said, "in spite of interference from a Warwick bomber approaching the field. Colonel Warburton was embarrassed to return the borrowed airplane with the damage we had inflicted, but the armor plate incident made the RAF people aware of a problem that could have been disastrous if it had happened in combat."

The duo produced a several hundred page report on their trip and the aircraft flown.

While in England, Ernest observed the operation of the RAF's Empire Test Pilot School at Boscombe Down. There were stringent requirements for pilots to be accepted in the school. The ground school part of the curriculum was strongly based on aeronautical engineering. There was a formal flying program that trained fledgling test pilots in the intricacies of precision test flying and data compilation in the air. Ernest decided the Air Force should have such a school. He arranged for test pilots Ralph Hoewing and Wallace A. Lien to attend the school. Lien was killed in an Oxford training aircraft while attending the school. When Hoewing returned, he set up and became the first Officer in Charge of the new test pilot school at Wright Field. The second Wright Field pilot to graduate from the British school was

Dick Muehlberg. On September 9, 1944 the Wright Field test pilot school officially became the Air Force Test Pilot School and Muehlberg was appointed Commandant.. The school is now located at Edwards AFB, California (formerly Muroc).

The Army had been using Muroc as a bombing range since the mid-Thirties. California aircraft manufacturers were the first to test aircraft there. The Army then followed suit and began testing on a sporadic basis, usually in the winter. But it was Ernest who realized that there should be a permanent, year 'round test base there. Nate Rosengarten took the initiative and composed a letter proposing a base be established at Muroc. It pointed out that, among other things, the weather was so good flying was possible 98 per cent of the time, and there were at least 100 square miles of take off and landing space, with eight good emergency landing fields within a 50 mile radius. Muroc's remote location made it relatively easy to maintain secrecy for special projects, and "when extra smooth air is required, tests could be flown over the ocean 100 miles from the base." There was plenty of space for heavyweight take offs, which required a very long ground roll. There was much more rationale in a three-page, single spaced letter. The letter sent to the Commanding General, Materiel Command, was signed by Colonel S.A. Gilkey, who became Chief of Flight Test when Ernest was reassigned. Ernest's initials "EKW" are affixed next to Gilkey's signature. By the time the new base was established, Ernest was in the Southwest Pacific war zone. Col. Gilkey became the first commander at Muroc. Had Ernest not gone off to war, he undoubtedly would have been Muroc's first commander.

In December 1943, Ernest took his first two flights in the brand-new Boeing YB-29, which as the B-29 was mass produced and later was used to end World War Two by dropping two atomic bombs on Japan. In February 1944, he flew the Bell XP-59 jet fighter four times, having flown it once before in August 1943 (The primary test pilot was Maj. Wally Lien). Ernest didn't think much of the airplane. For one thing, it was underpowered. The aircraft was powered by two General Electric GE-1A engines. The GE-1A was a copy of the first version of the British Whittle engine, so the XP-59 flew a lot like the first model of the Meteor. The report on the aircraft, written by Nate Rosengarten, concluded "At present, the YP-59A is definitely not satisfactory as a combat fighter; at best, it could be utilized as a transitional trainer to familiarize pilots with the operating characteristics of jet type power plant.

The YP-59 quickly became irrelevant because Lockheed had already turned out the first copy of the XP-80, which became the first successful U.S. operational jet fighter, the famous P-80 "Shooting Star." It performed sensationally and was the first jet to hit 500 mph in level flight. Ernest flew it in March 1944.

Over the summer and fall, he continued to fly a wide variety of aircraft including the P-38, P-51, B-26, B-19, B-24, B-17, B-25, B-29, C-46 AT-7, the Y4B helicopter, and an experimental attack aircraft, the XA-41. In September 1944, he was alerted that, at last, he was being transferred to the combat zone. His final Wright Field flight was in an RB-17E on September 29. He had logged a career total of 6,582 hours. Included in that total were more than 2500 hours of test flying in 250 types of aircraft at Wright Field.

When Ernest was transferred overseas, the Warburton family was required to vacate the big house and move off base. Anna decided to move back to Massachusetts. Until Ernest returned a year and a half later, they lived on the Ward Farm, which her parents owned in Westboro.

CHAPTER THIRTY-SEVEN

Wasting no time going to war, Ernest was assigned as Assistant Chief of Staff, Far East Air Service Command in Australia, effective October 5, 1944. Leaving Hamilton Field, California on October 2, he flew by C-54 to Hawaii and then island-hopped to Australia, making the trip in 35 hours and 55 minutes, stopping to rest for only one day enroute. He then spent two weeks on the ground, working into his new job. While in Darwin, he found time for a day of duck hunting, so he was able to briefly indulge his favorite pastime.

Ernest didn't want to stay at headquarters in Australia. He demanded to be transferred to the combat zone. Prior to the invasion of the Philippines, he became Commander of the V Air Force Service Command, Philippine Islands. This was the first service unit to land in the Philippines. They went ashore on Leyte, the main island, under enemy fire, October 20, 1944.

Ernest sent home a copy of the Manila Tribune published on October 24, when the Japanese still held the city. He obtained it after the fall of Manila. A front page story read "Scores of American tanks have already been blasted and disabled on the beach by the intensifying Japanese defense fire on the landing points near Tacloban, according to frontline reports received in Manila. The fighting in this area continues unabated as columns of heavy black smoke shoot skyward from stranded tanks among the coconut groves....The Japanese garrison, the dispatches revealed, were exacting heavy tolls in men and materiel as enemy forces tried frantically to establish beachheads under enemy fire."

"For about a week," a Boston newspaper reported, "the service command troops remained dug in on the beach, undergoing Jap bombing and strafing raids." At the same time, "the unit helped build Tacloban air strip for Fifth Air Force fighter planes. Work was carried on under constant enemy aerial attack and adverse weather conditions.. Upon completion of the strip, the troops began to service and maintain all aircraft in performance of the mission of Fifth Air Force Service Command."

Ernest found time for flying, and logged his first flight in the Combat Zone on October 24, 1944 in a B-25 over a Japanese-controlled part of New Guinea. Although not required to fly combat missions, he flew many.

He missed his family. On October 30, 1944, he wrote letters to his children. "Dear Darby," he wrote. "Well, big boy, how are you and the farm

150

getting along? Do you like the new bed? Is the bicycle still running? Be sure to keep off the big road. Tell Mommie to give you some candy. Be a good boy. Love, Daddy."

To Sally, he wrote "Just a note to my precious little blonde girl who is growing up so fast. Bet you must be big now. I am now in the tropics and enjoy it very much except for not being with my family. A lot of work to be done here. Tell Mommie to kiss you for me. Lovingly, Daddy."

To Ward, he wrote, "Just a line to say hello. Tell Mommie that you can use some of Daddy's tools—also Darby. Tell Mommie that you can have some candy." Before leaving California, he had written "Dear Ward and Darby, Mommie will read this to you. You are both big, healthy boys and Daddy loves you and wants you to grow up to be healthy and honest. Don't get into too much mischief in the meantime, though. Love, Daddy."

To Anna, he at first sent telegrams. Even in terse "telegramese, " his love for her was obvious. The first one read, simply, "AM WELL AND FIT. SEND ME A LATE PHOTO. BEST LOVE FROM DADDY." Another telegram read "AM WRITING REGULARLY. YOU ARE MORE THAN EVER IN MY THOUGHTS AT THIS TIME. ALL MY LOVE. " A third read "LETTERS ARRIVING REGULARLY. VERY HAPPY TO HEAR FROM YOU DEAREST. ALL MY LOVE." Often, Ernest sent Anna short notes, usually scrawled on the back of the mimeographed menus from the Officers' Mess. They usually said he was fine, sleeping well, and thinking of her. They always began "Darling," and ended with "All my love."

On December 5, 1944, he became Commanding Officer of the 46th Air Service Group, one of several Air Service Groups he would command setting up forward bases in support of the air war as General MacArthur's forces island-hopped across the Southwest Pacific. Air bases were of paramount importance in MacArthur's advance towards Japan because he never had much naval support for invasions of the islands he used as stepping stones. Most of his "naval gunfire support" came from Air Force General George C. Kenney's Far East Air Forces. Kenney's planes needed air bases from which to fly. Ernest's service groups, and others, provided them along with needed support.

Service groups were in the advance echelon as U.S. and Allied forces moved forward through the Southwest Pacific, pushing the Japanese back towards their homeland. They had a big and important job, which was to rehabilitate destroyed Japanese or Allied bases, or build new bases from which U.S. warplanes could operate, and then service and maintain those warplanes. Ernest's people built new runways, operations buildings, barracks, mess halls, aircraft repair facilities, chapels, hangars, and anything else required to make a base operational. They were then responsible for maintenance of these bases, including buildings, roads, taxiways, runways, parking areas and revetments as well as repair support for aircraft. Service groups built and supported base hospitals, and provided morale building events like movies, visits from show business people, Army stage shows, as well as the publishing of local base newspapers.

Sometimes, Ernest would have to do some "horse trading" to get things done. On one island, his people had repaired and were operating an ice making plant that provided the only ice for all the U.S. troops on the island. One of the runways needed extensive repairs which required heavy equipment that Ernest's unit did not possess at the time. There was an Army Corps of Engineers unit on the island, so he asked the engineer Commanding Officer for men and machinery to do the job. the C.O. replied that the engineers were too busy to carry out the runway project. Immediately, Ernest ordered his ice plant people to stop issuing ice to the engineers. The next day, the engineer Commanding Officer called on Ernest in his office and asked if there was anything he could do to help. Ernest repeated his request for runway repair equipment, the request was granted, and the engineers began receiving ice again.

As a service group commander, Ernest was not required to fly. Nevertheless, he did fly, averaging 30 or 40 hours a month. He logged most of his time in the B-25 bomber and the L-5 liaison aircraft, but also flew P-38 and P-51 fighters, C-47, C-46 and C-54 transports, A-20 and P-61 night-fighters, B-17 and B-24 bombers and C-64 liaison aircraft. He made one short flight in the Sikorsky R-4 helicopter, like the one in which he had hovered over Anna in the front yard of the big house at Wright Field. In the war zone, the Air Force logged flying time as either "Combat Zone" or "Combat Mission." The former was time logged flying around the combat zone. The latter was logged by pilots on actual combat missions against the enemy. Overall, Ernest logged 238 hours of Combat Zone time and 121 hours on actual Combat Missions. He flew many of these combat missions in the B-25H, which was equipped with a 75 mm cannon and fourteen heavy machine guns for dangerous low level attack of Japanese shipping and ground units.

On January 16, 1945, Ernest wrote to Ward, Sally and Darby to thank them for the Christmas presents they had sent, even though he had not as yet received them. He hoped they all liked their sweaters. He said it was a hot day in the tropics and he was going swimming. A few days later, he sent twelve tiny seashells scotch taped to a sheet of paper captioned "To Keeling, Joanne, Sally, Ward and Darby from the shores of Leyte."

After the invasion of the Philippines, his service command unit followed the ground advance from Leyte to the main island of Luzon and reached Clark Field, the huge prewar U.S. air base. The Japanese had occupied it during the war and had almost completely destroyed it when they pulled out prior to the Americans' return. Buildings were burned down, hangars were reduced to girder skeletons, planes, automobiles and trucks were disabled, craters were punched into ramps and runways. Ernest's people set to work on the biggest job they had faced in the war. They had the runways open in less than a week and then concentrated on building new structures. At the same time, they serviced the scores of U.S. fighters and bombers that began to fly in and out of the base.

For a long time after the Americans retook Clark Field from the Japanese, a large number of Japanese troops held out in the mountains near Clark. Ernest flew bombing missions against them.

As the Americans fought their way through the Philippines, Ernest became responsible for several bases. To get from place to place, he utilized three aircraft which were "his," but could be flown by other pilots when he did not need them. He named a C-47 "Anna," after his wife, and a B-25 "Joanne," after his eldest daughter. The third plane was an L-5, which he named "Sally," after his second daughter.

At Clark Field, Ernest temporarily got back into the testing business.

The Japanese had abandoned and nearly destroyed many types of their combat aircraft when they left. Several were so new they had not been seen in combat. But there were enough intact parts left to rebuild at least one copy of each plane and Ernest volunteered to test fly them. The war was still going on and information on their performance would be valuable to U.S. airmen meeting these new aircraft in air combat.

The Frank, George, Jack II, Judy fighters as well as the Nick I and Betty bombers were among those reconstructed. Ernest tested them all, one by one, and wrote a report on each. Generally, he concluded the Japanese had produced some very good planes. The Associated Press reported "Col. Ernest K.Warburton, one who should know, thinks the Japanese have produced a number of good combat planes and their latest fighters rank with those of the United States.

"The husky, regular army colonel, whose home is at Westboro, Mass., is a test pilot for captured Japanese aircraft. He has flown more than half a dozen types, both bombers and fighters, of Nippon's best planes. "The old idea that the Japanese couldn't invent anything is all wrong, in aircraft, at least,' he said. 'In design and thinking they are up to us.' "

This kind of test work was particularly dangerous. The planes were completely unfamiliar to Ernest and the quality of the reconstruction work, since it was done under austere field conditions, was unknown. For example, when he tested the George II fighter, he reported, "The right oleo leg (landing gear) collapsed on this airplane at the end of the landing roll and the airplane was badly damaged." If the collapse had taken place at a higher speed, Ernest might have been injured. There were in-air emergencies while other aircraft were being tested.

Ernest received a special commendation for this test work from General George C. Kenney, Commander Far East Air Forces:

> "1. It has come to my attention that you accepted the dangerous task of test-flying the captured Japanese airplanes recently rebuilt at Clark Field and that on two

occasions you risked your life to save these aircraft when a mechanical failure occurred in flight.

"2. In each case, by courageously deciding to try to land the enemy plane rather than to parachute out, you preserved a valuable source of technical intelligence.

"3. I wish to commend you highly for the bravery, skill, and devotion to duty which you displayed. "

CHAPTER THIRTY-EIGHT

Ernest performed other heroic exploits. In May, 1945, while the battle for the Philippines still raged, a P-51 pilot returning from a mission ran into bad weather and, rather than fly through it, made a forced landing on a flat, grassy plain on a small island in the archipelago. Following standard procedure for a forced landing on a strange, unpaved field, he bellied his plane in with landing gear up. He was soon surrounded by a band of Filipino guerrillas, who informed him the Japanese still held the island. Fortunately, the enemy was in a different part of the island.

The pilot switched his radio to the standard U.S. emergency channel, explained what he had done, stated his plane was practically undamaged, and asked to be rescued. His call was heard by the tower at one of Ernest's airstrips located on an island nearby. Ernest responded by flying his little L-5, "Sally," to the island, where he landed on the same grassy plain. He examined the P-51 and determined all it needed was a new propeller and some sheet metal work. He directed the guerrillas to begin cutting down some of the high grass on the plain to make a crude runway. Then he flew the pilot back to the base in "Sally."

There, he rounded up some mechanics, a P-51 propeller, and all the equipment needed to replace the prop and jack up the P-51 so its wheels could be lowered for takeoff. The next day, he loaded the people and equipment into his C-47, "Anna" and flew to the island. The work took three days. "Anna" flew Ernest's people into the little field each morning and flew them out each night. The guerrillas continued to cut the grass, and provided lookouts and protection in case the Japanese began to wander in the P-51's direction. When the work was done, Ernest started up the P-51, another pilot flew "Anna," with people and equipment back to the base, and Ernest flew the fighter to safety. The Japanese, apparently, never realized what happened.

155

Chapter Thirty-nine

On June 25, 1945, the "Coral Courier" newspaper published by Ernest's 46th Air Service Group, announced the battle for Okinawa was over. Ernest surmised he would soon be moving there to take over a new service group.

Soon he moved to Ie Shima, a small island off the coast of Okinawa, and established a base there in July, 1945. He and his troops lived in tents and portable buildings. Ernest awaited further orders.

On August 6, the B-29 "Enola Gay" dropped an atomic bomb on Hiroshima, Japan. A second atomic bomb was dropped on Nagasaki on August 9. The war was all but over. On August 15, the Emperor of Japan formally surrendered, against the wishes of fanatical Japanese Imperial Army leaders, who wanted the Japanese to fight to the last man, woman and child.

Ernest's next set of orders contained a big surprise. On August 21, 1945, he received orders making him Commander of all U.S. Air Force troops in the Tokyo, Japan area. He was to take the first Americans into Tokyo to prepare for General MacArthur's arrival on the Japanese mainland. They read:

HEADQUARTERS
FIFTH AIR FORCE
APO 710

"TO: Colonel Ernest K. Warburton, 017401, Headquarters, V Air Force Service Command, APO 710

1. You have been appointed Commander of all Army Air Forces troops in the Tokyo area.

2. Upon arrival in that area you will immediately notify Far East Air Forces and this Air Force that you have arrived and assumed command.

3. At the proper time you will be notified as to when you will proceed to Tokyo.

K.B. Wolfe
Major General, USA
Chief of Staff"

A few days later, a Japanese Betty bomber painted white with big cross-
es on the fuselage and vertical stabilizer to mark it as a neutral aircraft
touched down at Ernest's airfield. On board were several Japanese military
envoys who had come to work out the details of the American arrival in
Japan. Ernest learned that he was to lead his advance party into Atsugi airfield, near Tokyo. He and his communications and maintenance troops were
to land in Japan on August 26, 1945.

After the Japanese envoys left, an officer from MacArthur's headquarters
handed him an envelope marked "Urgent Secret," which contained his operational orders. He opened the envelope and read, "The Commanding
Officer of the advance party of the Supreme Commander for the Allied
Powers is charged with the following mission:

(1) Reconnaissance of the Atsugi airdrome to determine its
    suitability for the airborne operation to follow.

(2) Establishment of required air installations and supplies
    to support initial phases of the air operations in the area
    as provided by the Commanding General FEAF (Far
    East Air Forces).

(3) Supervision and coordination of improvements required
    at the Atsugi Airdrome.

(4) Establishment of communications with GHQ, AFPAC
    (General Headquarters, Air Forces Pacific) without
    delay and report on suitability or non-suitability of the
    Atsugi airdrome for the purpose intended. All messages
    to be transmitted in code. Report over signal commu-
    nications net additional information desired by the
    Commanding General, FEAF."

Atsugi airfield, Ernest was informed, happened to be the home base of
the fanatical Kamikaze pilots who flew their suicide planes into U.S. Navy
ships and Army landing craft right up to the end of the war. Although their
government had surrendered, nobody knew positively how these fanatics felt
about the idea of giving up. Ernest was aware the Japanese army opposed
surrender until finally overruled by the Emperor. Therefore, Ernest and his
men were told to go into Atsugi fully armed.

He led an airborne armada of 48 transports and bombers utilized as transports. Under his command were 150 airmen whose job was to set up communications and make sure the runway and other parts of the airfield were suitable for the arrival of MacArthur's entourage two days later, on August 28.

When they landed there was no opposition, much to everyone's relief. Ernest and his troops, dressed in flying suits and work uniforms, were met by Japanese officers in full dress uniforms with sashes and medals. There was no bowing, but everyone was very polite. The Americans were invited to sit down for tea and a lunch of turtle soup and sandwiches, served at tables that had been set up outdoors on the ramp. There were scores of Japanese combat aircraft at the field, but they had been disabled by the Japanese, either by removing their propellers or landing gear, or both.

So, at 12:10 P.M., August 27, 1945, before lunch was served, the American flag flew over a defeated Japan for the first time. Ernest's men had the first radio antenna erected in less than three hours. He reported his presence on Japanese soil and declared the two usable runways, which measured 5,600 and 5,100 feet in length, respectively, were long enough for MacArthur's C-54s to land, with some room to spare.

Ernest and his men took over Japanese facilities for offices and dormitories. They quickly established billeting facilities, mess halls, a chapel, and a dispensary. His sleeping quarters were in a building resembling a quonset hut. Other facilities soon followed as Americans began to arrive by the planeload.

On the second day, a supply officer offered to let Ernest choose a staff car for his own use from a group that had been commandeered from the Japanese General Staff. He chose a prewar era Rolls Royce with a convertible top. That afternoon, he was informed by a higher ranking officer on MacArthur's advance staff that the car was reserved for the General himself. Ernest chose another car. When the surrender ceremony took place on the battleship USS Missouri, anchored in Tokyo Bay, Ernest was one of the officers invited to observe. He appears in the front row of officers in a picture that ran on the first page of the New York Times and newspapers across America.

After MacArthur officially arrived and Americans were firmly in control, Ernest flew an L-5 much like "Sally" on exploratory trips over the countryside. He took along a crew chief as a passenger. One day, they decided to land in a field near one of the many palaces that dotted the area. As they taxied towards the edifice, palace guards began shooting at them (the Americans had not disarmed Japanese civilians). Calmly, Ernest told the crew chief to get out, lift the tail and turn the airplane around. Acting with the alacrity that comes from the sheer terror of being under fire, the crew chief complied, jumped back in, Ernest shoved the throttle forward, and they took off safely.

Ernest was respected and liked by his men in the service group as much as he had been by his subordinates at Wright Field. On August 25, 1945, while Ernest was preparing to fly into Tokyo, Anna received this telegram from Major Roy A. Davidson, one of his subordinates who had returned to the United States: "YOUR HUSBAND SENDS ALL HIS LOVE. HE IS THE BEST C.O. I EVER HAD. HEALTHY AND IN GOOD SPIRITS."

When the war had ended but Ernest was still in Japan, Anna got this telegram from a Major Jackson: "LEFT COLONEL WARBURTON 21 OCTOBER IN ATSUGI JAPAN. WAS IN GOOD HEALTH AND ANXIOUS TO GET HOME. HE WAS FLYING RESCUE MISSIONS FOR COLONEL JOHNSON." (Colonel Johnson was a friend who disappeared on a flight out of Japan after the war ended. He was never found).

On another occasion, Anna received a beautiful bouquet of flowers with a small card reading: "Greetings—to the wife of the finest gentleman in the U.S. Air Force. Major F. Vecchio." Major Vecchio had been Ernest's Chief Flight Surgeon at Ie Shima.

Ernest wrote as often as he could, using whatever paper was available. Once, he sent the front page of the Aug. 30, 1945 Nippon Times with a note scrawled above the headline at the top: "Darling—All fine. Write tomorrow. Busy as a bee. All my love, Ernest."

As time went on, Ernest began to make inspection trips to some the major bases he had set up along the chain of islands used for the invasion route. In November, he sent Anna and the children each an undated V-mail Christmas Card. A few days later, his bad back flared up with a vengeance and he was confined to bed in the hospital. This time, his condition was serious. He was shipped home on medical leave aboard the hospital ship "Comfort."

CHAPTER FORTY

On November 20, 1945, writing on American Red Cross stationary, he sent Anna a short note from the ship. "Darling," he wrote, "We expect to hit Guam tomorrow and I am very much improved. Much pleased with progress now. I really was in bad shape—not out of bed for two weeks. Doc gave me a spinal injection and it sure helped. All pain gone except hip and leg—get around okeh (sic) now. Expect to be able to skip rope by the time we get to Los Angeles. Will let you know when I get there. If all goes well, I'll be home in plenty of time for Christmas. Sure will be wonderful—hope to be sent to Cushing General Hospital at Framingham so I'll be close to home. Wish you could see the improvement in my figure—lost about ten pounds. Only trouble is, I've lost a lot in my face.

"This is a Liberty ship and it's not very fast—about fifteen knots—but it's pleasant. Getting good care and should be almost well when I get there. One of the docs thinks I may have had siacitca (sic) but it is diagnosed as scariliac (sic) acute. We're quite a ways south so it is nice and warm out. All my love."

Ernest sent this telegram from California: "ARRIVED OKEH. DEPARTING FOR DAYTON TOMORROW. BOSTON BY SUNDAY." As he hoped, he was attached to Cushing General Hospital in Framingham, Massachusetts, where he was examined and then temporarily sent home to Westboro. The Warburton family was together again for Christmas.

Ernest was assigned to Cushing for five long months, undergoing treatment, rehabilitation and evaluation of his physical condition. At one time, the doctors were on the verge of issuing a medical discharge. He commuted frequently each weekend between Cushjing and Westboro until May, 1946. Then, he was returned to flying status and temporarily reassigned to Wright Field, which by that time had been designated Wright Patterson Air Force Base. Ernest had been informed this was a temporary assignment, so he left his family back in New England.

At Wright-Pat, Ernest became Deputy for Operations of Air Materiel Command's Air Weather Division. He logged some flying time, but not much, in the L-5, B-25, XB-19, C-47, and B-24. He was only at Wright for three months before he was selected to be a member of the first class in the newly established Air War College at Maxwell Air Force Base, Alabama. He reported there in September, 1946. This was another prestigious assignment.

But getting to Maxwell was a real adventure for Anna and the children. Ernest left Massachusetts and drove to Alabama with Keeling, their eldest son. The plan was for Anna to fly down with the rest of the children to Montgomery, and Ernest would meet them at the airplane. She got on the airliner with the children in Boston and started the flight. The plane made some stops along the way.

When they reached Savannah, Georgia, after dark, the pilot announced, "The airfield at Montgomery, Alabama, is closed because of bad weather. We will not be able to land there. Everyone going to Montgomery, please disembark here." Anna, with the five children and all their traveling paraphernalia, luggage, toys, books and dolls, found herself stranded in Savannah. The only alternative was an uncomfortable all-night bus ride to Montgomery. The trip was a nightmare but it didn't end when they got to Montgomery. The family arrived there early in the morning, took a taxi from the bus terminal to Maxwell, and found Ernest sick in bed with the flu. "We had our furniture, which was placed all wrong," she remembers, "We were shoehorned into very small quarters, Ernest was sick, and I was seven months pregnant. Not a very good start for a new assignment."

Student officers and their families lived in quarters that had been converted from World War Two cadet quarters. "They were one story, with cement floors, "rooms just strung together," Anna commented. Mark was born November 24, 1946, in the Maxwell base hospital (Mark is the only one of the Warburton children to be born on base). Now there were six Warburtons. The base civil engineer had to cut a door through a wall, which gave them what amounted to one and a half quarters to accommodate their large brood.

As a student officer, Ernest was able to get only eight or ten flying hours a month. For a change, he was home most of the time.

He graduated from Air War College in June, 1947 and was transferred to Langley Air Force Base, Virginia. He got a plum assignment, Chief of Operations, Tactical Air Command. TAC was the fighter and troop transport arm of the U.S. Air Force and Ernest was in charge of all operations. He had accumulated just over 7,000 flying hours.

Unfortunately, his job at first kept him pretty well confined to his desk, except for short trips to TAC bases, so his flying time stayed relatively low, compared to his past assignments. He got most of his time in the Douglas A-26, which was a fast twin engine, single pilot, attack aircraft.

On weekends during hunting season, he was able to pursue his favorite pastime. The Army owned a huge wooded maneuver area, Camp A.P. Hill, less than a two-hour drive from Langley, which had a large deer population. There were also pheasant. Ernest and his sons hunted there frequently in season, and with much success. Langley, near the coast of Chesapeake Bay, was under a major wildlife flyway, and Ernest was able to get all the weekend duck hunting he wanted.

Anna was very happy at Langley. They had a large brick colonial style house on Back River, which ran along one edge of the base. The five oldest Warburton children of school age walked to their elementary school, just a few blocks away on the base.

Langley was an old, established base, with tree-shaded streets and an historic Officers Club which had hosted early Air Corps heroes like Billy Mitchell and Hap Arnold. Anna was able to obtain help caring for the children, and the many varied social activities on the base kept her busy. There were frequent formal dinners for visiting military dignitaries from Washington and from other country's air forces. Anna and Ernest made short vacation trips back to Massachusetts, a long day's drive away.

Their seventh child, Frank, was born at Langley on January 22, 1950.

Soon, Ernest was on frequent temporary duty visiting TAC bases all over the United States. He believed that the only sensible way to know what is going on in the units in the field is to see them personally. In June 1948, the Commander of TAC acquired a B-17 to be used as an "executive transport." It was stripped of guns and armor and seats were installed in what formerly had been the bomb bay and waist gunners' areas. Ernest began to log considerable pilot and instructor pilot time in the B-17, accompanying the TAC Commander to bases as far away as Muroc Field or the Navy's Moffett Field in California.

He also logged time in the Lockheed F-80, which at that time was still Tactical Air Command's first line fighter. It was rapidly being replaced by the Republic F-84. He also logged much time in the C-47, visiting bases as far away as Brookley and Albrook Air Bases in the Panama Canal Zone, as well as TAC units based in Haiti, Puerto Rico, Nicaragua, and Guatemala. From January to June 1950, Ernest was the acting Vice Commander of Tactical Air Command.

In July 1950, Ernest was transferred to Pope Air Force Base, at Fort Bragg, North Carolina, where he became Vice Commander of Ninth Air Division, a troop carrier command. The base was in a rural area, the largest nearby town being Fayetteville. The hunting was superb. After a month, while still a Colonel, he became temporary acting Commander of Ninth Air Force. Only six months later, General Edward Timberlake was named Commander of Ninth, and Ernest became his Deputy Commander . Timberlake was notorious as a very hard man to work for.

At that time, Strategic Air Command was getting most of the money Congress was appropriating for the Air Force. Tactical Air Command ran a distant second, and of the money appropriated for TAC, Ninth Air Force got the least. This did not sit well with General Timberlake. His staff, starting with Ernest at the top, felt his wrath almost every day. Being able to get away in the woods for some hunting was a good way for Ernest to relax.

Nevertheless, he weathered the storm. On July 28, 1951, he was promoted to Brigadier General.

CHAPTER FORTY-ONE

Then, in January 1952, with only one week's notice, Ernest was ordered to Korea, where the Korean conflict was in high gear. He departed on New Years Day, to be Deputy Chief of Staff, Fifth Air Force. Normally, at this point, the family would have been required to move off base. General Timberlake allowed Anna and the children to remain in Pope base quarters until the children finished the school year in May.

Moving back to Massachusetts in June presented Anna with a dilemma. The Ward Farm, where the family had lived while Ernest was away in World War Two, had been struck by a tornado the previous spring and was not habitable. Just then, a farm in Hardwick was put up for sale. "Ernest and I had seen this farm years ago," Anna said. "just driving by, and had seen the owner out front and she asked us in, and we looked at it. The farm house was large and well built, and quite a story was connected with it.

"It was an historic house, built on a tract of land deeded in colonial times to Daniel Ruggles by the King of England. Daniel's brother, Timothy, was also given a tract of land in Hardwick. Timothy was famous (or infamous) for being a Tory before and even after the American Revolution. He was ultimately banished from Massachusetts to Nova Scotia.

"Timothy's daughter, Bathsheba, was also famous in Massachusetts history—she was the last woman in the state to be hanged. She and her lover, an Army Captain, connived to kill her elderly husband. They hired two Army deserters to murder him and stuff his body down his well—which they did! But they got caught. A lengthy, famous trial ensued.

"Bathsheba, her husband and one of the deserters were hanged in Worcester, Massachusetts. Afterward, She was found to be 'with child'—if she had revealed that beforehand, she could not have been hanged under Massachusetts law. We were fascinated by the story, but of course, at that time, we were not interested at all in buying the place." Now, with Ernest away for at least a year, was a different time. Anna had seven children, some with her mother, some with Ernest's mother, some with his aunt, and this was a time, with Ernest gone, when they should all have been together.

"I wrote to Ernest and told him this farm was for sale for a very, very reasonable price. He wrote back, 'We don't need it. Don't buy it unless you've sold the farm in Westboro.' But I needed a house NOW. So, after my mother and father looked it over, they said 'Buy it, Anna. We'll help you.' So I borrowed some money from them and from Ernest's parents and bought the house in Hardwick. After I sold the house in Westboro, I paid them back."

The house required a lot of work before it would be modernized. The kitchen had an old-fashioned stove that burned wood or coal. There were no bathrooms. Anna quickly moved to rectify the situation. She located three brothers in Gilbertville, carpenters, who helped and advised her. She put in two bathrooms, drilled a new well and installed a septic tank. She modernized the kitchen and improved the heating system. "We moved in in September," she said, "and we had a very, very snowy winter, but I dressed the children warmly, and we survived."

Arriving in Korea as Deputy Chief of Staff, Operations, in January 1952, Ernest was soon given a new title, Deputy Commander for Administration, as well as Commanding General, Taegu Area. In this new job, he was in charge of the same kind of activities he had been associated with in service commands in World War Two.

One of his most auspicious accomplishments was the construction of airfield K-6, which was built under his supervision by the men of the 1903rd Engineer Aviation Battalion, starting the day after they arrived in Korea. This involved the largest earthmoving job undertaken during the entire Korean war and one of the largest jobs attempted by any military unit. The concrete runway was built, an Air Force report said, "in spite of terrific rains in November, and early severe winter commencing in December, and very cold, bitter weather throughout."

Ernest was responsible for U.S. Air Force facilities all over the lower part of South Korea and spent most of his time traveling from installation to installation.

Ernest continued to fly as often as possible, logging virtually all his flying time in the C-47, averaging 20 to 30 hours a month. He flew one combat mission in a T-6 "Mosquito" on a forward air controller flight. He continued his aerial exploits and was nominated for a second Distinguished Flying Cross by demonstrating that a stretch of ice-covered beach on a remote island could be used for a runway.

On this island, Americans were engaged in a vital, year-round intelligence gathering mission. Well above the demilitarized zone marking the border between North and South Korea, it was deep in North Korean controlled waters, and could only be supplied by air. Several attempts by experienced pilots had been made to land an aircraft on the ice-covered beach, which had high cliffs at either end, but the attempts had been aborted. Ernest devised an approach and succeeded in landing there and then taking off, showing the way for others.

The Distinguished Flying Cross citation read: "Brigadier General Ernest K. Warburton, Fifth Air Force, distinguished himself by extraordinary achievement while participating in aerial flight over enemy territory.

164

Flying as pilot in an unarmed C-47 aircraft, General Warburton proceeded from a forward air base in Korea to a friendly-held island deep in enemy territory for the purpose of determining the feasibility of landing an aircraft on the beach, which was covered with ice and had high, rocky cliffs at each end. The location and the facilities at this island necessitated that delivery of vitally needed supplies be made by air.

"General Warburton, as pilot, succeeded in making the difficult landing on the icy beach. Prior to this landing, there had been numerous attempts to land aircraft on the beach, but all were aborted. Upon completion of a survey of facilities on this island, the aircraft was successfully taken off, flown across enemy lines and safely landed at a friendly base. Throughout the entire flight, enemy interception was probable and expected. The success of this mission demonstrated that operation of transport aircraft in and out of this island was practicable and has resulted in daily scheduled flights carrying supplies and personnel.

"These flights have since made possible a tenfold enlargement of this island installation in personnel and equipment. Through General Warburton's superior airmanship and determination, this historic mission was successfully completed and reflects great credit upon himself and the United States Air Force." For unknown reasons, higher headquarters downgraded the Distinguished Flying Cross to an Air Medal.

Ernest spent 14 months in Korea. He departed there at the end of February 1953, carrying with him a personal commendation from General Mark W. Clark, Commander in Chief, United Nations Command and Commanding General, Far East Command. It read: "Upon completion of your tour of duty in this theater, I take this means to convey to you my personal appreciation of your eminent accomplishments in discharging your important responsibilities as Deputy Commanding General of the Fifth Air Force.

"During your distinguished service in the combat zone you formulated broad, effective programs which have firmly influenced the operational brilliance through which Fifth Air Force has achieved and maintained air supremacy for the United Nations Command and insured constant and effective support for the ground forces.

"Your organizational ability, singular professional competence and resourceful leadership have assured tremendous personnel, administrative and logistical advantages in attaining the United Nations objective in the Far East Command.

"I offer heartiest wishes that your journey home will be pleasant and your forthcoming assignment successful. "

Ernest also was awarded a U.S. Legion of Merit and two Korean medals, the Military Merit Ulchi Medal with Gold Star and the Republic of Korea Presidential Unit Citation. He now had a total of 8,944 hours of flying time.

He returned to the United States in March 1953 and spent a month's leave with his family at the farm Anna had bought. "Ernest," Anna said, "fell in love with the farm!" He liked the farm so much it became the family homestead for the next 45 years. During summers, when the children were out of school, Anna lived there full time, while Ernest flew in on weekends and holidays. Eventually, it became their retirement home.

CHAPTER FORTY-TWO

Ernest's next assignment, once again, was to Langley Air Force Base, Virginia, where on May 19, 1953, he was appointed Special Assistant to the Commander, Tactical Air Command. TAC at that time was commanded by General O. P. Weyland. Back in 1927, Weyland was the Instructor Lieutenant who had caught Cadet Ernest K. Warburton and his two friends off base one night while they were attending flying school at Brooks Field, Texas. When Ernest mentioned the incident to General Weyland, he recalled that evening and they enjoyed a laugh together.

Anna had enjoyed their previous assignment at Langley very much. This one was to be just as enjoyable. They had spacious brick quarters, as before, and the children this time attended school off base. Camp A.P Hill was still available for hunting in season on weekends, and Ernest enjoyed taking his sons along for deer, duck and game hunting.

Ernest was not a special assistant very long. On July 31, 1953, he became TAC's Chief of Staff.

This was an exciting time for TAC. The command was now all-jet, with the F-100 fighter replacing the F-84. The North American F-100 Supersabre was the hottest fighter in the world and the first jet to break the sound barrier in level flight. Langley hosted a wing of F-84s, soon to be replaced by F-100s, and a wing of B-57 Canberra light bombers.

Most of the TAC Headquarters staff were flying officers who held desk jobs but who were still required to comply with Air Force annual flying requirements. When Ernest arrived, these pilots were assigned for flying to Langley Air Force Base Operations. The base, of course, had its own corps of flying desk officers. There was difficulty keeping many of the TAC officers "up to snuff" because their administrative duties did not permit much time away from their desks.

Ernest soon realized there was a need for an organization dedicated to administrative and operational support of TAC headquarters. From a flying viewpoint, a unit of instructors was needed to check out each new officer, keep track of his flying time, schedule him to fly on a regular basis and keep him current in both contact and instrument flying. Ernest decided to form the 4500th Support Squadron to do just that. After interviewing several officers, he selected Major Ellis J. (Skinny) Wheless, a former WWII

F-51 piot who subsequently had tactical airlift experience, to be Commander.

With Major Wheless as his point man, Ernest created a squadron of 35 officers and 600 men, dedicated to supporting TAC headquarters in all administrative areas, and especially operationally. All the 4500th pilots were instructors who flew with the headquarters pilots. They also gave annual proficiency and instrument checks. The squadron was assigned 46 aircraft, most of them different types of World War Two aircraft such as the B-25, B-26, C-45, C-47, C-54, and Dehavilland L-20 Beaver. A B-17 "executive aircraft, " was eventually replaced by a C-131 (Convair 340). There were also T-33s, the trainer version of the P-80 jet fighter.

Major Wheless ran the squadron, but Ernest monitored operations closely. "He requested frequent briefings on what we in the squadron were doing," Skinny said. "He let me command the squadron, but he had almost daily briefings on what was going on." In reminiscing about the Warburtons, Wheless said "The Air Force was extremely fortunate to have had a career officer of General Warburton's stature. He was an architect of today's Air Force, providing the foundation for today's combat forces. There is an old adage that behind every superior General Officer there is a strong, dedicated, highly efficient, and diplomatic wife. Mrs. Warburton fulfilled all of those prerequisites, plus many more."

During the summer vacations, Anna took the children up to the farm in Massachusetts. Ernest frequently got his required flying time by flying back and forth on weekends between Langley and Massachusetts, landing at the Air Force Reserve base in Boston, or at one of the two small private fields near Hardwick. His favorite mode of transportation was the Douglas B-26, a fast, twin engine, single pilot aircraft.

On one of his trips in a C-47, when he landed at small Hiller Airport, he created a stir because it was the largest aircraft ever flown into that field. He chose Hiller on that particular flight because it was close to Gilbertville, where a Civil Defense emergency storage facility was located; his task was to determine whether a transport with Civil Defense supplies could be flown into and out of the rather short dirt runway. Even though the field had poor approaches, he made an uneventful landing, stopping with a little room to spare. He spent the weekend with the family.

When he was departing, Anna went to the field to see him off. She stood by the airport's owner, Mrs. Hiller, as Ernest ran up the engines for pre-takeoff checks. To gain extra takeoff room, he had maneuvered the C-47 so that its tail was practically in the woods at the end of the runway. Above the roar of the engines, Mrs. Hiller, a pilot and instructor, startled Anna by saying, "He will never make it!" Anna's reaction was a confident "He WILL make it!" As if he had heard her words, Ernest released brakes, rolled down the runway, slowly at first, then faster and faster, and took off with room to spare. He leveled off above the treetops, made a wide 360 degree turn back to the field, and swept triumphantly overhead before setting a southerly course for Langley. Years later, Ernest and Anna's youngest son, Frank, would take flying lessons from Mrs. Hiller.

As Chief of Staff, Ernest's job primarily was administrative. His staff kept the paperwork flowing into, through and out of the headquarters, no mean task in such a large and important organization. Because of the constant flow through Langley of distinguished visitors such as Congressmen and Senators, officials of foreign governments and high ranking officers from countries all over the world, there was a heavy emphasis on protocol, for which Ernest was responsible.

Naturally, the many social affairs at Langley involved Anna, who entertained dignitaries both at the Officers Club and at home. Their most distinguished visitor, Anna remembers, was England's Queen Mother Elizabeth. Almost 4,000 people were at Langley to greet her on November 17, 1954, and Ernest and Anna were among the relative few who met her personally.

Doris Wheless remembers Anna well: "Mrs. Warburton was a very talented person. She knitted, she crocheted, she sewed, she made her own hats. She was a wonderful cook and baker—she did beautiful breads. She entertained 50 or more people for dinner routinely and it seemed just nothing for her to do. With seven children to care for. And absolutely one of the nicest ladies I have ever known. "

CHAPTER FORTY-THREE

In June 1957, Ernest was reassigned to Eglin AFB Florida, as Commander of the Air Force Operational Test Center, under the Air Proving Command. At that time, the family had two cars, a Studebaker and a Buick. Ernest took Keeling along and drove to Eglin in the Studebaker. Anna was to follow with the rest of the children in the Buick. Less than 50 miles from Langley, the Buick broke down. The garage mechanic said the problem was serious, and it would take some time to fix because parts had to be ordered from the factory. Anna decided immediately to buy a new car.

When the family arrived at Eglin, Ernest was surprised to see them in a Mercury, and all the children garbed in T-shirts imprinted with the slogan "My Dad owns a Mercury." The Buick had been Ernest's favorite car, and he had enjoyed working on it with the boys in their garage. Unfortunately for Anna, the Mercury turned out to be a "lemon" for which Anna received many admonitions from "the Boss."

In December, the Air Proving Ground Command merged with the Air Force Armament Center to become the Air Proving Ground Center, with Ernest as Deputy Commander for Development and Test. Ernest's boss was Maj. Gen. Robert Burns, who was the same "Bobby" Burns referred to in Ernest's flight log back when they flew together in "The Three Musketeers."

Eglin, in northwest Florida on the Gulf of Mexico, was the largest U.S. Air Force installation on the globe. Famous throughout the world, it hosted a constant procession of world leaders, military and civilian, who visited there to observe operations. Once again, Anna found herself immersed in the social responsibilities she had shouldered at Langley, playing hostess to high ranking military and civilian visitors who came to Eglin. The quarters were "good, but a little small for us," she said. "The base was small, and friendly." The children loved the Gulf coast beaches, and the boys enjoyed hunting with their father.

Ernest had a big job. The mission of the Air Proving Ground Center, he explained in a speech, was "To conduct, participate, in and/or support systems evaluation tests and operational evaluation tests as directed." He was back in his favorite business, testing, only on a much larger scale. The mission of his command also encompassed " the research and development of non-nuclear munitions, aerial targets and scorers, instrumentation, and ballistics."

While the base proper was small, the Eglin testing areas covered an 800-mile square reservation, including a main base, 465,000 acres of land ranges on which were located ten auxiliary flying fields, as well as another 15,000 square miles of water ranges over the Gulf of Mexico.

Eglin had (and still has) the unique Climatic Laboratory, a huge building 250 feet long and 200 feet wide, in which the largest aircraft in the world could be subjected to temperatures ranging from 65 degrees below zero(F) to 165 degrees above. When a new aircraft such as the F-104 Starfighter, at that time the fastest airplane in the world, was received at Eglin, it would first be placed in the Climatic Laboratory to be sure its systems would operate in the heat and humidity of the tropics and the extreme cold of the Arctic or at high altitudes.

After that, Ernest's people would develop weapons for the aircraft, establish weapons attachment points, manufacture the weapons or have them manufactured, and then test fire them. Targets over the Gulf of Mexico were drones, that is, operational aircraft which are remotely controlled by radio. All tests were documented by telemetry and photos, including movies.

Three or more times a year, Ernest was responsible for putting on a huge live firepower demonstration that showcased every unclassified aircraft and weapon the U.S. Air Force possessed. These demonstrations took place on Range 52, on which was a grandstand seating more than 5,000 people. The spectators were Congressmen, Senators, other high ranking U.S. officials, foreign heads of state, high ranking officers from the armed forces of countries all over the world, state, city and local dignitaries, student and faculty members from the U.S. and foreign war colleges, cadets from West Point, Midshipmen from Annapolis, AFROTC cadets, movie stars, invited citizens and the press.

Each demonstration required months of preparation, planning, and rehearsals. More than 100 aircraft appeared in each show, which lasted two hours. The logistics challenges were monumental. Timing was crucial. Ernest demanded that pilots hit their targets on time, plus or minus three seconds. An "event" was scheduled every minute. One show included an F-102 interceptor shooting down a target with air-to-air rockets, a high altitude interception of a B-47 bomber by F-104s, an F-100 attack using napalm, an F-104 destroying an aircraft on the ground with the 20 mm "Gatling Gun," F-101s dropping 1,000 pound bombs, 16 F-100s attacking a railroad marshalling yard with bombs, rockets and napalm, three F-100s refueling in the air from a KB-50 tanker aircraft, a simulated nuclear bomb drop, and ended with a precision flying demonstration by the USAF "Thunderbirds" flying team.

These demonstrations were always well received by the press and people in the grandstand. Despite the large quantities of live munitions used, there was never an accident. For one of Ernest's shows, General Burns wrote: "The firepower demonstration of 8 October 1957 was superior to any conducted during the past two years. The skill displayed by the pilots and crews in their introduction of aircraft missiles was one of the highlights. General White (USAF Chief of Staff) expressed to me his personal praise and appreciation for the outstanding manner in which the entire demonstration was conducted. The 100% in-commission rate and the fact that each mission went off as scheduled is evidence of the superior maintenance which is so necessary to this operation."

One big advantage the Eglin reservation had was the wide variety of wildlife that populated its woods. Ernest and his sons spent many happy hours hunting deer and gamebirds in season.

When Ernest arrived at Eglin, he had logged 9,132 flying hours. He particularly enjoyed flying there because of the many different aircraft assigned to the base, most of which he flew. His first flight was in a T-33, the trainer version of the P-80 he had flown at Muroc, and his second was in an H-19 helicopter. During his assignment there, he flew the KC-135 tanker, B-57 light bomber, F-100 fighter, B-52 heavy bomber, B-47 medium bomber, F-104 fighter, C-131 transport, F-102 interceptor, C-54, and C-47. Finally, he flew his 10,000th hour in the F-104, which at that time was the fastest aircraft in the world.

Ernest knew that because of his age and his rank, he would never again be assigned to a primary flying job in the Air Force. After 33 years, he decided to retire. On April 11, 1959, he was officially retired in a ceremony that included a parade and full military honors.

His total flying time at retirement was 10,059 hours, during which he had progressed from the old JN-4 "Jenny," which flew at 75 miles an hour, to the supersonic, Mach 2, F-104 Starfighter, "the missile with a man it," which topped 1,200 mph. His career bridged the growth of the Air Service branch of the Army Signal Corps into the world's mightiest fighting organization, the United States Air Force, and his career mirrors that change and symbolizes the progress made.

CHAPTER FORTY-FOUR

Ernest had decided to retire from the Air Force, but not from life. Because of his injured back, he had been retired with a medical disability, but after all, he was only 55 years old. Before retiring, he had been contacted by an old friend, retired Major General Blair Garland, who was finishing up a tour as U.S. Advisor to the SHAPE Air Defense Technical Center, in the Netherlands (SHAPE stands for Supreme Headquarters, Allied Powers Europe. It is the military arm of NATO, the North Atlantic Treaty Organization).

General Garland suggested Ernest might enjoy taking on the job for a year or two. The center was located in The Hague, in Holland, where the family would live. Ernest consented and a contract was written by SHAPE and signed by Ernest. Anna was pleased, because she had never been stationed overseas, and being in Europe sounded exciting.

A particularly good part of the job was that Ernest had his own plane, a C-47, and crew and he was permitted to take her with him when he traveled. They traveled extensively through Europe, visiting the capitals of all twelve European nations that were members of NATO, and many other places on side trips. On a typical trip, in March 1960, the Warburtons visited Paris, Madrid, Lisbon, Majorca, Weisbaden, Edinburgh, Aberdeen, London, Evreux, and finally, back to the Hague

Anna liked the assignment in The Hague. They lived in "a very nice apartment in a modernized part of the city." They had five of the children with them. The younger ones attended the International School in the Hague. Sally traveled a lot and attended school in Weisbaden, Germany. Keeling was in medical school in the States and Darby first tried attending the University of Maryland at Munich, but didn't like it, and transferred to the University of Michigan. Joanne had trained as a physical therapist and remained in the United States, at Portland, Maine.

Ernest's new job at the Technical Center involved providing technical advice and assistance to SHAPE in the field of air defense of all NATO nations. His staff did research, both at The Hague and in the field, on air defense measures such as early warning radar. The center developed equipment specifically for European use and took the lead in developing data transmission between air defense centers at several locations in each country. His staff also developed NATO standards for data handling.

The staff produced several important evaluation studies for SHAPE, including the employment of nuclear warheads in the air defense of NATO Europe, survival of Allied Command Europe forces under enemy attack, ballistic missile warning, and many, many, other subjects. Ernest knew the center could do a better job on these studies than could individual nations.

Ernest realized that the capabilities of the SHAPE Air Defense Technical Center extended far beyond air defense. For example, it could act as central systems engineering agency for implementing special military communications systems. It could exert influence in developing a ship-to-shore communications system, something that did not exist in NATO at that time. He felt the mission should be broadened to include operations research and systems evaluation assistance in all military planning areas, such as air strike operations, training and logistics. He recommended more scientists be put on the center's staff and its mission statement be changed to reflect his views. He said the organization should be called simply "SHAPE Technical Center," with air defense only one of its responsibilities.

Ernest put his ideas in writing and made several speeches reflecting his ideas at a number of high level NATO meetings. He said the staff should be increased to at least 125. Ernest left The Hague to retire again on June 28, 1960. A year later, his ideas were totally accepted by the NATO authorities. The organization today has a staff of about 140. The staff carries out the tasks he put forth while he headed it. Today, its name is "SHAPE Technical Center."

CHAPTER FORTY-FIVE

Ernest returned to the farm at Hardwick in July 1960, and became a gentleman farmer. "He decided to retire, period," Anna said. "He had offers to teach at several schools, and a number of aircraft manufacturers made offers, but he turned them down. He was through."

His decision to become a gentleman farmer was not surprising. After all, he had always kept a garden wherever the Warburtons were stationed. As early as 1953, he had ordered U.S. Department of Agriculture pamphlets and booklets on all sorts of plants. Among them were "Why Fruit Trees Fail to Bear," "Control of Apple Borers," "Propagation of Trees and Shrubs," "Strawberry Culture," "Home Utilization of Muscadine Grapes," "Peach Growing East of the Rocky Mountains," "Growing Mushrooms in the U.S." "Production of Pumpkins and Squashes," "Production of Carrots," and many, many more.

In Hardwick, Ernest planted a very large plot on part of their land across the road from the home and spent much of each day in season working in his garden. It bore prodigiously. The farm had once had many grapevines. He reestablished grape arbors and produced his own wine. Reflecting his mechanical bent, he set up an authentic blacksmith's forge in the barn and used if for keeping the family vehicles in good repair and for making many useful implements. Anna ran a small antiques business. Retirement was sweet.

"But I did get him off the hill," Anna said. "We visited Florida, Mexico, Nova Scotia and Hawaii. But he'd seen enough of the world. He really loved being on the farm."

All the Warburton children were successful in life. Keeling and Mark are doctors, Joanne is a Physical Therapist, Sally is married to a veterinarian in Hawaii, Darby has a successful air conditioning business, Ward has an appliance repair business and Frank is an aerodynamic engineer with Sikorsky Aircraft Co. Of all the boys, Frank is the only one who took up flying. He owns a Cessna 150 and enjoys frequent flights.

As time went on, grandchildren were produced. Ernest loved them all. They, in turn, loved visiting the farm, where in the spring and summer he would teach them to take care of the garden. Family Christmases in the big farmhouse were warm, enjoyable and memorable.

Then, in 1979, Ernest suffered a heart attack. He recovered and fought his way back to reasonably good health. Then, in 1984, he was diagnosed with cancer. He fought hard and it took a long time for the disease to defeat him. At his memorial service, one of his grandsons, David Smith, delivered this eulogy, which he wrote during the last early springtime before Ernest died:

"The Gardener"

"His was a military garden. Not a plant stepped out of line. No weed infiltrated his ranks. He took command as soon as the ground thawed, and relinquished it to Jack Frost each fall. The General, as my father refers to him, maintained an orderly garden.

As a child, I was not allowed to wander far inside the garden's stone walls. Once beyond the civilian strawberries, I walked where he walked. He gave detailed orders where to step when I fetched a bucket. Pointing out each row, he maneuvered me through his garden. A wrong step meant a quick reprimand.

I would sit on the wall and watch him work. He moved from row to row, pulling weeds and thinning the ranks. In time, he allowed me to help with the garden. We worked our way through each row, pulling weeds and hilling up plants, but the weeds broke in my hand. "Grab the weed just below the dirt and pull," he said. Each day became a gardening lesson.

As we both grew older, the garden changed. He tired more easily, so I worked and he supervised. Now his orders were how to work as he watched me pull and hill my way through a row.

After he had heart surgery, I was sure he wouldn't have a garden. But, about mid-February, he ordered his seeds for the coming year. By April, the hotbeds were full of seedlings, and by May the garden was planted. As his strength returned, he worked more and more in the garden, relieving me of my duties. He reluctantly came in for dinner with barely enough time to wash his hands. I returned to watching and fetching, but I didn't mind.

He has cancer now. The garden looked sad last summer. It was much smaller, and I wasn't there enough to keep up with the weeds. We propped up the peas one day. He sat in the chair I had brought out for him while I drove the crowbar into the dirt. He told me to make sure the poles were in deep so they wouldn't blow over. When I finished we walked slowly back to the house, his hand resting on my shoulder.

My grandfather has never been a quitter. He crashed four planes during his career, but never stopped flying. He seldom asks for help, refusing to be defeated.

He has ordered the seeds for his garden."

Ernest died April 28, 1986. He was buried with full military honors at Hardwick.

As part of the research for this book, Nate Rosengarten was asked for his recollections of Ernest at Wright Field. "Almost a half century has gone by," Rosie wrote to Anna Warburton. "In retrospect, he was of the old Army Air Corps. He was not an armchair pilot. He never failed to do his duty in the best way he knew how. He was a commander who set the pace and an example for all he commanded by actively engaging in all aspects of the mission to be accomplished. He was a genuine 'stick and rudder man.' General Warburton played a very important part in military aviation and those who survive must never let his memory fade away."

He left his impression on the people of his hometown area. The editor of one weekly publication, Robie's Kaleidoscope, wrote "We met Ernest Warburton, Brig. Gen., USAF (Ret.) several times and were always impressed by his exuberant, outgoing personality. But we were somewhat overawed by the record he had compiled during his military career. It was an abundantly distinguished one. While perhaps not a member of the first wave of the leaders of military aviation, he certainly was a key figure in the second generation, which were responsible for the growth and accomplishments of the air arm from the 1930s through World War II, Korea and into the Cold War period. General Warburton died Sunday at the age of 82. It will be a long time before any other area resident can match the record of the General, in peace and war, and wear his laurels as gracefully. We extend our sympathy to his family."

During his career, Ernest had flown 474 models and types of aircraft (see list at Appendix 5). Among his many decorations were the Distinguished Flying Cross, the Bronze Star, four Air Medals and four Legion of Merits.

Anna has returned to live in Hardwick. The house on Ruggles Hill was too large for one person. She sold it and lives in town, not far from Ward and Darby. Anna and Ernest were blessed with fifteen grandchildren and fourteen great grandchildren, scattered from Maine to Hawaii. Anna sees them all regularly.

THE END

Note: The list of aircraft flown by Brigadier General E.K. Warburton was originally compiled in 1959 using his official military flight records, which identified the aircraft only by numbered designation. Robert Sopher, a friend and Sikorsky Aircraft associate of General Warburton's youngest son, Frank, compiled the extensively detailed expanded list in Appendix 5. Bob Sopher was in China during part of World War II and developed a lifelong passion for aircraft. He possesses an extensive aircraft reference library upon which he drew for the expanded list. While he used many references, he relied most heavily on "U.S. Army Aircraft (Heavier Than Air) 1908-1946," by James C. Fahey (editor) which was published in 1946.

APPENDIX 1

Established 1841.

George H. Gilbert Mfg. Co.

of Ware & Gilbertville, Mass.

Incorporated 1867.

Address all
correspondence to Ware.

GILBERTVILLE *Ware* Mass Oct. 8, 1929——191—

Mr. Earnest Warburton,

    28 Newton St.,Brighton,Mass.

My Dear Earnest,

        You will ,no doubt, be surprised to receive a letter from me as I haven't seen you since you were a rather small boy,that is to speak to,but to-day you surely did announce your comming as well as your presence in town,and beleive me you have no reason to be ashamed to enter your birth town in such a noisy mahner.

        It is needless for me to say that the entire town's people had the thrill of their lives and that your name is on the tongues of all of the residents this afternoon,your aunt Jane is no doubt the proudest of them all but we all share her pride in you and hope that some day you will again pay us a visit.

        Perhaps you noticed that in your honor I had all of the children in the Gilbertville Schoold dismissed so that they could see you in you excellent performance ov r the town and that they could realize that you once attended the same schools and roamed in the same streets and woods

        In the last hour I have talked with a large number of our people and the subject is always avation with you playing the leading roll and I am quite sure that you would pile up a big score in a popularity contest just now.

        I could go on but i would only repeat myself and I am taking the liberty,in behalf of the town's people,to say nothing of the school children,to congratulate you on your ability and wish you a long an succesful career

                Yours very truly,

                        Walter H. Holt

APPENDIX 2

Robt. Jenkins, Propr.

Greytown, Nicaragua
Oct. 24, 1889

Dear Brother:

I wrote you from Baracoa de Cuba some three or four months ago, so that you will be cognizant up to that date of my proceedings. You will, no doubt, have seen how we were burnt up at sea and of the mutiny on board through the papers. It was a fearful time. The Captain was killed, and some of the officers. All but most of the crew are now serving a life sentence in Havana in the chain gang.

I am at present employed as Chief Engineer of Menocal's yacht, "The Elizabeth." I have been all through this country with him, all over Lake Nicaragua prospecting with him.

The climate is very deleterious to white men. The hospitals are full of sick men languishing their life out with low malarial fever. Singular to say, it does not affect me, but I mind to keep pretty full all the time with a little old Rye or Duffy's malt, which I think is a very good preventative.

At home I am nobody. Out here I am Mr. Whitehead, and when I propose to say anything I am listened to with respect. My pay as Chief is $150. a month and board, and if I don't make a show leave me alone.

We are on a little bender today. We cut the first sod and had a great day on the 22nd, champagne ad lib. I am laid off for a few days because I had the audacity to tap the President of this glorious republic on the shoulder, in the cabin of the yacht, and tell him that between him and me I thought we should bring the canal to a successful issue. There is a big laugh here, and I am pointed out in the streets as the man who is next in turn for President.

Give my respects to all my admiring friends, and, if we don't meet on earth, if there is any meeting we may meet in a warmer clime.

Be kind as you can to my poor children as I don't think I shall ever put eyes on them again, as when I left England I made a resolution never to return. My wife and children I found had lost all love or regard for me, so that finishes everything with me. She will never be troubled with me in this world again.

I will write you again in the course of twelve months. It is no use you to write me as I don't know where I may be a month hence, and perhaps I may die in some of these outlandish places, but what a man craves for seldom comes. I can assure you I am tired and sick of it. Look at the thousands of miles I have travelled during the last twelve months, never finding root, continually on the move—talk about the Wandering Jew, he was no worse.

I was with Joe Speak in Jacksonville for two months. I was working in a diving bell at the bottom of the St. Johns River and then joined Goinaya as engineer. I left her in Jamaica and then joined the Nicaragua adventurers. She was a wreck such as I never want to put my eyes on again when we towed into Kingston Harbour.

I am well known in Jamaica, and I flatter myself pretty well known wherever I have travelled.

Give my respects to Luke Speak and Bob Smith and all the rest of the crowd, including Cheetham, the Taylors and Jack and all of them.

I must now conclude as I hear them calling for Whitehead and swearing they will have his life if he doesn't come up to the bar and take his medicine, so goodbye dearest of brothers, and believe me to be your own loving brother

                                        Mark

April 9, 1987

The original of this letter was found in the desk of Job Whitehead of Milnrow, Lancashire, England, after his death, and was forwarded by Job's son Percy to Frank Whitehead in America. He let his sister Betty Warburton borrow it, and while it was in her possession I copied it. The original letter has since disappeared, and no one knows what happened to it.

Muriel Johnson

APPENDIX 3

Wed. 4:10
Somewhere

Dear Folks

Am having a fine time. I
haven't been sick at all. The sea
is quite calm. There are 6 Tech
students on board, 4 sophs & 2 juniors.
We played the juniors at whist and
gave them a good trimming. We
ran into a fog last night and
we are still in it. Can just
see about 20 ft in front of boat.
Have inspected engine room.
They gave us a supper Tues. night.
They give us some fine feeds. Have
your pick of a whole menue
card. Didn't sleep very well
last night as the whistle
whistle goes off every 2 minutes
but expect to sleep tonight.

I will mail this when I get off the boat. I did not get in with John but have a bunk to myself. Had chicken, tomato sauce, buttered beets, peas fish, ice cream, short cake, malted milk, potatoes, pickles, iced water, dressing, fancy bread with cream, etc. for dinner. You ought to be here dad.

lovengly
Ernest

APPENDIX 4

Mount Clemens,Michigan,
April 12,1929.

Mrs. Warburton,
28 Newton St.,
Brighton, Mass.

My Dear Mrs.Warburton:

I wish to allay your fears as to the condition of
your son Ernest, he has apparently contracted an infection resembling Typhoid Fever, undoubtly from drinking water while
visiting a relative, Mrs. Metcalf of Roseville, Michigan.

He is not critically ill, but is of course as uncomfortable as one is who is suffering with typhoid. I don't
think there is any thing to cause you untold alarm,at present we
have day and night special nurses for him and have given him
every aid and comfort obtainable.

We will keep you informed of his progress as he does
not feel very ambitious about writing to you himself.

He will be in the hospital for quite some time, as
the convalescence is usually a lenghty one.

Donot be worried unduly about Ernest. I shall be
quite frank with you and you may be assured you will hear from
me frequently.

Sincerely

L. W. Ballantyne,
Captain, M. C.,
Surgeon.

190

APPENDIX 5

The following pages list all of the types and models of aircraft flown by Bridagier General Ernest K. Warburton during his career spanning the years 1926 thru 1959. The total is 474.

Acknowledgement: List format is based on Ref. 1

Designation	Name	Builder	Type	Years 1st Delivered	Gross Weight (lbs)	Engines	HP/Each	Thrust/Each (lb)	Top Spd, mph	Remarks	Ref. #
A-3	Falcon	Curtiss	Attack	27-28	4378	1-Curtiss V-1150-3	435		141	Biplane	1
A-3B	Falcon	Curtiss	Attack	30-30	4458	1-Curtiss V-1150-5	435		139	Biplane	1
A-11	P-25	Consolidated	Attack	33-33	5490	1-Curtiss V-1570-59	675		225	Low wing monoplane	1
A-12	Shrike	Curtiss	Attack	33-34	5745	1-Wright R-1820-21	690		177	Low wing monoplane	1
A-17	Nomad	Northrop	Attack	35-36	7405	1-P&W R-1535-11	750		206	Low wing monoplane	1
A-17A	Nomad	Northrop	Attack	36-37	7550	1-P&W R-1535-13	825		220	Low wing monoplane	1
A-18		Curtiss	Attack	39	13170	2-Wright R-1820-47	930		240		1
A-20	Havoc	Douglas	Attack	39-40	19050	2-Wright R-2600-7	1700		390		1
A-20A	Havoc	Douglas	Attack	39-40	19605	2-Wright R-2600-3	1600		349	No supercharger	1
A-20C	Havoc	Douglas	Attack	41-41	25600	2-Wright R-2600-23	1600		342	Models manufactured by Douglas or Boeing	1
A-24	Dauntless	Douglas	Attack	41-41	8295	1-Wright R-1820-52	1000		250	As SBD for Navy	1
A-26	Invader	Douglas	Attack	41-43	30000	2-P&W R-2800-27	2000		350	Data are for XA-26	1
A-26B	Invader	Douglas	Attack	42-44	30000	2-P&W R-2800-27	2000		350	Later designated B-26	1
A-26C	Invader	Douglas	Attack	44-45	29700	2-P&W R-2800-71	2100		330	Later designated B-26. Bombardier nose.	1
A-29	Hudson	Lockheed	Attack	41-42	21700	2-Wright R-1820-27	1200		253	Target tug	1
RA-29										Designation unknown	1
A-30	Baltimore	Martin	Attack	41-42	27100	2-Wright R-2600-19	1600		305		1
A-36	Apache	North-Amer.	Attack	43	10700	1-Allison V-1710-87	1325		356	Attack version of Mustang P-51	1
OA-1B		Loening	Amphibian	27-28	5200	1-Liberty V-1650-1	435		120	Biplane	1
OA-2		Loening	Amphibian	29-29	5414	1-Wrigh V-1460-1	480		112	Biplane	1
OA-3	Dolphin	Douglas	Amphibian	33	8563	2-Wright R-975-3	350		140	High wing monoplane	1
OA-4A	Dolphin	Douglas	Amphibian	34	8571	2-P&W R-985-9	350		141	Practically identical to OA-3	1
OA-4C	Dolphin	Douglas	Amphibian	36	9070	2-P&W R-985-9	350		137	Practically identical to OA-3	1
OA-8		Sikorsky	Amphibian	37	20271	2-P&W R-1690-23	750		126	Sikorsky S-43. Designated Y1OA-8. High wing monoplane. Used as transport.	1

Designation	Name	Builder	Type	Years 1st Delivered	Gross Weight (lbs)	Engines	HP/Each	Thrust/Each (lb)	Top Spd, mph	Remarks	Ref. #
OA-9	Goose	Grumman	Amphibian	38	7932	2-P&W R-985-17	450		190	High wing monoplane	1
OA-10	Catalina	ConVair	Amphibian	41	30300	2-P&W R-1830-92	1200		185	High wing monoplane	1
B-6A		Keystone	Bomber	32-32	13334	2-Wright R-1820-1	575		125	Biplane	1
B-10B		Martin	Bomber	34-34	14731	2-Wright R-1820-3	740		242	Midwing monoplane	1
B-10BM		Martin	Bomber	34-34	14731	2-Wright R-1820-3	740		242	Differences from B-10 not known	1
B-12		Martin	Bomber	33-34	12824	2-P&W R-1690-11	775		218	As B-10. Data are for YB-12	1
B-17	Flying Fortress	Boeing	Bomber	36-37	43650	4-Wright R-1820-39	930		256	Monoplane. Data are for YB-17	1
B-17A	Flying Fortress	Boeing	Bomber	37-39	45650	4-Wright R-1820-51	1000		311	Data are for YB-17A	1
B-17B	Flying Fortress	Boeing	Bomber	38-39	47921	4-Wright R-1820-51	1000		292		1
B-17C	Flying Fortress	Boeing	Bomber	40-40	49650	4-Wright R-1820-65	1200		323		1
B-17D	Flying Fortress	Boeing	Bomber	40-41	49650	4-Wright R-1820-65	1200		323	Self sealing tanks.	1
B-17E	Flying Fortress	Boeing	Bomber	41-42	54000	4-Wright R-1820-65	1200		317	New tail and turrets.	1
RB-17E	Flying Fortress	Boeing	Bomber							Designation unknown.	
B-17F	Flying Fortress	Boeing	Bomber	41-42	55000	4-Wright R-1820-97	1200		323	New nose. Version also made by Douglas and Vega.	1
B-17G	Flying Fortress	Boeing	Bomber	42-43	55400	4-Wright R-1820-97	1200		313	Chin turret added. Versions also made by Douglas and Vega.	1
VB-17G	Flying Fortress	Boeing	Bomber	42-44	55401	4-Wright R-1820-98	1201		313	Staff transport. Other data assumed from B-17G.	2
B-18	Bolo	Douglas	Bomber	36-37	25130	2-Wright R-1820-45	930		217	Descended from DC-3 airliner.	1,3
B-18A	Bolo	Douglas	Bomber	37-38	25746	2-Wright R-1820-53	1000		214	Pointed nose, power top turret.	1
B-18AM										B-18 variant not known	
B-18M										B-18 variant not known	
B-23	Dragon	Douglas	Bomber	39-39	30475	2-Wright R-2600-3	1600		282	Improved B-18A. First tail turret on U.S. Bomber.	1,3

Designation	Name	Builder	Type	Years 1st Delivered	Gross Weight (lbs)	Engines	HP/Each	Thrust/Each (lb)	Top Spd, mph	Remarks	Ref. #
B-24	Liberator	Consolidated	Bomber	39-40	46400	4-P&W R-1830-33	1200		273	This is assumed to be the XB-24.	1,3
B-24A	Liberator	Consolidated	Bomber	40-41	53600	4-P&W R-1830-33	1200		275	First production bomber with tricycle landing gear.	1,3
B-24C	Liberator	Consolidated	Bomber	40-41	54000	4-P&W R-1830-41	1200		313	Turbo-supercharging. 3 power turrets.	1,3
B-24D	Liberator	Consolidated	Bomber	40-42	56000	4-P&W R-1830-43	1200		303	First large scale production version. Normal combat take-off weight increased to 64000 lb in late versions.	1,4
B-24J	Liberator	Consolidated	Bomber	42-43	60000	4-P&W R-1830-65	1200		290	Armament increased to power operated nose turret and Sperry ball turret.	1,3,4
B-24L	Liberator	Consolidated	Bomber	44-44	64500	4-P&W R-1830-65	1200		300	As -J with hand held tail guns to reduce weight and widen field of fire.	1,4
B-24M	Liberator	Consolidated	Bomber	44-44	64500	4-P&W R-1830-65	1200		300	Light weight tail turret	1
B-25	Mitchell	North Amer.	Bomber	40-40	27310	2-Wright R-2600-9	1700		322	No XB-25. First 9 had constant dihedral. Later models had gull wing.	1,4
TB-25	Mitchell	North Amer.	Bomber	44-45	38000	2-Wright R-2600-43	2000		283	Trainer, target tug.	1
B-25A	Mitchell	North Amer.	Bomber	40-41	27100	2-Wright R-2600-9	1700		315	Self-sealing tanks	1
B-25B	Mitchell	North Amer.	Bomber	40-41	28460	2-Wright R-2600-9	1700		300	Two power turrets, no tail gun.	1
B-25C	Mitchell	North Amer.	Bomber	41-41	33000	2-Wright R-2600-13	1700		284	Autopilot, external bomb racks.	1,4
B-25C1	Mitchell	North Amer.	Bomber							Designation not known. May be Company designation.	
B-25D	Mitchell	North Amer.	Bomber	41-42	33000	2-Wright R-2600-13	1700		282	Bomb bay tanks. Max. take off weight=41800 lb.	1,4
B-25H	Mitchell	North Amer.	Bomber	43-43	35000	2-Wright R-2600-13	1700		278	One 75 mm cannon + 14 50-cal. guns.	1,4

Designation	Name	Builder	Type	Years 1st Delivered	Gross Weight (lbs)	Engines	HP/Each	Thrust/Each (lb)	Top Spd, mph	Remarks	Ref. #
B-25J	Mitchell	North Amer.	Bomber	43-43	35000	2-Wright R-2600-13	1700		272	Glazed bombardier nose.	1
B-26	Marauder	Martin	Bomber	40-41	30035	2-P&W R-2800-5	1850		315	Ordered "off drawing board". No XB-26.	1,4
B-26A	Marauder	Martin	Bomber	41-41	32200	2-P&W R-2800-5	1850		310	50 cal nose and tail guns vs 30 cal.	1,4
B-26A1	Marauder	Martin	Bomber							Designation not known. May be Co. designation.	
B-26B	Marauder	Martin	Bomber	41-42	34000	2-P&W R-2800-41	2000		282	Seven 50-cal. guns. 12 50-cal. in B-26B-10	1,4
RB-26B	Marauder	Martin	Bomber							Restricted use - not for combat missions.	1
TB-26B	Marauder	Martin	Bomber							Trainer, target tug. Other data not known.	1
VB-26B	Marauder	Martin	Bomber							Staff transport.	
B-26B-10	Marauder	Martin	Bomber	41-42	38200				282	Increased wing area. Twelve 50-cal. guns.	4
B-26B-20	Marauder	Martin	Bomber	41-42						As B-26B-10 with power operated Martin-Bell tail turret.	4
B-26C	Marauder	Martin	Bomber	41-42						Various versions of B and C models manufactured in Baltimore and Omaha were designated B-26C.	4
TB-26C	Marauder	Martin	Bomber							Trainer, target tug.	
B-26F	Marauder	Martin	Bomber	42-43	38200	2-P&W R-2800-41	2000		277	Wing incidence increased to improve take-off. Side package guns added.	1
B-29	Superfortress	Boeing	Bomber	42-44	133500	4-Wright R-3350-23	2200		357		1,5
B-29A	Superfortress	Boeing	Bomber	42-45	140000	4-Wright R-3350-57	2200		357	As B-29 with one foot increase in span and tail cannon removed.	1,5
B-34	Ventura	Lockheed/Vega	Bomber	41-42	27270	2-P&W R-2800-31	2000		315	Bomber version of Navy PV-1 patrol plane.	1,3
B-45	Tornado	North Amer.	Bomber	47-	82600	4-All. J35-A-4		4000	550	Weight and speed are for B-45C	6

Designation	Name	Builder	Type	Years 1st Delivered	Gross Weight (lbs)	Engines	HP/Each	Thrust/Each (lb)	Top Spd, mph	Remarks	Ref. #
B-47E	Stratojet	Boeing	Bomber	53-	220000	6-Ge.El. J47-GE-25A		6000	606	Swept wing bomber. Thrust = 7200 lb with water injection. Weight = max. overload.	6,8
KB-50J	Superfortress	Boeing	Bomber	57-	179500	4-P&W R-4360-35	3500			Aerial refueling tanker version of B-50.	7
B-52C	Stratofortress	Boeing	Bomber	56-	400000	8-P&W J57-P-29W		10900	630	Thrust with water injection = 12,500 lb	2
B-57E	Intruder	Martin	Bomber	55-	55000	2-CurtissWr. J65-W-5		7220	580	Based on English Electric "Canberra".	9
C-1		Douglas	Cargo/Tr.	25-25	6483	1-Lib V-1650-1	420		119	Biplane	1
C-1C		Douglas	Cargo/Tr.	26-27	6483	1-Lib V-1650-1	420		121	Improved C-1.	1
C-2		Atlantic	Cargo/Tr.	26-27	9715	3-Wright R-790-1	225		116	Fokker trimotor high-wing monoplane.	1
C-2A		Atlantic	Cargo/Tr.	28-28	9715	3-Wright R-790-1	225		112	Increased wing area.	1
C-4A		Ford-Stout	Cargo/Tr.	31-31	13500	3-P&W R-1340-11	450		148	All metal high-wing trimotor	1
C-7		Atlantic	Cargo/Tr.	29	10565	3-Wright R-975-1	300		127	Former C-2A with engine change.	1
C-7A		General	Cargo/Tr.	30	11026	3-Wright R-975-1	300		139	Improved C-7A.	1
C-8A		Fairchild	Cargo/Tr.	31	5500	1-P&W R-1340-0	450		142	High wing monoplane.	1
ZC-9A		Fairchild	Cargo/Tr.	31	5500	1-P&W R-1340-0	450		142	Z indicates model has been classified obsolete. Other data assumed as for C-8A.	
C-9		Ford-Stout	Cargo/Tr.	29	9984	3-Wright R-975-1	300		131	High wing trimotor.	
C-14		General	Cargo/Tr.	31-31	7200	1-Wright R-1750-3	525		133	High wing Fokker monoplane. Data are for Y1C-14	1
C-14A		General	Cargo/Tr.	32	7204	1-Wright R-1820-7	575		144	Last Y1C-14 with engine change. Data are for Y1C-14A.	1
C-15A		General	Cargo/Tr.	32	7200	1-Wright R-820-5	575		147	As Y1C-14A. 4 litter ambulance.	1

196

Designation	Name	Builder	Type	Years 1st Delivered	Gross Weight (lbs)	Engines	HP/Each	Thrust/Each (lb)	Top Spd, mph	Remarks	Ref. #
C-19		Northrop	Cargo/Tr.	31-31	4500	1-P&W R-1340-7	450		158	Northrop Alpha low wing monoplane. Data are for YC-19	1
C-21		Douglas	Cargo/Tr.	32-32	8583	1-Wright R-975-3	350		140	As OA-3 Dolphin amphibian. Data are for Y1C-21.	1
C-24		American Pilgrim	Cargo/Tr.	32-32	7070	2-Wright R-1820-1	575		136	High wing monoplane. Data are for Y1C-24.	1
C-32		Douglas	Cargo/Tr.	36-36	18200	2-Wright R-1820-25	750		210	Commercial DC-2. Larger tail.	1
C-33		Douglas	Cargo/Tr.	36-36	18500	2-Wright R-1820-25	750		202	Commercial DC-2. Data are for XC-32.	1
C-38		Douglas	Cargo/Tr.	37	18500	2-Wright R-1820-45	920		208	Commercial DC-2. DC-3 tail (DC-2 1/2).	1
C-39		Douglas	Cargo/Tr.	38-39	18500	2-Wright R-1820-55	975		210	Commercial DC-2. DC-3 tail. Cargo.	1
C-40		Lockheed	Cargo/Tr.	38-38	9200	2-P&W R-985-17	450		218	Commercial 12-A Electra Junior. 10 place in commercial version.	1
C-40A		Lockheed	Cargo/Tr.	38-39	9600	2-P&W R-985-17	450		220	As C-40. 5 place.	1
C-40B		Lockheed	Cargo/Tr.	38-39	9720	1-P&W R-985-17	450		218	Radio test ship. Tricycle gear.	1
C-43	Traveler	Beech	Cargo/Tr.	39-39	4696	2-P&W R-985-17	450		198	Beech Model 17 Staggerwing biplane. Retractable gear. Service to 1942 in other versions. Data are for YC-43	1,10
C-45	Expeditor	Beech	Cargo/Tr.	40-40	7659	2-P&W R-985-17	450		225	Staff transport. Commercial B-18S.	1,10
UC-45	Expeditor	Beech	Cargo/Tr.	42-42	7659	2-P&W R-985-17	450		225	C-45 became UC-45.	1
C-45A	Expeditor	Beech	Cargo/Tr.	41-41	8300	2-P&W R-985-AN-1	450		221	Improved C-45A. 8 place.	1
C-45B	Expeditor	Beech	Cargo/Tr.	42-42	8727	2-P&W R-985-AN-1	450		218	As C-45A. Revised interior.	1
UC-45B2	Expeditor	Beech	Cargo/Tr.	42-42	8727	2-P&W R-985-AN-1	450		218	Utility transport version. Data are for C-45B.	

197

Designation	Name	Builder	Type	Years 1st Delivered	Gross Weight (lbs)	Engines	HP/Each	Thrust/Each (lb)	Top Spd, mph	Remarks	Ref. #
C-45F	Expeditor	Beech	Cargo/Tr.	43-44	8725	2-P&W R-985-AN-1	450		206	Data are for UC-45F.	1
C-46	Commando	Curtiss	Cargo/Tr.	41-41	50675	2-P&W R-2800-43	2000		264	Development of commercial 36-place CW-20	1
C-46A	Commando	Curtiss	Cargo/Tr.	41-43	49600	2-P&W R-2800-51	2000		270	Cargo. Large loading door. Data are for C-46-CU (Curtiss-Wright, Buffalo).	1
C-46D	Commando	Curtiss	Cargo/Tr.	43-44	51900	2-P&W R-2800-51	2000		241	New nose. Double doors. Data are for C-46D-CU (Curtiss-Wright, Buffalo).	1
C-47	Skytrain	Douglas	Cargo/Tr.	41-41	29300	2-P&W R-1830-92	1200		220	Militarized DC-3. Data are for C-47-DL(Douglas Long Beach, CA).	1
C-47A	Skytrain	Douglas	Cargo/Tr.	42-42	29300	2-P&W R-1830-92	1200		220	24 volt electrical system. Data are for C-47A-DL(Douglas Long Beach, CA).	1
VC-47A	Skytrain	Douglas	Cargo/Tr.		29300	2-P&W R-1830-92	1200		220	Administrative aircraft.	1
C-47B	Skytrain	Douglas	Cargo/Tr.	43-43	30000	2-P&W R-1830-90	1200		224	For China over the Hump operations. Data are for C-47B-DL(Douglas Long Beach, CA).	1
C-47D	Skytrain	Douglas	Cargo/Tr.	46	30000	2-P&W R-1830-90	1200		224	As C-47B. Blowers deleted.	1
VC-47D	Skytrain	Douglas	Cargo/Tr.	46	30000	2-P&W R-1830-90	1200		224	Administrative aircraft.	1
C-49	Skytrain	Douglas	Cargo/Tr.	41-41	23400	2-Wright R-1820-71	1200		218	Commercial DC-3 with Wright Cyclone 9's	1
C-50	Skytrain	Douglas	Cargo/Tr.	41-41	29300	2-Wright R-1820-85	1100		212	Commercial DC-3 with chairs, doors on left.	1
C-53	Skytrain	Douglas	Cargo/Tr.	41-41	29300	2-P&W R-1830-92	1200		212	Troop transport.	1
C-54	Skymaster	Douglas	Cargo/Tr.	41-42	65800	4-P&W R-2000-3	1350		275	DC-4A Skymaster. Data are for C-54-DO(Douglas Santa Monica, CA).	1
C-54A	Skymaster	Douglas	Cargo/Tr.	42-43	65800	4-P&W R-2000-7	1350		275	As C-54. 6 crew. 30-50 passengers.	1

Designation	Name	Builder	Type	Years 1st Delivered	Gross Weight (lbs)	Engines	HP/Each	Thrust/Each (lb)	Top Spd, mph	Remarks	Ref. #
C-54B	Skymaster	Douglas	Cargo/Tr.	43-43	73000	4-P&W R-2000-7	1350		270	As C-54A. Modified fuel system. Data are for C-54B-DO(Douglas Santa Monica, CA).	1
C-54D	Skymaster	Douglas	Cargo/Tr.	43-44	73000	4-P&W R-2000-11	1350		270	As C-54B with engine change. Data are for C-54D-DC(Douglas Chicago, IL).	1
C-54G	Skymaster	Douglas	Cargo/Tr.	45-45	73000	4-P&W R-2000-9	1450		275	Long range, cargo or 20 passengers. Data are for C-54G-DO(Douglas Santa Monica, CA).	1
VC-54G	Skymaster	Douglas	Cargo/Tr.	45-45	73000	4-P&W R-2000-9	1450		275	Administrative aircraft.	1
C-55	Commando	Curtiss	Cargo/Tr.	41-41	40000	2-Wright R-1820-87	1700		235	C-46 prototype. Data are for C-55-CS(Curtiss-Wright, St Louis).	1
C-60	Lodestar	Lockheed	Cargo/Tr.	41-41	17000	2-Wright R-2600-87	1200		259	Commercial Lodestar.	1
C-60A	Lodestar	Lockheed	Cargo/Tr.	42-42	18500	2-Wright R-2600-87	1200		257	Paratroop benches.	1
C-64A	Norseman	Noorduyn	Cargo/Tr.	43-43	7440	1-P&W R-1340-AN-1	600		170	Light transport. High wing.	1
UC-64A	Norseman	Noorduyn	Cargo/Tr.	43-43	7440	1-P&W R-1340-AN-1	600		170	Utility transport.	1
C-67	Dragon	Douglas	Cargo/Tr.	42	26400	2-Wright R-2600-3	1600		282	B-23 fast transport. Glider tug. Data are for UC-67	1
C-69	Constellation	Lockheed	Cargo/Tr.	42-45	82000	4-Wright R-3350-35	2200		329	Model 49-10 Constellation.	1
C-72		Waco	Cargo/Tr.	42-42	4200	1-P&W R-985-33	400		200	Commercial SRE. 5-place biplane. Other versions powered by Jacobs, Wright, Continental, and Lycoming engines. Data are for UC-72.	1
C-76	Caravan	Curtiss	Cargo/Tr.	42-43	28000	2-P&W R-1830-92	1200		200	All wood high wing monoplane. Data are for C-76-CS(Curtiss St. Louis).	1
C-78	Bobcat	Cessna	Cargo/Tr.	42-42	5700	2-Jacobs R-755-9	225		175	Cessna T-50. Similar to AT-17. Data are for YC-78.	1

Designation	Name	Builder	Type	Years 1st Delivered	Gross Weight (lbs)	Engines	HP/Each	Thrust/Each (lb)	Top Spd, mph	Remarks	Ref. #
UC-78	Bobcat	Cessna	Cargo/Tr.	42-42	5700	2-Jacobs R-755-9	225		175	Utility transport. Cessna T-50. Similar to AT-17.	1
C-82A	Packet	Fairchild	Cargo/Tr.	44-46	42000	2-P&W R-2800-85	2100		223	Twin boom cargo transport. Data are for C-82-FA(Fairchild, Hagerstown MD).	1
C-87	Liberator Express	Convair	Cargo/Tr.	42	56000	4-P&W R-1830-43	1200		306	B-24D. 5 crew. 20 passengers.	1
C-87B	Liberator Express	Convair	Cargo/Tr.	43	58000	4-P&W R-1830-43	1200		**	Armed version. Project canceled.	1
C-93	Conestoga	Budd	Cargo/Tr.	42	32000	2-P&W R-1830-92	1200		165	Stainless steel aircraft with rear loading ramp and upswept tail. Data are for C-93A.	1,10
C-117C	Skytrain	Douglas	Cargo/Tr.	45-45	30000	2-P&W R-1830-90C	1200		224	Staff transport with plush seats. 21 seats. Generally similar to C-47B with two stage high altitude blowers removed. Designation of VC-117.	1,10
C-118A	Liftmaster	Douglas	Cargo/Tr.	-65	107000	4-P&W R-2800-52W	2500		372	Similar to DC-6A. 74 passengers, or 27000 lb of cargo, or 60 stretchers.	7,10
C-130A	Hercules	Lockheed	Cargo/Tr.	54-	135000	4-Allison T56-A-7A	4050		376	High wing transport. Data are for C-130B.	7
C-131B	Samaritan	Convair	Cargo/Tr.	51-	47000	2-P&W R-2800-103W	2500		305	Based on commercial CV-340. 48 passenger transport and flying labs.	7
JC-131B	Samaritan	Convair	Cargo/Tr.	51-	47000	2-P&W R-2800-103W	2500		305	Data as for C-131B. J designation not known.	7
C-131D	Samaritan	Convair	Cargo/Tr.	51-	47000	2-P&W R-2800-103W	2500		305	Essentially similar to C-131B.	7
VC-131D	Samaritan	Convair	Cargo/Tr.	51-	47000	2-P&W R-2800-103W	2500		305	Staff transport.	7
KC-135A	Stratotanker	Boeing	Cargo/Tr.	56-	297000	4-P&W J57-P-59W		13750	624	Boeing 707. Refueling tanker.	7

Designation	Name	Builder	Type	Years 1st Delivered	Gross Weight (lbs)	Engines	HP/Each	Thrust/Each (lb)	Top Spd, mph	Remarks	Ref. #
Bellanca			Civilian							Designation insufficient. Bellanca manufactured at least 4 aircraft types: CH-300 Pacemaker; 31-55A Skyrocket; 66-75 Aircruiser; Cruisair.	
BG (NC 18469)			Civilian							Designation unknown.	
Cub Coupe	Cub Coupe	Piper	Civilian	38-42	1400	Continental A-75-8	75		100	Improved Cub with side-by-side seating and hydraulic brakes, and navigation lights. Used in Civilian Air Training Program.	7
Erco	Ercoupe	Erco	Civilian	37-	1450	Continental C90-16F	90		120	Designed by Fred Weick to be spin-proof. First manufactured by Erco (Engineering and Research Corporation) and later by Alon until 1964.	7, 11
Fairchild			Civilian							Designation insufficient.	
Menasco			Civilian							Cannot find any aircraft so designated.	
Piper Cub	Piper J-3 Cub	Piper	Civilian	40-	1220	Continental A-65-8	65		100	Data are for J-3C-65 Cub Trainer.	7
Rearwin			Civilian	35-						Data insufficient. There are 4 Rearwins.	
S-1A-65FO			Civilian							Designation unknown.	
Stearman	Stearman Kaydet	Stearman	Civilian	34-	2635	Continental R-670-5	124		220	Biplane. Primary trainer.	7
Stinson	Voyager	Stinson	Civilian	39-	1580	Continental A75	75		115	Data are for Stinson 105 (HW-75).	7
Timm	Tutor	Timm	Civilian	40-	2725	Continental W-670-K	220		144	Two-seat primary trainer. Structure entirely of plastic-bonded plywood.	7
Vega Ventura	Ventura	Lockheed/Vega	Civilian	41-42	27270	2-P&W R-2800-31	2000		315	Data are for B-34 Bomber version. Re-manufactured as executive versions for 8-15 passengers.	7

Designation	Name	Builder	Type	Years 1st Delivered	Gross Weight (lbs)	Engines	HP/Each	Thrust/Each (lb)	Top Spd, mph	Remarks	Ref. #
Ventura 37	Ventura	Lockheed/Vega	Civilian	42	29500	2-Wright R-2600-1	1700		298	Data are for B-37 Bomber.	1
7-W	Spartan 7-W Executive	Spartan	Civilian	36-42	4400	1-P&W R-985-SB3	450		212	Five-seat cabin monoplane. Also used by USAAF in WWII as UC-71.	7
Lockheed Jetstar	Jetstar	Lockheed	Civilian	57-	130000	4-P&W J60-P5		3000	573	Jet utility transport and trainer. Data are for C-140.	7
XA-8	Shrike	Curtiss	Exptl	30-31	5413	1-Curtiss V-1570-23	600		196	Low wing monoplane	1
XA-19B		Vultee	Exptl	40	16805	1-P&W R-2800-1	1800		232	Low wing monoplane. Speed is for XA-19A.	1
XA-21		Stearman	Exptl	40-40	18230	2-P&W R-2180-7	1400		257		1
XA-22		Martin	Exptl	40-40	18192	2-P&W R-1830-37	1200		280	Marin Maryland.	1
XA-26	Invader	Douglas	Exptl	41-43	30000	2-P&W R-2800-27	2000		355	Attack bomber with bomb aimer's position. Redesignated B-26 (Original B-26 was the Marauder). Speed is for A-26B.	1,10
XA-26A	Invader	Douglas	Exptl	41-43	29000	2-P&W R-2800-27	2000		355	Night fighter version. Speed is for A-26B.	1,10
XA-41		Vultee	Exptl	43-44	23359	1-P&W XR-4360-9	3000		353	Dive bomber.	1
XAT-13		Fairchild	Exptl	41-42	12401	2-P&W 1340-AN-1	600		202	Duramold structure.	1
XB-7		Douglas	Exptl	31	10537	2-Curtiss V-1570-25	600		169	High wing monoplane with inverted gull wing.	1
XB-15		Boeing	Exptl	35-37	70700	4-P&W R-1830-11	1000		197		1
XB-19		Douglas	Exptl	37-41	160332	4-Wright R-3350-5	2200		204		1
XB-19A		Douglas	Exptl	43	140230	4-Allison V-3420-11	2600		265	Inline engines.	1
XB-21		North Amer.	Exptl	38	27255	2-P&W R-2180-1	1200		220		1
XB-24K	Liberator	Consolidated	Exptl	43	62000	4-P&W R-1830-75	1350		294	Single tail version of B-24D	1
XB-26F	Marauder	Martin	Exptl	42-43	38200	2-P&W R-2800-41	2000		277	Wing incidence increased to improve take-off. Side package guns added. Data are for B-26F.	4
XB-28		North Amer.	Exptl	40-41	35763	2-P&W R-2800-11	2000		372	High altitude bomber.	1, 10
XC-35	Electra	Lockheed	Exptl	36-37	10500	2-P&W XR-1340-33	550		240	High altitude version.	1

Designation	Name	Builder	Type	Years 1st Delivered	Gross Weight (lbs)	Engines	HP/Each	Thrust/Each (lb)	Top Spd, mph	Remarks	Ref. #
XFM-1	Airacuda	Bell	Exptl	36-38	17933	2-Allison V-1710-13	1150		271	Long range bomber destroyer (FM=Fighter-Multiplace). Pusher engines with guns in nacelles.	1,12
XO-16		Curtiss	Exptl	28-29	4305	1-Curtiss V-1570-9	600		161	Biplane.	1
XO-25A		Douglas	Exptl	30	4800	1-Curtiss V-1570-27	600		158	Biplane.	1
XO-60		Kellett	Exptl	42	2640	1-JacobsR-915-3	300		127	Autogyro.	1
XP-6E	Hawk	Curtiss	Exptl	32	3842	1-Curtiss V-1570-23	600		205	Biplane. Data are for XP-6F (with turbo-supercharged engine).	1
XP-16		Berliner-Joyce	Exptl	29-30	3927	1-Curtiss V-1570-25	600		185	Biplane.	1
XP-36D	Hawk	Curtiss	Exptl	39	6420	1-P&W R-1830-13	1050		291	Low wing all-metal monoplane. 4 .30 cal. wing guns. Shares name with biplane.	1
XP-36F	Hawk	Curtiss	Exptl	40	6850	1-P&W R-1830-13	1050		265	P-36A with 2-20mm cannon.	1
XP-37		Curtiss	Exptl	37	6643	1-Allison V-1710-17	1150		340	Low wing all-metal monoplane. Turbo-supercharger.	1
XP-39	Airacobra	Bell	Exptl	38-39	6204	1-Allison V-1710-11	1150		390	Low wing all-metal monoplane. Engine behind cockpit.	1
XP-39B	Airacobra	Bell	Exptl	40	6450	1-Allison V-1710-37	1090		375	As XP-39. No turbo-supercharger.	1
XP-40	Warhawk	Curtiss	Exptl	38	6870	1-Allison V-1710-19	1160		342	Tenth P-36A. Inline engine.	1
XP-40N	Warhawk	Curtiss	Exptl	43	8850	1-Allison V-1710-81	1200		378	Data are for P-40N-1-15 (Blocks 1-15).	1
XP-40Q	Warhawk	Curtiss	Exptl	44-45	9000	1-Allison V-1710-81	1425		422	Bubble canopy, wing radiators, square tips.	1
XP-41		Seversky	Exptl	38	7200	1-P&W R-1830-19	1200		323	Last P-35. Engine change. Turbo-supercharger.	1
XP-46A		Curtiss	Exptl	42	7081	1-Allison V-1710-39	1150		357	Improved P-40. No guns, radio.	1
XP-47F	Thunderbolt	Republic	Exptl	42	13500	1-P&W R-2800-21	2000		420	P-47B with laminar flow wings.	1

Designation	Name	Builder	Type	Years 1st Delivered	Gross Weight (lbs)	Engines	HP/Each	Thrust/Each (lb)	Top Spd, mph	Remarks	Ref. #
XP-51	Mustang	North Amer.	Exptl	42	8400	1-Allison V-1710-39	1150		382		1
XP-59A	Airacomet	Bell	Exptl	42-43	10500	2-GE-Model I-A		1250	404	First US Jet. Designation XP-59 was given to a canceled pusher interceptor.	2 1
XP-60		Curtiss	Exptl	41-42	9961	1-Packard V-1650-1	1300		380	Improved P-40.	1
XP-77		Bell	Exptl	43-44	3940	1-Ranger XV-770-7	520		330	Lightweight interceptor.	1
XP-80	Shooting Star	Lockheed	Exptl	43-44	8620	1-De havilland Goblin H-1B		2460	502		2 1
XPT-14		Waco	Exptl	39-39	2842	1-Continental R-670-3	220		138	Biplane.	1
XPT-15		St. Louis	Exptl	40-40	2766	1-Wright R-670-1	225		124	Biplane.	1
XPT-16		Ryan	Exptl	39-39	1600	1-Menasco L-365-1	125		131	Low-wing wire-braced monoplane.	1
XR-4		Sikorsky	Exptl	41-42	2449	1-Warner R-500-3	165		102	Helicopter.	1
F-80B	Shooting Star	Lockheed	Fighter	46	15336	2-GE-J33-A-21		4000	594	Thinner wing than P-80A. Engine thrust is 5200 lb with water injection. Weight and speed are for F-80C. "F" replaced "P" for Fighters on June 11th, 1948.	6
F-100F	Super Sabre	North Amer.	Fighter	57	30700	2-P&W J57-P-53		11700	846	Tandem two-seat version. Thrust with afterburning is 16950 lb.	7
F-101B	Voodoo	McDonnell	Fighter	57	46673	1-P&W J57-P-21		11990	1220	Thrust with afterburning is 14990 lb.	7
TF-102	Delta Dagger	Convair	Fighter	55	27778	1-P&W J57-P-23		11700	646	Side-by-side two-seat combat trainer. Speed is at 38000 ft.	7
F-104B	Starfighter	Lockheed	Fighter	57	22420	1-GE-J79-GE-3B		9600	1254	Tandem two-seat operational trainer derivative of F-104A. Weight, speed, and thrust data are for F-104A. Thrust with afterburning is 14800 lb.	7
P-1	Hawk	Curtiss	Fighter	25-25	2846	1-Curtiss V-1150-1	435		163	Biplane.	1
P-1B	Hawk	Curtiss	Fighter	27-27	2932	1-Curtiss V-1150-3	435		157	Improved with larger wheels.	1
P-1C	Hawk	Curtiss	Fighter	29-29	2846	1-Curtiss V-1150-3	435		154	Wheel brakes.	1

Designation	Name	Builder	Type	Years 1st Delivered	Gross Weight (lbs)	Engines	HP/Each	Thrust/Each (lb)	Top Spd, mph	Remarks	Ref. #
P-3A		Curtiss	Fighter	28-28	2788	1-P&W R-1340-3	450		153	Biplane.	1
P-5		Curtiss	Fighter	27-28	3360	1-Curtiss V-1570-1	600		182	Biplane.	1
P-6	Hawk	Curtiss	Fighter	29-29	3150	1-Curtiss V-1570-17	600		180	Biplane.	1
P-6A	Hawk	Curtiss	Fighter	30	3172	1-Curtiss V-1570-23	600		176		1
P-6D	Hawk	Curtiss	Fighter	31	3200	1-Curtiss V-1570-23	600		180		1
P-6E	Hawk	Curtiss	Fighter	32-32	3436	1-Curtiss V-1570-23	600		197		1
P-6G	Hawk	Curtiss	Fighter	33	3450	1-Curtiss V-1570-51	600		195		1
P-6H	Hawk	Curtiss	Fighter	34	3520	1-Curtiss V-1570-51	600		193		1
P-12		Boeing	Fighter	29-29	2536	1-P&W R-1340-7	450		171	Biplane. Navy F4B series.	1
P-12B		Boeing	Fighter	29-30	2638	1-P&W R-1340-9	525		166		1
P-12C		Boeing	Fighter	31-31	2615	1-P&W R-1340-9	525		178		1
P-12D		Boeing	Fighter	31-32	2648	1-P&W R-1340-17	525		188	High compression engine.	1
P-12E		Boeing	Fighter	31-32	2660	1-P&W R-1340-17	525		189	Monocoque fuselage.	1
P-12F		Boeing	Fighter	32-32	2726	1-P&W R-1340-19	600		194		1
P-12K		Boeing	Fighter	33	2720	1-P&W R-1340-17	525		190	As P-12E with fuel injection. Data are for YP-12K.	1
P-16		Berliner-Joyce	Fighter	32	4298	1-Curtiss V-1570-25	600		170		1
P-26		Boeing	Fighter	32-33	2789	1-P&W R-1340-21	550		227	Low wing monoplane. Data are for Y1P-26.	1
P-26A		Boeing	Fighter	33-33	3012	1-P&W R-1340-27	600		234		1
P-26B		Boeing	Fighter	33-34	3030	1-P&W R-1340-33	600		230	As -A. Fuel injection.	1
P-26C		Boeing	Fighter	34	3015	1-P&W R-1340-27	600		230		1
P-29		Boeing	Fighter	34	3312	1-P&W R-1340-39	600		240	Low-wing monoplane.	1
P-30		Consolidated	Fighter	33-34	5092	1-Curtiss V-1570-57	675		239	Low-wing 2-place monoplane. Became PB-2 (Pursuit Biplace).	1
P-35		Seversky	Fighter	36-37	5600	1-P&W R-1830-9	950		251	All metal low-wing monoplane.	1
P-36	Hawk	Curtiss	Fighter	38	5460	1-P&W R-1830-13	1050		294	All metal low-wing monoplane. Shares name with biplane.	1
P-36A	Hawk	Curtiss	Fighter	38-38	6010	1-P&W R-1830-13	1050		294		1
P-36B	Hawk	Curtiss	Fighter	39	6010	1-P&W R-1830-25	1100		294		1
P-36C	Hawk	Curtiss	Fighter	39	6128	1-P&W R-1830-17	1200		294	Two .30 wing guns.	1
P-36D	Hawk	Curtiss	Fighter	39	6429	1-P&W R-1830-13	1050		294	Four .30 wing guns. Data are for XP-36D.	1
P-36E	Hawk	Curtiss	Fighter	40	6576	1-P&W R-1830-13	1050		294	8 .30 wing guns. Data are for XP-36E.	1

Designation	Name	Builder	Type	Years 1st Delivered	Gross Weight (lbs)	Engines	HP/Each	Thrust/Each (lb)	Top Spd, mph	Remarks	Ref. #
P-36F	Hawk	Curtiss	Fighter	40	6850	1-P&W R-1830-13	1050		294	Two 23mm wing cannon. Data are for XP-36F.	1
P-38	Lightning	Lockheed	Fighter	40-41	15340	2-Allison V-1710-27	1150		395	Production version. Also equipped with Allison V-1710-29.	1
P-38D	Lightning	Lockheed	Fighter	40-41	14456	2-Allison V-1710-27	1150		390	Leak proof tanks. One 37 mm cannon plus two .50 cal and two .30 cal. In nose. Also equipped with Allison V-1710-29.	1
P-38E	Lightning	Lockheed	Fighter	41-41	14424	2-Allison V-1710-27	1150		395	One 20 mm replaced 37mm cannon. Also equipped with Allison V-1710-29.	1
P-38G	Lightning	Lockheed	Fighter	42-42	15800	2-Allison V-1710-51	1325		400	Long range version with racks under wings for bombs or fuel tanks. Also equipped with Allison V-1710-55.	1,13
P-38G1	Lightning	Lockheed	Fighter	42-42	15800	2-Allison V-1710-51	1325		400	Data given are for -G.	1,13
P-38GL	Lightning	Lockheed	Fighter	42-42	15800	2-Allison V-1710-51	1325		400	Data given are for -G.	1,13
P-38J	Lightning	Lockheed	Fighter	43-43	17500	2-Allison V-1710-89	1425		420	Beard radiator. Ferry range increased to 2260 miles. Also equipped with Allison V-1710-91.	1,13
P-38L	Lightning	Lockheed	Fighter	45	17500	2-Allison V-1710-111	1475		414	Power boosted ailerons and dive flaps. Also equipped with Allison V-1710-113.	1,13
P-39	Airacobra	Bell	Fighter	40	7235	1-Allison V-1710-37	1090		368	1-37 mm cannon in nose, 2-.50 cal. guns, and 2-.30 cal. guns. Data are for YP-39.	1,14
P-39C	Airacobra	Bell	Fighter	40	7180	1-Allison V-1710-35	1150		375	Virtually identical to YP-39.	1,14
P-39D	Airacobra	Bell	Fighter	41-41	8200	1-Allison V-1710-35	1150		379	37 mm cannon in nose, two .50 cal. guns, and 4 wing-mounted .30 cal. guns. Self-sealing fuel tanks and armor.	1,14

Designation	Name	Builder	Type	Years 1st Delivered	Gross Weight (lbs)	Engines	HP/Each	Thrust/Each (lb)	Top Spd, mph	Remarks	Ref. #
P-39Q	Airacobra	Bell	Fighter	44-44	8300	1-Allison V-1710-85	1200		385	Wing mounted guns replaced by underwing two .50 cal. guns. Manufactured in largest numbers.	1,14
P-40	Warhawk	Curtiss	Fighter	39-39	7215	1-Allison V-1710-33	1040		357	As XP-40 with engine change.	1
P-40B	Warhawk	Curtiss	Fighter	41-41	7645	1-Allison V-1710-33	1040		352	Armor added.	1
P-40C	Warhawk	Curtiss	Fighter	41-41	8058	1-Allison V-1710-33	1040		340	Self-sealing tanks.	1
P-40E	Warhawk	Curtiss	Fighter	41-41	8840	1-Allison V-1710-39	1150		354	Six .50 cal. guns.	1
P-40F	Warhawk	Curtiss	Fighter	41-41	9870	1-Packard V-1650-1	1300		365	Engine change.	1
P-42	Hawk	Curtiss	Fighter	38	6260	1-P&W R-1830-31	1050		315	As P-36A. Engine change. Data are for XP-42.	1
P-43A	Lancer	Republic	Fighter	40-41	7850	1-P&W R-1830-49	1200		355	Development of XP-41.	1
P-47B	Thunderbolt	Republic	Fighter	41-42	13356	1-P&W R-2800-21	2000		429		1
P-51	Mustang	North Amer.	Fighter	41-42	8800	1-Allison V-1710-39	1150		387		1
P-51A	Mustang	North Amer.	Fighter	42-42	9000	1-Allison V-1710-81	1200		390	Bomb racks.	1
P-51B	Mustang	North Amer.	Fighter	41-42	11800	1-Packard V-1650-3	1150		436	Engine change to Packard built Rolls-Royce Merlin. This version inaugurated the premier strategic fighter of WW2.	1
P-61	Black Widow	Northrop	Fighter	42-43	27614	2-P&W R-2800-10	2000		369	Dedicated night fighter.	1
P-61A	Black Widow	Northrop	Fighter	43-43	27600	2-P&W R-2800-65	2250		355	Four .50 cal. dorsal turret removed.	14
P-61B	Black Widow	Northrop	Fighter	43-44	29700	2-P&W R-2800-65	2250		352	Dorsal turret reintroduced in 201st -B.	14
P-63	Kingcobra	Bell	Fighter	42-43	8800	1-Allison V-1710-93	1325		410	XP-63 developed from XP-39E with laminar flow wing. Data are for P-63A-10.	14
P-66	Vanguard	Vultee	Fighter	42-42	7100	1-P&W R-1830-33	1200		340		14
P-70	Havoc	Douglas	Fighter	42	21264	2-P&W R-2600-11	1600		329	Night fighter conversion of A-20.	14

Designation	Name	Builder	Type	Years 1st Delivered	Gross Weight (lbs)	Engines	HP/Each	Thrust/Each (lb)	Top Spd, mph	Remarks	Ref. #
PB-2		Consolidated	Fighter	33-34	5092	1-Curtiss V-1570-57	675		239	Pursuit Biplace. Also designated P-30.	1
PB-2A		Consolidated	Fighter	33-34	5092	1-Curtiss V-1570-57	675		239	Data are for PB-2.	1
PB-16			Fighter							Designation unknown.	
PC-5			Fighter							Designation unknown.	
PC-6A			Fighter							Designation unknown.	
TF-86F	Sabre	North Amer.	Fighter	53-54	14836	1-GE-J47-GE-27		5910	692	Two seat trainer based on F-86F. Designation is TF-86.	15
Avro Anson	Anson	Avro	Foreign	34-52	8000	2-Armstrong -Siddeley Cheetah IX radial	350		188	British. Civil airliner, Coastal reconnaisance aircraft, trainer. Data are for Mark I.	10
Beaufighter	Beaufighter	Bristol	Foreign	39-60	20800	2-Bristol Hercules XI radial	1590		323	British. Night-fighter, long range day-fighter, anti-shipping aircraft. Data are for Night-fighter IF.	16
British Lightning	Lightning	Lockheed	Foreign	42-42	15800	2-Allison V-1710-51	1325		400	Lightning Mark II data, same as for P-38G. Did not reach squadron service in RAF.	1,13
Defiant	Defiant	Boulton-Paul	Foreign	37-42	8318	1-Rolls-Royce Merlin III Vee engine	1030		304	British. Turret fighter. Day- and night-fighter. Data are for Mark I.	16
DH-89A	Dragon Rapide	De Havilland	Foreign	34-	6000	2-De havilland Gipsy Queen inline engines	200		150	British. Biplane. Light transport. Data are for DH 89A Mark 4.	10
Fairey Battle	Battle	Fairey	Foreign	36-	10792	1-Rolls-Royce Merlin I Vee engine	1030		257	British. Day bomber, target tug. Data are for Mark I.	10
Firebrand	Firebrand	Blackburn	Foreign	42-	17500	1-Bristol Centaurus IX radial	2520		340	British. Naval fighter, torpedo-fighter (TF). Data are for TF-5.	10
Gladiator	Gladiator	Gloster	Foreign	34-	4864	1-Bristol Mercury IX radial	830		257	British. Biplane fighter. Data are for Mark II.	10
Halifax	Halifax	Handley-Page	Foreign	39-	54400	4-Bristol Hercules XVI radials	1455		282	British. Bomber. Data are for B. Mark III.	5

Designation	Name	Builder	Type	Years 1st Delivered	Gross Weight (lbs)	Engines	HP/Each	Thrust/Each (lb)	Top Spd, mph	Remarks	Ref. #
Hurricane	Hurricane	Hawker	Foreign	35-	8470	1-Rolls-Royce Merlin XX Vee engine	1460		342	British. Single seat fighter monoplane, ground attack fighter. Data are for Mark IIB.	16
Lancaster	Lancaster	Avro	Foreign	39-	53000	4-Packard Built Rolls-Royce Merlin 28 or 38 Vee engines	1390		270	British. Bomber. Data are for Lancaster III. Take off power.	4
Meteor	Meteor I	Gloster	Foreign	43-	11800	2-Rolls-Royce Welland I turbojets		1700	410	British. Jet Fighter.	16
Mosquito	Mosquito	De havilland	Foreign	40-	19500	2-Rolls-Royce Merlin 25 Vee engine	1635		380	British. Fighter, bomber. Data are for FB Mark VI.	16
Rapide	Dragon Rapide	De Havilland	Foreign	34-	6000	2-de havilland Gipsy Queen inline engines	200		150	British. Biplane. Light transport. Data are for DH 89A Mark 4.	10
Spitfire	Spitfire	Supermarine	Foreign	36-	7500	1-Rolls-Royce Merlin 66 Vee engine	1720		404	British. Single seat fighter. Data are for L.F. IXE.	16
Stirling	Stirling	Short	Foreign	39-	59400	4-Bristol Hercules XI radials	1460		260	British. Bomber. Data are for Mark I Series I. Max. power for 5 min.	5
Tempest	Tempest	Hawker	Foreign	42-	11800	1-Napier Sabre IIB Horizontal H liquid-cooled engine.	2200		435	British. Fighter. Used thinner high speed airfoil than Typhoon. Data are for Tempest V Series 2.	16
Typhoon	Typhoon	Hawker	Foreign	40-	11400	1-Napier Sabre IIA Horizontal H liquid-cooled engine.	2180		405	British. Fighter, fighter bomber.	16
Welkin	Welkin	Westland	Foreign	42-	17500	2-Rolls-Royce Merlin 76/77 Vee liquid-cooled engines.	1250		382	British. Two-seat high-altitude day-and night-interceptor. Data are for Welkin I.	16

Designation	Name	Builder	Type	Years 1st Delivered	Gross Weight (lbs)	Engines	HP/Each	Thrust/Each (lb)	Top Spd, mph	Remarks	Ref. #
Warwick	Warwick	Vickers	Foreign	39-	51250	2-Bristol Centaurus VI sleeve radials	2500		262	British, Bomber, Air/Sea Rescue, General Reconnaissance (GR). Geodetic construction fuselage. Max. take off weight. Data are for GR Mark II.	1 0
Wellington	Wellington	Vickers	Foreign	36-	31500	2-Bristol Centaurus VI radials	1585		255	British, Bomber. Geodetic construction fuselage. Take off power. Data are for B. Mark X.	4
Focke Wulf, FW-200-C3	Condor	Focke Wulf	Foreign	37-	50045	4-BMW-Bramo Fafnir 9-cylr. radials	1000		224	Designation "Focke-Wulf" is insufficient. FW-200-C3 is assumed. German long-range reconnaissance bomber.	5
FW-190	Wurger	Focke Wulf	Foreign	39-						German fighter. Sub-designation needed. See data for FW-190A. The name "Wurger" (Shrike) was virtually never used.	
FW-190A	Wurger	Focke Wulf	Foreign	43-	10800	1-BMW 801D-2 14-cylr. 2-row radial.	1440		408	Outstanding German fighter. Data are for Fw-190A-8. The name "Wurger" (Shrike) was virtually never used.	13, 17
Ju-88		Junkers	Foreign	42-	31000	2-Junkers Jumo 211-J1 12-cylr. inline engines	1350		273	German bomber. Data are for Ju-88A-4/R. Earlier versions were first flown in 1939.	4
Me-109E		Messerschmitt	Foreign	39-	5523	1-Daimler-Benz DB 601A 12-cylr. inverted Vee inline engine.	1100		354	German fighter. Data are for Bf 109E-1. ("Bf" is the correct modern designation. "Me" was used as the popular designation.)	1 8
Me-109F		Messerschmitt	Foreign	42-	6054	1-Daimler-Benz DB 601E-1 12-cylr. inverted Vee inline engine.	1300		390	German fighter. Data are for Bf 109F-3. ("Bf" is the correct modern designation. "Me" was used as the popular designation.)	1 8

Designation	Name	Builder	Type	Years 1st Delivered	Gross Weight (lbs)	Engines	HP/Each	Thrust/Each (lb)	Top Spd, mph	Remarks	Ref. #
Betty. G4M2a Type 1 Model 24	Betty	Mitsubishi	Foreign	44-	33070	2-Mitsubishi MK4T Kasei 25 14-cylr. radials.	1680		272	Japanese bomber. Late model. Early models 1st flown in 1939.	5
Frank. Ki.84-1a	Frank, "Hayate" (Gale).	Nakajima	Foreign	43-	9194	1-Nakajima Ha.45/11 Type 4 18-cylr. radial.	1900		388	Outstanding Japanese fighter. Take-off power specified.	13
George. N1K1-J	George, "Shiden" (Violet Lightning).	Nakajima	Foreign	43-	9526	1-Nakajima Homare 21 18-cylr. radial.	1990		362	Japanese fighter. Model described was test flown by US Army in S.W. Pacific in late war years.	19
Jack. J2M2-3	Jack, "Raiden" (Thunderbolt).	Mitsubishi	Foreign	43-	8699	1-Mitsubishi MK4R-A Kasei 23a 14-cylr. raidial.	1820		371	Japanese fighter. Fast-climbing interceptor.	19
Judy. DAY3 Model 33	Judy, "Susei" (Comet).	Yokosuka	Foreign	44-	10267	1-Mitsubishi MK8P Kinsei 62 14-cylr. radial.	1340		357	Japanese carrier-based dive bomber and reconnaisaance aircraft. Some versions had inline engines.	20
Nick. Ki.45-KAlc	Nick, "Toryu" (Dragon Killer).	Kawasaki	Foreign	42-43	12125	2-Mitsubishi Ha.102 Type 1 14-cylr. radiate.	1080		340	Japanese night fighter. Armament included 2 forward firing 12.7 mm guns aft of pilot firing forward at 30 deg.	19
Zero. A6M6c Model 53c	Zeke.	Mitsubishi	Foreign	44-	6047	1-Nakajima Sakai 31 14-cylr. radial.	1130		346	Famous Japanese Navy fighter. Early model flew in 1939.	19
L-4H	Grasshopper	Piper	Liason	43-43	1300	1-Lycoming O-170-3	65		85	Piper Cub.	
L-5	Sentinel	Vultee-Stinson	Liason	42	2200	1-Lycoming O-435-1	185		115	Stinson Sentinel. Data are for L-5A.	1
L-5E	Sentinel	Vultee-Stinson	Liason	42	2200	1-Lycoming O-435-1	185		118	Provison for K-20 camera. Drooping ailerons.	1
L-20A		Vultee-Stinson	Liason							Designation unknown.	
BC-1		North Amer.	Misc.	37-38	5223	1-P&W R-1340-47	600		207	Basic combat. Ancestor to AT-6 and T-6 trainers.	1,1,10

Designation	Name	Builder	Type	Years 1st Delivered	Gross Weight (lbs)	Engines	HP/Each	Thrust/Each (lb)	Top Spd, mph	Remarks	Ref. #
BC-2		North Amer.	Misc.	38-38	5290	1-P&W R-1340-45	600		212	Modified BC-1. 3-bladed prop.	1
BC-3		Vultee	Misc.	39-40	5700	1-P&W R-1340-45	600		223	Basic combat. Low wing. Retractable gear.	1
BM-10			Misc.							Designation unknown.	
CQ-1			Misc.							Designation unknown.	
CW-21			Misc.							Designation unknown.	
DH-4		Boeing	Misc.	23-23	4510	1-Liberty 12-A	420		123	Modernized version of British DH-4 biplane bomber of World War I. Aircraft was also built by other US builders.	1
F-2		Beech	Misc.	40-40	7725	2-P&W R-985-19	375		225	Photo-reconnaisance version of C-45.	1
F2A-3	Buffalo	Brewster	Misc.	41-	6321	1-Wright R-1820-40	1200		321	Navy monoplane fighter. Take-off power cited.	22,23
F4F-3	Wildcat	Grumman	Misc.	41-	6876	1-P&W R-1830-90	1200		312	Navy monoplane fighter. Take-off power cited. Data are for F4F-3A.	
F4U-1	Corsair	Vought	Misc.	42-	12694	1-P&W R-2800-8	2000		395	Outstanding Navy fighter. Take-off power cited. Data are for F4U-1A.	24
F-46A			Misc.							Designation unknown.	
GI-80			Misc.							Designation unknown.	
G-15			Misc.							Designation unknown.	
H-5D		Sikorsky	Misc.	46-	5500	1-P&W R-985-AN-7	450		104	S-51 helicopter.	7
H-5G		Sikorsky	Misc.	46-	5500	1-P&W R-985-AN-7	450		104	S-51 helicopter. USAF Air Rescue Service version.	7,10
H-19B		Sikorsky	Misc.	49-	7900	1-P&W R-1340	550		101	S-55 helicopter for US Army. Data are for Navy HRS-2.	10,22
JH-19B		Sikorsky	Misc.	49-	7900	1-P&W R-1340	550		101	S-55 helicopter for US Army. J-designation not known. Data are for Navy HRS-2.	10,22
H-81A			Misc.							Designation unknown.	
JNS			Misc.							Designation unknown.	
LB-30			Misc.							Designation unknown.	

Designation	Name	Builder	Type	Years 1st Delivered	Gross Weight (lbs)	Engines	HP/Each	Thrust/Each (lb)	Top Spd, mph	Remarks	Ref. #
N-9M		Northrop	Misc.	43-	7000	2-Menasco C6S4	290		257	0.35 flying-wing scale model of XB-35 bomber.	25
NS-1			Misc.							Designation unknown.	
PQ-8		Culver	Misc.	41-42						Man-carrying aerial target.	1
R-5D	Skymaster	Douglas	Misc.	41-	65000	4-P&W R-2000-7	1350		281	Navy version of C-54.	2 2
SB2C-1	Helldiver	Curtiss	Misc.	42-	13674	1-Wright R-2600-8	1700		281	Navy bomber.	22,26
SB2U-2	Vindicator	Vought	Misc.	38-	9421	1-P&W R-1535-02	825		243	Navy scout bomber. Data are for SB2U-3. Delivery date is for SB2U-2.	2 2
SBD-1	Dauntless	Douglas	Misc.	40-	10360	1-Wright R-1820-32	1000		252	Navy bomber.	2 6
SU-2	Corsair	Vought	Misc.	32-34	4451	1-P&W R-1340-12	550		164	Navy scout biplane. Data are for O3U-3.	2 2
TF-8D	Mustang	North Amer.	Misc.	44-	11000	1-Packard V-1650-7	1490		436	Training version assumed.of photo-recon version of P-51D (F-6D).	1
TG-2			Misc.							Designation unknown.	
WT-1			Misc.							Designation unknown.	
ZB-21		North Amer.	Misc.	38-38	27255	2-P&W R-2180-1	1200		220	Classified obsolete. Data assumed for XB-21 (NA-21 with Twin Hornets).	
415-C			Misc.							Designation unknown.	
O-1G	Falcon	Curtiss	Observation	31-31	4488	1-Curtiss V-1150-5	435		142	Biplane	1
O-2		Douglas	Observation	25-25	4753	1-Lib. V-1650-1	435		128	Biplane	1
O-2B		Douglas	Observation	25-26	4852	1-Lib. V-1650-1	435		121	Biplane	1
O-19B		Th. Morse	Observation	30-30	3800	1-P&W R-1340-7	450		137	Biplane	1
O-19C		Th. Morse	Observation	31-31	3990	1-P&W R-1340-7	450		142	Biplane	1
O-19E		Th. Morse	Observation	31-32	3938	1-P&W R-1340-15	575		156	Biplane	1
O-25A		Douglas	Observation	30-30	4805	1-Curtiss V-1570-7	600		158	Biplane	1

Designation	Name	Builder	Type	Years 1st Delivered	Gross Weight (lbs)	Engines	HP/Each	Thrust/Each (lb)	Top Spd, mph	Remarks	Ref. #
O-25C		Douglas	Observation	32-32	4816	1-Curtiss V-1570-27	600		161	Biplane	1
O-33		Th. Morse	Observation	30-	4291	1-Curtiss V-1570-11	600		165	First O-19B with engine change.	1
O-38		Douglas	Observation	31	4270	1-P&W R-1690-3	525		145	Improved O-25. Engine change.	1
O-38B		Douglas	Observation	31-31	4458	1-P&W R-1690-5	525		149	New tail, landing gear.	1
O-38E		Douglas	Observation	33-33	4600	1-P&W R-1690-13	625		154		1
O-38F		Douglas	Observation	33-34	4650	1-P&W R-1690-9	625		158		1
O-39		Curtiss	Observation	32-32	4725	1-Curtiss V-1570-25	600		173	As O-1G. Engine and canopy change.	1
O-46A		Douglas	Observation	35-36	725	1-P&W R-1535-7	725		200	High-wing monplane.	1
O-47A		North Amer.	Observation	37-37	7636	1-Wr. R-1820-49	975		223	3-pl. mid-wing monoplane.	1
O-47B		North Amer.	Observation	39-39	8092	1-Wr. R-1820-57	1060		227		1
RO-47B		North Amer.	Observation	39-39	8092	1-Wr. R-1820-57	1060		227	R-restricted - not for combat use.	1
O-49		Stinson	Observation	40-40	3725	1-Lycoming R-680-9	295		129	Became L-1.	1
O-52		Curtiss	Observation	40-41	5585	1-P&W R-1340-51	600		208	High-wing monoplane.	1
O-59A	Owl	Piper	Observation	42-42	1300	1-Continental O-170-3	65		87	Cub. Became L-4.	1
YA-19		Vultee	Serv. Test	38-39	16285	1-P&W R-1830-17	1200		230	Low-wing attack monoplane.	1
YB-10		Martin	Serv. Test	33-33	14192	2-Wright R-1820-25	675		196	Became B-10M.	1
YB-29	Superfortress	Boeing	Serv. Test	41-43	120000	4-Wright R-1350-13	2200		357	Bomber. Data are for YB-29BO (Boeing manufactured). Speed is for B-29A.	1,5
YBT-5		Stearman	Serv. Test	32-	2802	1-P&W R-985-1	300		140	Basic trainer. Biplane.	1
Y-1C			Serv. Test							Designation unknown.	
Y-1C-14			Serv. Test							Designation unknown.	

214